Lecture Notes in Computer Science

Edited by G. Goos, J. Hartmanis and J. van L

Springer
Berlin
Heidelberg
New York
Barcelona
Hong Kong
London
Milan
Paris
Singapore
Tokyo

Isabelle Attali   Thomas Jensen (Eds.)

Java on Smart Cards: Programming and Security

First International Workshop, JavaCard 2000
Cannes, France, September 14, 2000
Revised Papers

 Springer

Series Editors

Gerhard Goos, Karlsruhe University, Germany
Juris Hartmanis, Cornell University, NY, USA
Jan van Leeuwen, Utrecht University, The Netherlands

Volume Editors

Isabelle Attali
INRIA Sophia Antipolis
BP 93, 06902 Sophia Antipolis Cedex, France
Isabelle.attal@inria.fr

Thomas Jensen
IRISA/CNRS
Campus de Beaulieu
35042 Rennes, France
E-mail: Thomas.Jensen@risa.fr

Cataloging-in-Publication Data applied for

Die Deutsche Bibliothek - CIP-Einheitsaufnahme

Java on smart cards : programming and security ; first international
workshop ; revised papers / JavaCard 2000, Cannes, France, September
14, 2000. Isabelle Attali ; Thomas Jensen (ed.). - Berlin ; Heidelberg ;
New York ; Barcelona ; Hong Kong ; London ; Milan ; Paris ;
Singapore ; Tokyo : Springer, 2001
  (Lecture notes in computer science ; Vol. 2041)
  ISBN 3-540-42167-X

CR Subject Classification (1998): C.2, C.3, D.3.2, D.4.6, E.3, F.3, K.6.5, K.4.4

ISSN 0302-9743
ISBN 3-540-42167-X Springer-Verlag Berlin Heidelberg New York

Springer-Verlag Berlin Heidelberg New York
a member of BertelsmannSpringer Science+Business Media GmbH

http://www.springer.de

© Springer-Verlag Berlin Heidelberg 2001
Printed in Germany

Typesetting: Camera-ready by author, data conversion by PTP Berlin, Stefan Sossna
Printed on acid-free paper   SPIN 10782523   06/3142   5 4 3 2 1 0

Foreword

Smart cards are playing an increasingly important role in areas such as banking, electronic commerce, and telecommunications. The Java Card[1] language has been proposed as a high-level language for programming multi-application smart cards. The use of a high-level language can facilitate the development and verification of software for smart cards. The modest code size and the importance of the application areas implies that it is both possible and desirable to develop and apply formal methods in the construction of safe and secure Java Card software.

The present volume constitutes the proceedings of the Java Card workshop held in Cannes, 14 September 2000. The workshop grew out of the INRIA *Action de Recherche Coopérative* "Java Card" and was organized in collaboration with the Java Card Forum. A call for papers resulted in 14 submissions of which the program committee selected 11 papers for presentation at the workshop. In addition, the workshop featured an invited talk by Daniel Le Métayer, Trusted Logic, on formal methods and smart card security. We wish to thank Catherine Godest and Maryse Renaud for their help with preparing the proceedings for this workshop.

February 2001

Isabelle Attali
Thomas Jensen

---

[1] It should be noted that Java Card is a trademark of Sun Microsystems.

Organization

Program Committee

Program Chair: Isabelle Attali (INRIA, France)
Thomas Jensen (IRISA/CNRS, France)

Committee members: Christian Goire (Bull CP8, France)
Sebastian Hans (Sun Microsystems, USA)
Pieter Hartel (University of Southampton, UK)
Peter Honeyman (University of Michigan, USA)
Pierre Paradinas (Gemplus, France)
Joachim Posegga (SAP Corporate Research, Germany)

Table of Contents

Invited Talk

Contributed Papers

Formal Methods in Context: Security and Java Card

D. Bolignano, D. Le Métayer, and C. Loiseaux

Trusted Logic
www.trusted-logic.fr

1. Security and Java Card: An Ideal Application Area for Formal Methods

The benefits of formal methods for software engineering have been described at length in many research papers. They include among others:

- Better understanding and improved communication through unambiguous descriptions.
- Early bug detection thanks to the formalisation of specifications.
- Possibility of formal verifications of properties of software components and systems.
- Systematic testing from formal specifications.

The best way to turn formal methods to account is to use them as the basis of software engineering tools. A lot of effort has been put on this issue during the last decade, as evidenced by dedicated conferences like CAV (Computer Aided Verification) and TACAS (Tools and Algorithms for the Construction and Analysis of Systems). Despite this fact, the impact of formal methods on software engineering is still far from coming up to the expectations of their proponents. Our goal in this paper is not to dwell again on the advantages of formal methods but rather to highlight some key issues that have to be addressed to improve their acceptance in the industrial world. We take the case of Java Card to illustrate our arguments because we believe that it is an ideal area for the application of formal methods in industry:

- First, due to the scarce resources on smart cards and the specific needs in terms of applications, Java Card programs are less complex than typical PC or main-frame programs. As a consequence, they are more amenable to formal treatments (specification, computer assisted verification, systematic testing, etc.).

- In addition, the very strong requirements of the smart card industry in terms of security is an incentive for platform and software providers to have their products certified. Actually certification is even mandatory for certain kinds of applications (in the banking sector for example). Certification can play a significant role for the wider acceptance of formal methods because they require their use for the highest evaluation levels.

Most certifications are now conducted according to an international

I. Attali and T. Jensen (Eds.): Java Card 2000, LNCS 2041, pp. 1–5, 2001.
© Springer-Verlag Berlin Heidelberg 2001

standard called the Common Criteria for information technology security evaluation [CC] (Common Criteria in the sequel). In the next section, we provide an overview of a number of problems that have to be faced for the application of the Common Criteria and for which we believe further research in formal methods is needed.

2. Where Can Formal Methods Help and How Can They Do Better?

The application of the Common Criteria can be divided into two main stages: the security analysis and the development of the product (based on the security requirements stemming from the security analysis). We consider these two stages in turn.

2.1 Security Analysis

The security analysis leads to the definition of the *security target* in the Common Criteria terminology. The main steps of the security analysis are the following:

- Definition of the perimeter of the product to be evaluated (*target of evaluation*), its physical environment and the assumptions on this environment, the assets requiring protection, the threats against these assets and the nature and strength of the attackers, etc.
- Definition of the *security objectives*. The security objectives should be sufficient to counter the threats against the assets.
- Definition of *security functional requirements* of the product. The security functional requirements should satisfy the objectives.
- Definition of the *security assurance requirements*. The purpose of the security assurance requirements is to qualify the effectiveness of the functional requirements. They specify a minimum level of assurance that should be consistent with the security objectives. The assurance level is based on an estimation of the degree of rigour that is evidenced by the use of more or less formal methods or cryptographic keys of specific lengths.

Many formal models of security have been proposed and studied in the literature [ML]. They can be used for the definition of the *security policy model* that is required for the Common Criteria evaluations from level five upwards. Unfortunately, they are of little help for the security analysis itself. The notion of attack tree has been proposed to support threat analysis [SC] but it is hardly formal and, to our best knowledge, no connection has been established so far between attack trees and formal models of security. No model has been proposed either for security objectives, which means that the above analysis stages have to be carried out without much tool support. The only known existing tool in this category is the "CC toolbox" [NI] which makes it easier to access the Common Criteria catalogues for functional and assurance requirements, but does not rely on any security model. We believe that formal methods could bring a lot in this area, by providing ways to specify and check the notions of interest (actors, assets, product life cycle, rationale, etc.) and help the security designer to experiment with different sets of assumptions and evaluate their impact.

As an illustration of the problems to be solved for the security analysis of a Java Card system, let us mention the following. First, it should be decided whether the perimeter of the system should include the Java Card byte code verifier or not. This decision has a great impact on the rest of the security analysis. If the byte code verifier is not embedded on the card (which is the case up to now) then it is justified to exclude it from the target of evaluation, but further guarantees should then be provided to ensure that the code loaded on the card is indeed the code that has been checked outside the card. The actors of a Java Card system should include at least the issuer and applet providers, but the status of the smart card manufacturer and software developers should be made precise. They can either be considered as actors themselves or act on the behalf of the issuer. The assumptions on the environments at the different stages of the life cycle should also be described with great care. For example, it should be stated whether post-issuance loading and deletion of applets is considered or not (and if so, if native applets are excluded). Threats should include, among others, impersonation, unauthorised disclosure, modification and use of code as well as data. The choice of the appropriate security functional requirements in the Common Criteria catalogue is also far from straightforward. Let us consider for example an aspect of the strong typing property stating that the values manipulated by the virtual machine as references are always correct references. This property could be seen as an access control policy checking the references used at each access; it could also be seen as an information flow policy stating that only values of type "reference" can flow in locations expecting such a type; it could also be argued that this property expresses a form of integrity of values of "reference" type. Last but not least, all the choices made during the security analysis should be justified by a *rationale*. Such a justification would be made much easier to establish if the whole process could be based on an underlying formal model.

2.2 Development

The second stage for the application of the Common Criteria is the development of the product following the requirements established by the *security target* constructed in the first phase. The Common Criteria impose three levels of refinement for the development phase; they are called respectively the *functional specification*, the *high-level design*, the *low-level design* and the *implementation representation*. As mentioned above, the Common Criteria require the use of formal descriptions for certain documents, but only from level five upwards. Even level seven, which is the highest evaluation level, requires formal descriptions only for the functional specification, the high-level design, the correspondence between them (which has to be a formal proof) and the security policy model. The other documents are provided in an informal or semi-formal style. The important issue that we want to make here is that formal methods in this context will never be used in isolation. It is thus of prime importance to be able to establish links between formal methods and more "traditional" development methods. This issue has received more attention from the formal methods community in the last decade. One illustration is the design of tools for the automatic generation of test scripts from formal specifications [TC,VA]. Such tools bring a significant added value to formal methods and can help a lot to improve their benefit-cost ratio. However much progress has still to be made for a better integration of formal methods into traditional development environments. Let us just sketch some possible directions:

- Semi-formal methods (such as methods based on the UML notation) and formal methods (as exemplified by B [AB] or Coq [BA]) have emerged from very different contexts. They have been studied, developed and used by people with different backgrounds and motivations. They have a common goal though, which is to improve the quality of design and development through a higher level of rigour. The solutions they provide should thus be complementary rather than exclusive. Unfortunately they have led to environments which are far from being integrated. As interesting steps in the right direction, we can mention the effort initiated by the *Precise UML* group [PU], which aims at providing sound foundations to the UML notation, and proposals for complementing semi-formal specifications with formal descriptions [LE]. An important issue to this respect is to provide not only tool integration, but also a common methodology so that users can take advantage of both semi-formal and formal methods. TL-FIT [TF] is an example of such an environment which is dedicated to the design of products in the context of Common Criteria certifications.

- More research is also needed to find better ways for a non-expert to interact with a theorem prover. As an illustration, the complete proof of key security properties of a Java Card virtual machine is quite large and intricate. It involves among others type checking and properties of the firewall mechanism. The least that can be asked is to be able to provide the essence of a proof without getting into the idiosyncrasies of a specific theorem prover. This issue is especially important in the context of Common Criteria evaluations where the ultimate goal is to convince human evaluators that the product satisfies its security requirements.

- Another issue which is becoming increasingly important for the application of formal methods to security is compositionality. We have some ideas about specifying security properties of individual components; but what happens when these components are linked together to form a system? Is it possible to build on the work done at the level of components to derive useful information about the system? An interesting, and timely, question to this respect is the independent security evaluation of a system and its components. Again, we can take the example of a Java Card system and think of an individual evaluation of (1) the virtual machine with the runtime environment (JCRE), (2) the underlying platform and (3) applications.

3. Challenges: Enhanced Methodology and Better Integration

As a conclusion, we believe that the real challenge today is not to design new sophisticated specification languages or powerful proof techniques but rather to provide ways of integrating formal techniques in an otherwise informal or semi-formal environment. Such an objective should not be seen as a simple engineering problem: it is not clear whether anyone today can offer good enough solutions to problems such as proof explanations, traceability between informal and formal specifications, verifications on semi-formal documents, reusability of semi-formal descriptions to construct formal specifications, etc. It is also crucial to be able to provide a common methodology for the joined use of formal and more traditional methods.

Bibliography

[AB] J. R. Abrial, Assigning programs to meaning, Cambridge University Press, 1996.
[BB] B. Barras et al., The Coq proof assistant reference manual, Version V6.3, Technical Report, Inria, 1999.
[CC] The Common Criteria for Information Technology Security Evaluation, http://www.commoncriteria.org/docs/aboutus.html.
[LE] Y. Ledru. Complementing semi-formal specifications with Z. Proc. 11th Knowledge-Based Software Engineering Conference, IEEE, September 1996.
[ML] J. McLean, Security models, Encyclopedia of Software Engineering, Vol. 2, John Wiley and Sons, 1994.
[NI] NIAP, The CC toolbox, http://niap.nist.gov/tools/cctool.html.
[PU] The Precise UML (PUML) group, http://www.cs.york.ac.uk/puml/.
[SC] B. Schnier, Attack trees, modeling security threats, Dr Dobb's Journal, December 1999.
[TC] Trusted Logic, Computer Assisted Testing: The TL-CAT white paper, http://www.trusted-logic.fr.
[TF] Trusted Logic, From informal to formal development methods: The TL-FIT white paper, http://www.trusted-logic.fr.
[VA] L. Van Aertryck, M. Benveniste, D. Le Métayer, Casting: a formally based software test generation method, IEEE int. Conference on formal engineering methods, pp. 101-111, 1997.

A Dynamic Logic for the Formal Verification of Java Card Programs

Bernhard Beckert

Universität Karlsruhe
Institut für Logik, Komplexität und Deduktionssysteme
D-76128 Karlsruhe, Germany
i12www.ira.uka.de/~beckert

Abstract. In this paper, we define a program logic (an instance of Dynamic Logic) for formalising properties of JAVA CARD programs, and we give a sequent calculus for formally verifying such properties. The purpose of this work is to provide a framework for software verification that can be integrated into real-world software development processes.

1 Introduction

Motivation. The work that is reported in this paper has been carried out as part of the KeY project [1]. The goal of KeY is to enhance a commercial CASE tool with functionality for formal specification and deductive verification and, thus, to integrate formal methods into real-world software development processes. Accordingly, the design principles for the software verification component of the KeY system are:

- The programs that are verified should be written in a "real" object-oriented programming language (we decided to use JAVA CARD).
- The logical formalism should be as easy as possible to use for software developers (that do not have years of training in formal methods).

The ultimate goal of the KeY project is to facilitate and promote the use of formal verification as an integral part of the development process of JAVA CARD applications in an industrial context.

In this paper, after giving an overview of the KeY project in Section 2, we present a Dynamic Logic (a program logic that can be seen as an extension of Hoare logic) for JAVA CARD. It allows to express properties of JAVA CARD programs. The syntax of this logic is described in Section 3 and its semantics in Section 4. In Section 5, we present a calculus for this program logic that allows to reason about the properties of JAVA CARD programs and verify them. The main ideas and principles of the calculus are described and its most important rules are presented (due to space restrictions, we cannot list all the rules in this paper). In Section 6, we give an example for the verification of a small JAVA CARD program. As part of the KeY project we currently implement an interactive theorem prover for our calculus; this and other future work is described in Section 7, where we also compare our work with other approaches to the verification of JAVA CARD programs.

I. Attali and T. Jensen (Eds.): Java Card 2000, LNCS 2041, pp. 6–24, 2001.

Java Card. Since JAVA CARD is a "real" object-oriented language, it has features that are difficult to handle in a software verification system, such as dynamic data structures, exceptions, object initialisation, and dynamic binding. On the other hand, JAVA CARD lacks some crucial complications of the full JAVA language such as threads and dynamic loading of classes. JAVA smart cards are an extremely suitable application for software verification:

- JAVA CARD applications are small;
- at the same time, they are embedded into larger program systems or business processes which should be modeled (though not necessarily formally verified);
- JAVA CARD applications are often security-critical, giving incentive to apply formal methods;
- the high number of deployed smart cards constitutes a new motivation for formal verification, as arbitrary updates are not feasible.

Dynamic Logic. We use an instance of Dynamic Logic (DL) [14]—which can be seen as an extension of Hoare logic [3]—as the logical basis of the KeY system's software verification component. Deduction in DL is based on symbolic program execution and simple program transformations and is, thus, close to a programmer's understanding of JAVA CARD. DL is used in the software verification systems KIV [20] and VSE [12] (for a programming language that is not object-oriented). It has successfully been applied in practice to verify software systems of considerable size.

DL can be seen as a modal predicate logic with a modality $\langle p \rangle$ for every program p (we allow p to be any sequence of legal JAVA CARD statements); $\langle p \rangle$ refers to the successor worlds (called states in the DL framework) that are reachable by running the program p. In standard DL there can be several such states (worlds) because the programs can be non-deterministic; but here, since JAVA CARD programs are deterministic, there is exactly one such world (if p terminates) or there is no such world (if p does not terminate). The formula $\langle p \rangle \phi$ expresses that the program p terminates in a state in which ϕ holds. A formula $\phi \rightarrow \langle p \rangle \psi$ is valid if for every state s satisfying pre-condition ϕ a run of the program p starting in s terminates, and in the terminating state the post-condition ψ holds.

Thus, the formula $\phi \rightarrow \langle p \rangle \psi$ is similar to the Hoare triple $\{\phi\} p \{\psi\}$. But in contrast to Hoare logic, the set of formulas of DL is closed under the usual logical operators: In Hoare logic, the formulas ϕ and ψ are pure first-order formulas, whereas in DL they can contain programs. DL allows to involve programs in the descriptions ϕ resp. ψ of states. For example, using a program, it is easy to specify that a data structure is not cyclic, which is impossible in pure first-order logic. Also, all JAVA constructs are available in DL for the description of states (including while loops and recursion). It is, therefore, not necessary to define an abstract data type *state* and to represent states as terms of that type; instead DL formulas can be used to give a (partial) description of states, which is a more flexible technique and allows to concentrate on the relevant properties of a state.

In comparison to classical versions of DL that use a simple "artificial" programming languages, a DL for a "real" object-oriented programming language like JAVA CARD has to cope with the following complications:

- A program state does not only depend on the value of (local) program variables but also on the values of the attributes of all existing objects.
- The evaluation of a JAVA expression may have side effects; thus, there is a difference between an expression and a logical term.
- Language features such as built-in data types, exceptions, object initialisation, and dynamic binding have to be handled.

2   The KₑY Project[1]

While formal methods are by now well established in hardware and system design, usage of formal methods in software development is still (and in spite of exceptions [7,8]) more or less confined to academic research. This is true though case studies clearly demonstrate that computer-aided specification and verification of realistic software is feasible [10].

The future challenge for formal methods is to make their considerable potential feasible to use in an industrial environment. This leads to the requirements:

1. Tools for formal software specification and verification must be integrated into industrial software engineering procedures.
2. User interfaces of these tools must comply with state-of-the-art software engineering tools.
3. The necessary amount of training in formal methods must be minimised.

To be sure, the thought that full formal software verification might be possible without any background in formal methods is utopian. An industrial verification tool should, however, allow for *gradual* verification so that software engineers at any (including low) experience level with formal methods may benefit. In addition, an integrated tool with well-defined interfaces facilitates "outsourcing" those parts of the modeling process that require special skills.

Another important motivation to integrate design, development, and verification of software is provided by modern software development methodologies which are *iterative* and *incremental*. *Post mortem* verification would enforce the antiquated waterfall model.

The KeY project [1]) addresses the goals outlined above. In the principal use case of the KeY system there are actors who want to implement a software system that complies with given requirements and formally verify its correctness (typically a smart card application). In this scenario, the KeY system is responsible for adding formal detail to the analysis model, for creating conditions that ensure the correctness of refinement steps (called proof obligations), for finding proofs showing that these conditions are satisfied by the model, and for generating counter examples if they are not. Special features of KeY are:

---

[1] More information on the KeY project can be found at i12www.ira.uka.de/~key.

- We concentrate on object-oriented analysis and design methods (OOAD)—because of their key role in today's software development practice—, and on JAVA CARD as the target language. In particular, we use the Unified Modeling Language (UML) [18] for visual modeling of designs and specifications and the Object Constraint Language (OCL) for adding further restrictions. This choice is supported by the fact, that the UML (which contains OCL) is not only an OMG standard, but has been adopted by all major OOAD software vendors and is featured in recent OOAD textbooks [15].
- We use a commercial CASE tool as starting point and enhance it by additional functionality for formal specification and verification. The tool of our choice is TogetherSoft LLC's TOGETHERJ.
- Formal verification is based on a Dynamic Logic for JAVA CARD.
- As a case study to evaluate the usability of our approach we develop a scenario using smart cards with JAVA CARD as programming language.
- Through direct contacts with software companies we check the soundness of our approach for real world applications (some of the experiences from these contacts are reported in [4]).

A first KeY system prototype has been implemented, integrating the CASE tool TOGETHERJ and a deductive component. Work on the full KeY system is under progress. Although consisting of different components, the KeY system is going to be fully integrated with a uniform user interface.

3 Syntax of Java Card DL

As said above, a dynamic logic is constructed by extending some non-dynamic logic with modal operators of the form $\langle p \rangle$. The non-dynamic base logic of our DL is a typed first-order predicate logic. To define its syntax, we specify its types and the variable sets and signatures from which terms are built (which we often call "logical terms" in the following to emphasise that they are different from JAVA expressions). Then, we define which programs p are allowed in the operators $\langle p \rangle$, i.e., in the program parts of DL formulas. Finally, the syntax of DL formulas and sequents is defined.

Program Contexts. In order to reduce the complexity of the programs occurring in DL formulas, we introduce the notion of a *program context*. The context can consist of any legal JAVA CARD program, i.e., it is a sequence of class and interface definitions. Syntax and semantics of DL formulas is then defined with respect to a given context; and the programs in DL formulas are assumed to not contain class definitions.

A context must not contain any constructs that according to the JAVA language specification lead to a compile-time error or that are not available in JAVA CARD. An additional restriction is that a program context must not contain *inner classes* (this restriction is "harmless" because inner classes can be removed with a structure-preserving program transformation and are rarely used in JAVA CARD anyway).

Types. Given a program context, the set $\mathcal{T}$ of types contains:

- the primitive types of JAVA CARD (`boolean`, `byte`, `short`),
- the built-in classes `Object` and `String`,
- the classes defined in the program context,[2]
- an array type $T[\,]$ for each primitive type, each array type T, and each class,
- the type *Null*,
- abstract types.

Abstract types are not defined in the program context but are given separately. They can be declared to be generated by certain function symbols (called constructors), in which case they can be used for induction proofs (see Section 5). For example, a type *nat* may be declared to be generated by 0 and *succ*; and an abstract (data) type *list* may be declared to be generated by *cons* and *nil*. Axioms may be provided to specify the properties of abstract types. Since abstract types are not defined as JAVA classes, they can only be used in the non-program parts of a DL formula and not in programs (in particular not in the program context). Nevertheless, they can be used in DL formulas to describe the behaviour of programs (in particular they can be used as abstractions of object structures).

Note that there are three kinds of types in our DL: Built-in JAVA CARD types, types defined in the program context (classes), and abstract types defined separately from the program context. The classes, the array types, and *Null* are called *object types*.[3]

We assume that the methods and fields shown in Table 1 are implicitly defined for each class and each array type and can thus be used in DL formulas (but not in the program context). Note that they are not actually implemented, but only provide additional expressiveness for the logic. They allow to access information about the program state that is otherwise inaccessible in JAVA: a list of all existing objects of a class or array type and information on whether objects and classes are initialised (`classInitialised` is only available for classes and not for array types). The objects of a certain type are considered to be organised into an (infinite) ordered list; this list is used by `new` to "create" objects (intuitively, `new` changes the attributes `lastCreatedObj` of the class and sets the attribute `created` of the new object to `true`, see Section 5).

The sub-type relation $\preceq$ is transitive and reflexive. If C_1 is defined to be a sub-class of C_2 in the program context, then $C_1 \preceq C_2$ and $C_1[\,] \preceq C_2[\,]$. *Null* is a sub-type of all object types.

Variables. In classical versions of DL there is only one type of variables. Here however, to avoid confusion, we use two kinds of variables, namely *program variables* and *logical variables*.

Program variables are denoted with x, y, z, ... Their value can differ from state to state and can be changed by programs. They occur in programs as

---

[2] Interfaces defined in the context are not types of the logic.

[3] In JAVA, arrays are considered to be objects.

```
public static Cls firstObj;    // the first object in the list,
                               // whether already created or not
public static Cls lastCreatedObj;   // the last created object,
                                    // null if no object exists
public Cls prevObj;    // the previous object in the list,
                       // null for the first object
public Cls nextObj;    // the next object in the list
public boolean beforeObj(Cls obj);   // returns true if this
                                     // is before obj in the list
public boolean created;    // true if the object has already been
                           // created with new, and false otherwise
public static boolean classInitialised;    // true if the class resp.
public boolean objInitialised;             // the object is initialised
```

Table 1. Methods and fields that are implicitly defined for each class Cls.

local variables.[4] Program variables can also be used in the non-program parts of DL formulas (there they behave like modal constants, i.e., constants whose value can differ from state to state). They cannot be quantified. We assume the set of program variables to contain an infinite number of variables of each primitive type and each object type. In particular, it contains the special variable **this** of type **Object**.

Logical variables are denoted with x, y, z, ... They are assigned the same values in all states; a statement such as "$x = 1$;", which tries to change the value of the logical variable x, is illegal. Free occurrences of logical variables are implicitly universally quantified. The set of logical variables contains an infinite number of variables of each type.

Terms. Logical terms are constructed from program variables, logical variables, and the constant and function symbols of all types (observing the usual typing restrictions). The set of logical terms includes in particular all JAVA CARD literals for the primitive types, string literals, and the null object reference literal (which is of type *Null*).

In addition, (a) if o is a term of class type C (i.e., denotes an object) and a is a field (attribute) of class C, then $o.a$ is a term. (b) If $Class$ is a class name and a is a static field of $Class$, then $Class.a$ is a term. (c) If a is an array type term and i is a term of type byte, then $a[i]$ is a term.

Example 1. Assume class C has an attribute a of type C and an attribute i of type byte, and o is a variable of type C. Then o, o.a, o.a.a, etc. are terms of type C; and o.i, o.a.i etc. are terms of type byte. Also, 1+2 and o.i+1 are terms of type byte. The JAVA expression o.i++, however, is not a logical term

---

[4] In the JAVA language specification, certain more complex expressions such as x.a are called *variables* as well. According to our definitions, however, x.a is not a variable but a (complex) term.

because ++ is not a function symbol (it is an operator with side effects). The expression o.i==1 is a logical term of type boolean.

Programs. Basically, the programs in DL formulas are executable JAVA CARD code; as said above, they must not contain class definitions but can only use classes that are defined in the program context. There are two additions that are not available in pure JAVA CARD: Programs can contain a special construct for method invocation (see below), and they can contain logical terms. These extensions are not used in the input formulas, i.e., we prove properties of pure JAVA CARD programs. Extended programs only occur within proofs; they result from rule applications.

The basic, non-extended programs either are a legal JAVA CARD statement or a (finite) sequence of such statements:

- expression statements such as "x = 1;" (assignments), "m(1);" (method calls), "i++;", "new Cls;", local variable declarations (which restrict the "visibility" of program variables)—expressions with inner classes are *not* allowed;
- blocks and compound statements built with if-else, switch, for, while, and do-while;
- statements with exception handling using try-catch-finally;
- statements that abruptly redirect the control flow (throw, return, break, continue);
- labelled statements;
- the empty statement.

A basic program must not contain anything that would lead to a compile-time error (according to the JAVA language specification) if it were used as, for example, a method's implementation. The only exception to that rule is that program variables may be used as local variables in a program without being declared.

Example 2. The statement i=0; may be used as a program in a DL formula although i is not declared as a local variable.

The statement break 1; is not a legal program because such a statement is only allowed to occur inside a block labelled with 1. Accordingly, 1:{break 1;} is a legal program and can be used in a DL formula.

The purpose of our first extension of pure JAVA CARD is the handling of method calls. Methods are invoked by syntactically replacing the call by the method's implementation. To handle the return statement in the right way, it is necessary to record the program variable or object field that the result is to be assigned to and to mark the boundaries of the implementation when it is substituted for the method call. For that purpose, we allow statements of the form call(x){$prog$} resp. call{$prog$} to occur in DL programs, where $prog$ is considered to be the implementation of a method and x is the variable or object field that the return value of $prog$ is to be assigned to (if (x) is omitted, $prog$ must not return a value).

The second extension is that we allow programs in DL formulas (not in the program context) to contain logical terms. A JAVA expression of type T can be replaced by a logical term of type T. However, since the value of logical terms cannot and must not be changed by a program, a logical term can only be used in positions where a final local variable could be used according to the JAVA language specification (the value of local variables that are declared final cannot be changed either). In particular, logical terms cannot be used as the left hand side of an assignment.

Note that, according to our definitions, both program variables and logical variables can occur in the program parts as well as the non-program parts of a DL formula. Nevertheless, there is a difference between the two kinds of variables, as the following example demonstrates.

Example 3. If x is a program variable and y is a logical variable, then the formula $(\forall y)(\langle x=y \rangle x \doteq y)$ is syntactically correct. However, $(\forall y)(\langle y=x \rangle x \doteq y)$ is not a formula because logical variables must not be used as the left side of an assignment. And $(\forall x)(\langle x=y \rangle x \doteq y)$ is a not a formula because program variables cannot be quantified.

Formulas. Atomic formulas are built as usual from the (logical) terms and the predicate symbols of all the types, including the following special predicates:

- the equality predicate $\doteq$,
- the (unary) definedness predicate *isdef* (which, for example, is false for $x.a$ if the value of x is *null*),
- the (binary) predicate *instanceof*.

Complex formulas are constructed from the atomic formulas using the logical connectives $\neg$, $\wedge$, $\vee$, $\rightarrow$, the quantifiers $\forall$ and $\exists$ (that can be applied to logical variables but not to program variables), and the modal operator $\langle p \rangle$, i.e., if p is a program and ϕ is a formula, then $\langle p \rangle \phi$ is a formula as well.

Updates. One of the main problems of designing a program logic for JAVA CARD (or any other object-oriented language) is *aliasing*. That is, different object type variables o_1 and o_2 can be aliases for the same object, such that changing an attribute of o_1 changes the same attribute of o_2 as well. A considerable amount of literature has been published on this problem (see e.g. [6] for an overview), which is comparable to the problem of array handling. In the same way, as $o_1.a$ and $o_2.a$ are the same if o_1 and o_2 have the same object as their value and a is an attribute, $a[i_1]$ and $a[i_2]$ are the same if the byte variables i_1 and i_2 have the same value and a is the name of an array.

To handle aliasing in our calculus, we need a way of syntactically denoting what the value of $o_1.a$ (resp. $a[i_1]$) is in a state where the value $o_2.a$ (resp. $a[i_2]$) has been changed; the representation should be independent of whether o_1 and o_2 (resp. i_1 and i_2) have the same value or not. For that purpose, we allow *updates* of the form $v \leftarrow e$ to be attached as superscripts to terms, formulas, attributes, and array variables; v is either a local variable or of the form $o.a$, and e is a logical term of compatible type. Thus, if U is an update and t and ϕ are a term resp. a formula, then t^U and ϕ^U are a term resp. a formula as well. Moreover, $o.a^U$ is a term if $o.a$ is a term, and $a^U[i]$ is a term if $a[i]$ is a term.

The intuitive meaning of an update is that the term or formula that it is attached to is to be evaluated after changing the state accordingly, i.e., $\phi^{x \leftarrow e}$ has the same semantics as $\langle x = e \rangle \phi$ but is easier to handle because the evaluation of e is known to have no side effects. Note, that the terms $o.a^U$ and $(o.a)^U$ may have different values because in the former term the update does not apply to o (which is evaluated in the non-updated state) whereas in the latter term the update applies to o as well.

Rules for simplifying terms and formulas with attached updates are described in Section 5.

Example 4. The formula $(\langle i = j; \rangle (i \doteq j))^{i \leftarrow 1}$ is valid, i.e., true in all states. The formula $\langle i = j; \rangle ((i \doteq j)^{i \leftarrow 1})$ is only valid in states where the value of j is 1.

Sequents. A sequent is of the form $\phi_1, \ldots, \phi_m \vdash \psi_1, \ldots, \psi_n$ $(m, n \geq 0)$, where the ϕ_i and ψ_j are DL formulas. The intuitive meaning of a sequent is that the conjunction of the ϕ_i's implies the disjunction of the ψ_j's.

4   Semantics of Java Card DL

In the definition of the semantics of JAVA CARD DL, we use the semantics of the JAVA CARD programming language. The language specification [9], though written in English and not in a formal language, is very precise. In case of doubt, we refer to the precise semantics of JAVA (and, thus, of the subset JAVA CARD) defined by Börger and Schulte [5] using Abstract State Machines.[5]

The models of DL are Kripke structures consisting of possible worlds that are called states. All states of a model share the same universe containing a sufficient number of elements of each type. In particular, they contain infinitely many objects of all classes and all array types and the special value *null*, which is the only element of type *Null*.

The function and predicate symbols that are not user-defined—such as the equality predicate and the function symbols of the primitive JAVA CARD types— have a fixed interpretation. In all models they are interpreted according to their intended semantics resp. their meaning in the JAVA CARD language.

Logical variables are interpreted using a (global) variable assignment; they have the same value in all states of a model.

---

[5] Following another approach, Nipkow and von Oheimb have obtained a precise semantics of a JAVA sublanguage by embedding it into Isabelle/HOL; they also use an axiomatic semantics [16].

States. In each state a (possibly different) value (an element of the universe) of the appropriate type is assigned to:

- the program variables (including this),
- the attributes (fields) of all objects (including arrays),
- the class attributes (static fields) of all types,

Variables and attributes of type T can be assigned a value of type T' if $T' \preceq T$. In particular, variables and attributes of any object type can be assigned the value *null*, because *Null* is a sub-type of all object types.

Note, that states do not contain any information on control flow such as a program counter or the fact that an exception has been thrown.

Programs and Formulas. The semantics of a program p is a state transition, i.e., it assigns to each state s the set of all states that can be reached by running p starting in s. Since JAVA CARD is deterministic, that set either contains exactly one state (in case p terminates) or is empty (in case p does not terminate). The set of states of a model must be closed under the reachability relation for all programs p, i.e., all states that are reachable must exist in a model (other models are not considered).

The semantics of a logical term t occurring in a program is the same as that of a JAVA expression whose evaluation is free of side-effects and gives the same value as t.

For formulas ϕ that do not contain programs, the notion of ϕ being satisfied by a state is defined as usual in first-order logic. A formula $\langle p \rangle \phi$ is satisfied by a state s if the program p, when started in s, terminates normally in a state s' in which ϕ is satisfied.[6] A formula is satisfied by a model M, if it is satisfied by one of the states of M. A formula is valid in a model M if it is satisfied by all states of M; and a formula is valid if it is valid in all models.

We consider programs that terminate abruptly to be non-terminating. Examples are a program that throws an uncaught exception and a **return** statement that is not within the boundaries of a method invocation. Thus, for example, $\langle \text{throw } \mathtt{x}; \rangle \phi$ is unsatisfiable for all ϕ. Nevertheless, it is possible to express and (if true) prove the fact that a program p terminates abruptly. For example, the formula

$$\mathtt{e} \doteq \mathtt{null} \ \rightarrow \ \langle \mathtt{try}\{p\}\mathtt{catch}\{\mathtt{Exception\ e}\}\rangle(\neg\, \mathtt{e} \doteq \mathtt{null}) \ ,$$

is true in a state s if and only if the program p, when started in s, terminates abruptly by throwing an exception.

---

[6] According to the JAVA language specification, a program either terminates normally or terminates abruptly (or does not terminate at all). It terminates abruptly if the reason for termination is an uncaught exception, or the execution of a **break**, **continue**, or **return** statement.

Sequents. The semantics of a sequent $\phi_1, \ldots, \psi_m \vdash \psi_1, \ldots, \psi_n$ is the same as that of the formula $(\forall x_1) \cdots (\forall x_k)((\phi_1 \wedge \ldots \wedge \psi_m) \to (\psi_1 \vee \ldots \vee \psi_n))$, where $x_1, \ldots, x_k$ are the free variables of the sequent.

5   A Sequent Calculus for Java Card DL

In this section, we outline the ideas behind our calculus for JAVA CARD DL, and we present some of the basic rules. As JAVA CARD has many features and programming constructs, many rules are required. Due to space restrictions, we only present one or two typical representatives from each class of rules. No rules are shown for method invocations,[7] local variable declarations, and type conversions; and the rules for the classical logical operators (including the cut rule) and for handling equality and the predicates *isdef* and *instanceof* are omitted as well. Moreover, we present simplified versions of our rules that do not consider initialisation of objects and classes.[8]

All the rules shown in this section, except the induction rules, handle certain constructs of the JAVA CARD language. It is easy to see, that these rules basically perform a symbolic program execution.

The semantics of sequent rules is that, if all sequences above the line (the premisses of the rule) are valid, then the sequence below the line (the conclusion) is valid as well. The rules are applied from bottom to top. That is, the proof search starts with the original proof obligation at the bottom.

Notation. In the definition of the calculus, we assume that the programs are parsed, i.e., they are not given as a string but their syntax tree is available. Thus, the calculus needs not to know about operator priorities etc., and we can use notions like "immediate sub-expression" in the definition of our rules.

Many formulas in the rules are of the form $(\langle p \rangle \phi)^U$, where U is a sequence of state updates. Note, that the parentheses cannot be omitted, as the program p is to be executed in the updated state.

The rules of our calculus operate on the first *active* command p of a program $\pi p \omega$. The non-active prefix π consists of an arbitrary sequence of opening braces "{", labels, beginnings "try{" of try-catch blocks, and beginnings "call(...){" of method invocation blocks. The prefix is needed to keep track of the blocks that the (first) active command is part of, such that the commands **throw**, **return**, **break**, and **continue** that abruptly change the control flow can

---

[7] Method invocation is handled by syntactically replacing the method call by the implementation of the method. In case of dynamic binding, where the implementation that is to be used depends on the actual type that the value of an object variable has in the current state, method invocation leads to a case distinction in the proof, i.e., the proof tree branches.

[8] The complete rule set of our calculus for JAVA CARD DL can be found in a technical report that—at the date of submission of this paper—is in the process of being published. It will be publicly available before TACAS 2001; and I am happy to provide a draft of the report for the referees if they wish to have it.

be handled appropriatly.[9] The postfix ω denotes the "rest" of the program, i.e., everything except the non-active prefix and the part of the program that the rule operates on. For example, if a rule is applied to the following JAVA block operating on its first active command i=0;, then the non-active prefix π and the "rest" ω are the marked parts of the block:

$$\underbrace{\text{l:\{try\{}}_{\pi} \text{ i=0; } \underbrace{\text{j=0; \}finally\{ k=0; \}\}}}_{\omega}$$

Rules for Assignment and Expression Evaluation. Since assignments are the basic state changing statements of JAVA, the rule for assignments is one of the basic and most important rules of the calculus:[10]

$$\frac{\Gamma \vdash \mathit{isdef}(o.a^{U}) \quad \Gamma \vdash \mathit{isdef}(expr^{U}) \quad \Gamma \vdash (((\langle \pi\ \omega \rangle \phi)^{o.a \leftarrow expr})^{U}}{\Gamma \vdash (\langle \pi\ o.a\ =\ expr;\ \omega \rangle \phi)^{U}} \quad \text{(R1)}$$

Rule (R1) is not always applicable; it can only be used if the expression $expr$ is a logical term. Otherwise, other rules have to be applied first to evaluate $expr$ (as that evaluation may have side effects). An example is the following rule for evaluating expressions with the ++ prefix operator:

$$\frac{\Gamma \vdash \mathit{isdef}(v^{U}) \quad \Gamma \vdash (\langle \pi\ e=e+1;\ v=e;\ \omega \rangle \phi)^{U}}{\Gamma \vdash (\langle \pi\ v\ =\ ++e;\ \omega \rangle \phi)^{U}} \quad \text{(R2)}$$

where v and e are logical terms.

There are also rules for decomposing complex expressions that are not a logical term and whose evaluation, thus, potentially has side effects. An example is the following rule:

$$\frac{\Gamma \vdash \mathit{isdef}(v^{U}) \quad \Gamma \vdash (\langle \pi\ x_1=e_1;\ x_2=e_2;\ v=x_1+x_2;\ \omega \rangle \phi)^{U}}{\Gamma \vdash (\langle \pi\ v\ =\ e_1+e_2;\ \omega \rangle \phi)^{U}} \quad \text{(R3)}$$

where v is a logical term, and x_1 and x_2 are new local variables. This rule has to be applied in case the expression e_1+e_2 is not a term; for example, the expression (++i) + (++i) has to be decomposed because the evaluation of its sub-expressions changes the state.

The premisses of the form $\Gamma \vdash \mathit{isdef}(v)$ in the above rules ensure that the expression v is defined in the state, i.e., its evaluation does not lead to a null pointer exception being thrown. That, for example, happens if $v = o.a$ and the value of o is *null*. Other rules are available for handling this particular situation.

---

[9] In DL versions for 'simple artificial programming languages, where no prefixes are needed, any formula of the form $\langle p\ q \rangle \phi$ can be replaced by $\langle p \rangle \langle q \rangle \phi$. In our calculus, splitting of $\langle \pi p q \omega \rangle \phi$ into $\langle \pi p \rangle \langle q \omega \rangle \phi$ is not possible (unless the prefix π is empty) because πp is not a valid program; and the formula $\langle \pi p \omega \rangle \langle \pi q \omega \rangle \phi$ cannot be used either because its semantics is in general different from that of $\langle \pi p q \omega \rangle \phi$.

[10] A similar rule is defined for the case where the left side of the assignment is a local variable.

Rules for Update Simplification. In many cases, formulas and terms with an update can be simplified. For example, if x is a local variable, the term $x^{v \leftarrow e}$ can be replaced by x in case $x \neq v$ and by e in case $x = v$. Another rule allows to replace a term of the form $(f(o))^{v \leftarrow e}$ by $f(o^{v \leftarrow e})$ if the function f does not depend on the state.

When no further simplification of a formula $\phi(o' . a^{o . a \leftarrow e})$ is possible, because the terms o and o' may be aliases for the same object, the following branching rule has to be applied:

$$\frac{\Gamma, o \doteq o' \vdash \phi(e) \qquad \Gamma, \neg(o \doteq o') \vdash \phi(o' . a)}{\Gamma \vdash \phi(o' . a^{o . a \leftarrow e})} \qquad \text{(R4)}$$

where o and o' are terms of the same object type and a is an instance attribute, i.e., it is not declared `static`.

Rules for Creating Objects. The `new` statement is treated by the calculus as if it were a method implemented as follows (this implementation accesses the fields that are implicitly defined for all classes and array types, see the explanation in Section 3):

```
public static Cls new() {
   if (lastCreatedObj == null)
      lastCreatedObj = firstObj;
   else
      lastCreatedObj = lastCreatedObj.nextObj;
   lastCreatedObj.created = true;
   return lastCreatedObj;
}
```

Note, that this is a simplified version where object initialisation is not considered.

Rules for Loops. The following rule "unwinds" `while` loops. Its application is the prerequisite for symbolically executing the loop body. Similar rules are defined for `for` and `do-while` loops. These "unwind" rules allow to handle `while` loops if used together with induction schemata for the primitive and the user defined types (see below). Section 6 contains an example for the verification of a `while` loop.

$$\frac{\Gamma \vdash (\langle \pi \ l':\{\texttt{if}(c)\ l'':\{p'\} \ l:\texttt{while}(c)\{p\}\} \ \omega\rangle\phi)^{U}}{\Gamma \vdash (\langle \pi \ l:\texttt{while}(c)\{p\} \ \omega\rangle\phi)^{U}} \qquad \text{(R5)}$$

where l' and l'' are new labels, and p' is the result of (simultaneously) replacing in p (a) every `break` (with no label) that has the `while` loop as its target by `break` l', and (b) every `continue` (with no label) that has the `while` loop as its target by `break` l''.[11]

---

[11] The target of a `break` or `continue` statement with no label is the loop that immediately encloses it.

In the "unwound" instance p' of the loop body p, the new label l' is the new target for **break** statements and l'' is the new target for **continue** statements. This results in the desired behaviour: **break** abruptly terminates the whole loop, while **continue** abruptly terminates the current instance of the loop body.

Rule R5 only applies to unlabelled **while** loops, i.e., in case π is not of the form $\pi'\, l\, :$; another rule is defined for labelled **while** loops.

From the general **while** rule (R5), the following simpler rules can be derived. The two rules are applicable if (a) the loop condition is a logical term c (and, thus, its evaluation does not have side effects), and (b) the loop body p does not contain any **break** or **continue** statements.

$$\frac{\Gamma \vdash isdef(c^U) \qquad \Gamma \vdash c^U \doteq \mathbf{true} \qquad \Gamma \vdash (\langle \pi\ p\ \mathbf{while}\,(c)\ p\ \omega\rangle\phi)^U}{\Gamma \vdash (\langle \pi\ \mathbf{while}\,(c)\ p\ \omega\rangle\phi)^U} \quad \text{(R6)}$$

$$\frac{\Gamma \vdash isdef(c^U) \qquad \Gamma \vdash c^U \doteq \mathbf{false} \qquad \Gamma \vdash (\langle \pi\ \omega\rangle\phi)^U}{\Gamma \vdash (\langle \pi\ \mathbf{while}\,(c)\ p\ \omega\rangle\phi)^U} \quad \text{(R7)}$$

Induction Rules. Induction schemata are available for the primitive type **byte** and all abstract types that are declared to be generated by constructors. The following rules are the induction schemata for **byte** and for an abstract type *list* generated by *cons* and *nil*:

$$\frac{\Gamma \vdash \psi(0) \qquad \Gamma \vdash (\forall x : \mathbf{byte})(\psi(x) \to \psi(x+1))}{\Gamma \vdash (\forall x : \mathbf{byte})\psi(x)} \quad \text{(R8)}$$

$$\frac{\Gamma \vdash \psi(nil) \qquad \Gamma \vdash (\forall l : list)(\forall o : \mathbf{Object})(\psi(l) \to \psi(cons(o,l)))}{\Gamma \vdash (\forall l : list)\psi(l)} \quad \text{(R9)}$$

Rules for Conditionals. Two rules are available for handling **if-then-else** statements: One rule for the case where the condition evaluates to true and one for the case where the condition evaluates to false:

$$\frac{\Gamma \vdash isdef(c^U) \qquad \Gamma \vdash c^U \doteq \mathbf{true} \qquad \Gamma \vdash (\langle \pi\ p\ \omega\rangle\phi)^U}{\Gamma \vdash (\langle \pi\ \mathbf{if}(c)\ p\ \mathbf{else}\ q\ \omega\rangle\phi)^U} \quad \text{(R10)}$$

$$\frac{\Gamma \vdash isdef(c^U) \qquad \Gamma \vdash c^U \doteq \mathbf{false} \qquad \Gamma \vdash (\langle \pi\ q\ \omega\rangle\phi)^U}{\Gamma \vdash (\langle \pi\ \mathbf{if}(c)\ p\ \mathbf{else}\ q\ \omega\rangle\phi)^U} \quad \text{(R11)}$$

These rules are only applicable if the condition c is a logical term. Otherwise, rules for the decomposition and evaluation of c have to be applied first.

Similar rules are defined for **if-then** without **else** and for the **switch** statement.

Rules for Handling Exceptions. The following rules allow to handle **try-catch-finally** blocks and the **throw** statement. These are restricted versions of the actual rules, they apply to the case where there is exactly one `catch` clause and one `finally` clause. And again, these rules are only applicable if both the exception *exc* that is thrown and the variable *e* that it is bound by the `catch` clause are logical terms. If they are more complex expressions, they first have to be decomposed and evaluated by applying other rules.

$$\frac{\Gamma \vdash isdef(exc^U) \qquad \Gamma \vdash instanceof(exc^U, T) \qquad \Gamma \vdash isdef(e^U)}{\Gamma \vdash (\langle \pi \; \texttt{try\{e=exc; } q \texttt{\}finally\{}r\texttt{\} } \omega\rangle\phi)^U} \qquad \text{(R12)}$$

$$\frac{\Gamma \vdash isdef(exc^U) \qquad \Gamma \vdash \neg instanceof(exc^U, T)}{\Gamma \vdash (\langle \pi \; r\texttt{; throw } exc\texttt{; } \omega\rangle\phi)^U}}{\Gamma \vdash (\langle \pi \; \texttt{try\{throw } exc\texttt{; } p\texttt{\}catch(}T\;e\texttt{)\{}q\texttt{\}finally\{}r\texttt{\} } \omega\rangle\phi)^U} \qquad \text{(R13)}$$

$$\frac{\Gamma \vdash (\langle \pi \; r \; \omega\rangle\phi)^U}{\Gamma \vdash (\langle \pi \; \texttt{try\{\}catch(}T\;e\texttt{)\{}q\texttt{\}finally\{}r\texttt{\} } \omega\rangle\phi)^U} \qquad \text{(R14)}$$

Rule (R12) applies if an exception *exc* is thrown that is an instance of exception class *T*, i.e., the exception is caught; otherwise, if the exception is not caught, rule (R13) applies. Rule (R14) applies if the `try` block is empty and, thus, terminates normally.

Rules for the `break` Statement. The following rule handles `break` statements:

$$\frac{\Gamma \vdash (\langle \pi \; \omega\rangle\phi)^U}{\Gamma \vdash (\langle \pi\,l\texttt{:\{}\pi' \; \texttt{break } l\texttt{; } \omega'\texttt{\}}\omega\rangle\phi)^U} \qquad \text{(R15)}$$

where $\pi\,l\texttt{:\{}\pi'$ is a non-active prefix and $\{\pi' \; \texttt{break } l\texttt{; } \omega'\}$ is a block, i.e., the two braces in the conclusion of the rule are the opening and the closing brace of the same block.

Note, that according to the JAVA language specification, a label l is not allowed to occur within a block that is itself labelled with l. This ensures that the label l occurs only once in the prefix $\pi\,l\texttt{:\{}\pi'$.

Similar rules are defined for `break` statements without label and for the `continue` statement.

6   Example

As an example, we use the calculus presented in the previous section to prove that, if the while loop

```
while (true) {
  if (i==10) break;
  else i++;
}
```

is started in a state in which the value of the program variable i of type **byte** is between 0 and 10, then it terminates normally in a state in which the value of i is 10. That is, we prove that the sequence

$$0 \leq i \wedge i \leq 10 \vdash \langle p_{\text{while}} \rangle i \doteq 10 \tag{1}$$

is valid, where p_{while} is an abbreviation for the above while loop. Instead of proving (1) directly, we first use the induction rule (R8) to derive the sequence

$$\vdash (\forall n)((0 \leq n \wedge n \leq 10) \rightarrow (\langle p_{\text{while}} \rangle i \doteq 10)^{i \leftarrow 10 - n}) \tag{2}$$

as a lemma (the logical variable n is of type byte). It basically expresses the same as (1), the difference is that its form allows it to be proved by induction on n. The introduction of this lemma is the only step in the proof where an intuition for what the JAVA CARD program p_{while} actually does is needed and where a verification tools would require user interaction.

Due to space restrictions, we only show the proof for the induction base $n = 0$; the proof for the induction step is omitted. The proof obligation for the induction base is

$$\vdash (0 \leq 0 \wedge 0 \leq 10) \rightarrow (\langle p_{\text{while}} \rangle i \doteq 10)^{i \leftarrow 10 - 0}) \tag{3}$$

which simplifies to

$$\vdash (\langle p_{\text{while}} \rangle i \doteq 10)^{i \leftarrow 10}$$

An application of the rule for **while** loops (R5) results in the new proof obligation

$$\vdash (\langle \texttt{l1:\{if (true) l2:\{if (i==10) break l1; else i++;\}}} \\ p_{\text{while}}\rangle i \doteq 10)^{i \leftarrow 10}$$

Now, the rule for conditionals with a condition that evaluates to true (R10) can be applied. This results in three new proof obligations:

$$\vdash \mathit{isdef}(\texttt{true}^{i \leftarrow 10}) \tag{4}$$

$$\vdash \texttt{true}^{i \leftarrow 10} \doteq \texttt{true} \tag{5}$$

$$\vdash (\langle \texttt{l1:\{l2:\{if (i==10) break l1; else i++;\}}} \ p_{\text{while}}\rangle i \doteq 10)^{i \leftarrow 10} \tag{6}$$

Sequences (4) and (5) can easily be shown to be valid. To prove sequence (6), we apply rule (R10) again and derive the proof obligations

$$\vdash \mathit{isdef}((\texttt{i==10})^{i \leftarrow 10}) \tag{7}$$

$$\vdash (\texttt{i==10})^{i \leftarrow 10} \doteq \texttt{true} \tag{8}$$

$$\vdash (\langle \texttt{l1:\{l2:\{break l1; else i++;\}}} \ p_{\text{while}}\rangle i \doteq 10)^{i \leftarrow 10} \tag{9}$$

Sequence (7) can easily be shown to be valid, as well as sequence (8), which can be simplified to $\vdash (\texttt{10==10}) \doteq \texttt{true}$.

To prove (9) to be valid, the rule for **break** statements (R15) has to be applied. The result is $\vdash (i \doteq 10)^{i \leftarrow 10}$. This simplifies to $\vdash 10 \doteq 10$ and can thus be shown to be valid.

After the lemma (2) has been proved by induction, it can be used to prove the original proof obligation (1). First, we use a quantifier rule to instantiate n with $10 - i$. The result is

$$\vdash (0 \leq 10 - i \wedge 10 - i \leq 10) \rightarrow (\langle p_{\text{while}} \rangle i \doteq 10)^{i \leftarrow 10-(10-i)}$$

which can be simplified to

$$\vdash (0 \leq i \wedge i \leq 10) \rightarrow (\langle p_{\text{while}} \rangle i \doteq 10)^{i \leftarrow i} \tag{10}$$

And, since (10) is derivable, the original proof obligation (1) is derivable as well, because the trivial update $i \leftarrow i$ can be omitted.

7   Conclusion

Extensions and Future Work. We are currently implementing an interactive prover for our calculus as part of the KeY project. Such an implementation is a prerequisite for applying the calculus to more complex examples.

Further work is to prove soundness and relative completeness of the calculus w.r.t. a *formal* semantics. And we plan to extend the calculus with the concept of parameters (or meta-variables) that can be instantiated with logical terms "on demand" during the proof using unification. Meta-variables are the most important technique for automated deduction in classical logic, and this promises to make the automated proof search in JAVA CARD DL much more efficient as well.

Related Work. There are many projects dealing with formal methods in software engineering including several ones aimed at JAVA as a target language. Work on the verification of Java programs includes [19,13,11,17,21]. The main difference of all these approaches to our work is that they use a Hoare logic instead of full DL, i.e., formulas and programs remain separated.

In [19], states are represented as terms of an abstract data type, whereas in our approach the states correspond to "worlds" in the models. They are not represented as terms but described with formulas. This allows to use the full expressiveness of DL to formalise the properties of a state.

Another important difference to other approaches is that abrupt termination, in particular exception handling, is either not treated at all or is treated in a completely different way (e.g. [11] where the reason for abrupt termination is made a part of the states, which leads to a more complex notion of states and of method return values).

Acknowledgements. I thank B. Sasse for working out the details of some of the rules of the calculus, and W. Ahrendt, T. Baar, M. Giese, E. Habermalz, R. Hähnle, W. Menzel, and P. H. Schmitt for many fruitful discussions and comments on earlier versions of this paper.

References

1. W. Ahrendt, T. Baar, B. Beckert, M. Giese, E. Habermalz, R. Hähnle, W. Menzel, and P. H. Schmitt. The KeY approach: Integrating object oriented design and formal verification. In M. Ojeda-Aciego, I. P. de Guzman, G. Brewka, and L. M. Pereira, editors, *Proceedings, Logics in Artificial Intelligence (JELIA), Malaga, Spain*, LNCS 1919. Springer, 2000.
2. J. Alves-Foss, editor. *Formal Syntax and Semantics of Java*. LNCS 1523. Springer, 1999.
3. K. R. Apt. Ten years of Hoare logic: A survey – part I. *ACM Transactions on Programming Languages and Systems*, 1981.
4. T. Baar. Experiences with the UML/OCL-approach to precise software modeling: A report from practice. Available at i12www.ira.uka.de/~key, 2000.
5. E. Börger and W. Schulte. A programmer friendly modular definition of the semantics of Java. In Alves-Foss [2], pages 353–404.
6. C. Calcagno, S. Ishtiaq, and P. W. O'Hearn. Semantic analysis of pointer aliasing, allocation and disposal in Hoare logic. In *Proceedings, International Conference on Principles and Practice of Declarative Programming, Montreal, Canada*. ACM, 2000.
7. E. Clarke and J. M. Wing. Formal methods: State of the art and future directions. *ACM Computing Surveys*, 28(4):626–643, 1996.
8. D. L. Dill and J. Rushby. Acceptance of formal methods: Lessons from hardware design. *IEEE Computer*, 29(4):23–24, 1996. Part of: Hossein Saiedian (ed.). *An Invitation to Formal Methods*. Pages 16–30.
9. J. Gosling, B. Joy, G. Steele, and G. Bracha. *The Java Language Specification*. Addison Wesley, second edition, 2000.
10. M. G. Hinchey and J. P. Bowen, editors. *Applications of Formal Methods*. Prentice Hall, 1995.
11. M. Huisman and B. Jacobs. Java program verification via a Hoare logic with abrupt termination. In *Proceedings, Fundamental Approaches to Software Engineering (FASE), Berlin, Germany*, LNCS 1783. Springer, 2000.
12. D. Hutter, B. Langenstein, C. Sengler, J. H. Siekmann, and W. Stephan. Deduction in the Verification Support Environment (VSE). In M.-C. Gaudel and J. Woodcock, editors, *Proceedings, International Symposium of Formal Methods Europe (FME), Oxford, UK*, LNCS 1051. Springer, 1996.
13. B. Jacobs, J. van den Berg, M. Huisman, M. van Berkum, U. Hensel, and H. Tews. Reasoning about Java classes (preliminary report). In *Proceedings, Object-Oriented Programming, Systems, Languages and Applications (OOPSLA)*, pages 329–340. ACM Press, 1998.
14. D. Kozen and J. Tiuryn. Logic of programs. In J. van Leeuwen, editor, *Handbook of Theoretical Computer Science*, volume B: Formal Models and Semantics, chapter 14, pages 789–840. Elsevier, Amsterdam, 1990.
15. J. Martin and J. J. Odell. *Object-Oriented Methods: A Foundation, UML Edition*. Prentice-Hall, 1997.

16. T. Nipkow and D. von Oheimb. Machine-checking the Java specification: Proving type safety. In Alves-Foss [2], pages 119–156.

17. T. Nipkow, D. von Oheimb, and C. Pusch. μJava: Embedding a programming language in a theorem prover. In F. L. Bauer and R. Steinbrüggen, editors, *Foundations of Secure Computation*. IOS Press, 2000. To appear.

18. Object Management Group, Inc., Framingham/MA, USA, www.omg.org. *OMG Unified Modeling Language Specification, Version 1.3*, June 1999.

19. A. Poetzsch-Heffter and P. Müller. A programming logic for sequential Java. In S. D. Swierstra, editor, *Proceedings, Programming Languages and Systems (ESOP), Amsterdam, The Netherlands*, LNCS 1576, pages 162–176. Springer, 1999.

20. W. Reif. The KIV-approach to software verification. In M. Broy and S. Jähnichen, editors, *KORSO: Methods, Languages, and Tools for the Construction of Correct Software – Final Report*, LNCS 1009. Springer, 1995.

21. D. von Oheimb. Axiomatic semantics for Java^{light}. In S. Drossopoulou, S. Eisenbach, B. Jacobs, G. T. Leavens, P. Müller, and A. Poetzsch-Heffter, editors, *Proceedings, Formal Techniques for Java Programs, Workshop at ECOOP'00, Cannes, France*, 2000.

The PACAP Prototype: A Tool for Detecting Java Card Illegal Flow

P. Bieber[1], J. Cazin[1], A. El Marouani[2], P. Girard[2], J.-L. Lanet[2], V. Wiels[1], and G. Zanon[1]

[1]ONERA-CERT/DTIM
BP 4025, 2 avenue E. Belin,
F-31055 Toulouse Cedex 4, France
{bieber,cazin,wiels,zanon}@cert.fr
[2]GEMPLUS
avenue du pic de Bertagne, 13881 Gemenos cedex, France
{abdellah.el-marouani,pierre.girard,jean-louis.lanet}@gemplus.com

Abstract. This paper presents some practical issues of a joint project between Gemplus and ONERA. In this approach, a smart card issuer can verify that a new applet securely interacts with already loaded applets. A security policy has been defined that associates levels to applet attributes and methods and defines authorized flows between levels. We propose a technique based on model checking to verify that actual information flows between applets are authorized. In this paper, we focus on the development of the prototype of the analyzer and we present the first results.

1. Illegal Flow in Multi-applicative Smart Cards

Security is always a big concern for smart cards but it is more important with multi-application smart cards and post issuance code downloading. Opposed to mono-applicative smart cards where Operating System (OS) and application were mixed, multi-application smart cards have drawn a clear border between the OS, the virtual machine and the applicative code. In this context, it is necessary to distinguish the security of the card (hardware, operating system and virtual machine) from the security of the application. The card issuer is responsible for the card security and the application provider is responsible for the applet security, which relies necessarily on the card security. The physical security is obtained by the smart card media and its tamper resistance. The security properties that the OS guarantees are the quality of the cryptographic mechanisms (which should be leakage resistant, *i.e.*, resistant against side channel attacks such as Differential Power Analysis), the correctness of memory and I/O management.

A Java Card virtual machine relies on the type safety of the Java language to guarantee the innocuousness of an applet with respect to the OS, the virtual machine, and other applets. However, this is ensured by an off-card byte-code verifier, and extra mechanisms that have been added. A secure loader checks, before loading, that an applet that it has been signed (and therefore verified) by an authorized entity (namely the card issuer). Figure 1 shows the role of the different participants. The card issuer or a Trusted Third Party (TTP) is responsible in delivering the certificate indicating

I. Attali and T. Jensen (Eds.): Java Card 2000, LNCS 2041, pp. 25–37, 2001.

the correctness of the verified applet. This verification concerns the type correctness and the card issuer security policy correctness [5].

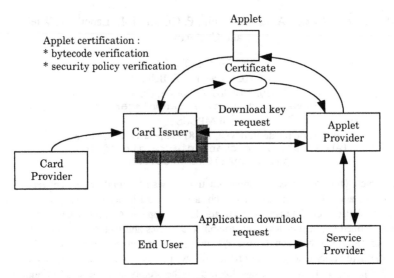

Fig. 1. Certification scheme

Applet providers and end users cannot control that their information flow requirements are enforced inside the card because they do not manage it. Our goal is to provide techniques and tools enabling the card issuer to verify that new applets respect existing security properties defined as authorized information flows. If the applet provider wants to load a new applet on a card, it provides to the card issuer or to the TTP the byte code for this applet. The card issuer has a security policy for the card and security properties that must be satisfied. This security policy should enforce the confidentiality while taking into account data exchange between applets.

Actually, most of multi-application smart cards, in order to build cooperative schemes and to optimize memory usage, allow data and service sharing (*i.e.*, objects sharing) between applications. Beyond this point, there is a need for a card-wide security policy concerning all applications. A small example should clarify this point. When an application provider A decides to share (or more probably to sell) some data with an application provider B, it asks for guarantees that B is not able to resell those data or to make them available world-wide. For example, in Java, if one decides to store the exchanged information in a public static variable, this datum becomes readable by every one. This point is important and difficult to verify using traditional means.

A mandatory security policy is necessary to solve the problem of re-sharing shared objects as mentioned above [4]. The security policy should model the information flows between the applications that, themselves, reflect the trust relationships between the participants of the applicative scheme. The best candidate for such a mandatory policy appears to be a multilevel policy. This security model uses a set of security levels ordered in a complete lattice. With this security model, each applet is assigned a security level and each shared data has a specific security level. This lattice represents all the legal flows. For example, consider that the configuration to be checked includes an Air France loyalty applet (level AF), an Hertz loyalty applet (level H) and an electronic purse (level EP). When buying a flight ticket with the purse, you add miles to your loyalty program. Shared information from Air France and the electronic purse (level EP+AF) may be received by the Air France applet and the electronic purse applet. The same operation can be done when renting an Hertz car. This is represented by the following lattice.

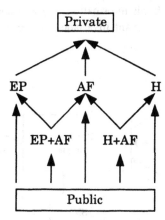

Fig. 2. The security policy lattice

To model that applets may only communicate through shared interfaces, direct flows between AF, H and EP are forbidden.

2. The PACAP Prototype

The PACAP project[1] aims to check the data flows between objects on the card by static analysis prior to applets downloading, for a given configuration. We verify information flows between applets that share data through shareable interfaces. The sharable interface is the means to transfer information from an applet to another one in Java Card. A sharable interface can be called by an applicative command (process APDU) or an external call. In all the interactions, we check if the level associated to all the variables (system and application) does not exceed the allowed sharing level.

Our tool verifies automatically if a set of applications correctly implements a given security policy. An application is composed of a finite number of interacting applets. Each applet contains several methods. For efficiency reasons, we want to limit the

[1] The PACAP project is partially founded by MENRT contract n°98B0252

number of applets and methods analyzed when a new applet is downloaded or when the security policy is modified.

Our method to verify the security property on the application byte code is based on three elements:

- abstraction: we abstract all values of variables by computed levels,
- sufficient condition: we verify an invariant that is a sufficient condition of the security property;
- model checking: we verify this invariant by model checking.

The abstraction mechanism and the invariant definition have been described in [13] and [14]. The tool needs as inputs, a representation of the lattice and the configuration (*i.e.*, the set of applets). With this information the tool transforms the byte code into a formal semantics, adds the relevant invariants and performs the verification of the invariants.

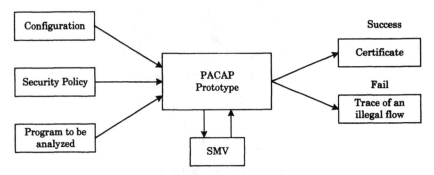

Fig. 3. Architecture of the prototype

The verification is done by an off the shelf model checker: SMV from Cadence Lab. If the verification fails (*i.e.*, an illegal flow has been discovered) a trace is provided in order to extract the proof of the illegal flow. In the case of a successful verification, a certificate can be provided as shown in the previous picture.

The transformation of the program into a formal model is automatic. The tool computes all the call graphs of the application and generates one SMV model per graph. Two kinds of methods interest us because they are the basis of applet interactions: interface methods that can be called from other applets and methods invoking external methods of other applets. We generate only call graphs that include an interface method, either as the root or as a leaf. A call graph that does not include such a method is not relevant here. Furthermore the call graph subset only contains methods that belong to the same applet. For a given program, we consider as inputs results from external invocations and read attributes. We take as outputs parameters of external invocations and modified attributes. We associate security levels with applet attributes and with method invocations between applets.

3. The PACAP Prototype

The first step was to specify the translation rules between the Java byte code and the SMV language. In order to ease the final transformation several treatments must be done on the byte code: for example, subroutine elimination and end of conditional branch computation.

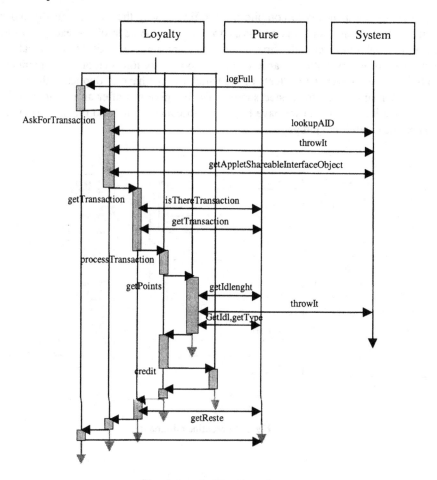

Fig. 4. Logfull call graph

The Call Graph

We build an SMV model for each call graph that includes an access to a method of a shareable interface. The previous figure shows the call graph of the logfull method. The purse calls this method through the Loyalty shareable interface.

The resulting call graph is a tree: for each invokeSpecial and invokeVirtual byte code we need to develop the sub-tree while the invokeStatic and invokeInterface are leaves of the tree.

Subroutine Elimination

Subroutines are a means to compile in an efficient way the Java try-finally blocks. Without this mechanism, it is necessary to duplicate the code of the exception treatment. In a subroutine call, the first action is to store the return address in a local variable. Unfortunately with our abstraction we loose this information. We manipulate only levels and never the contents of the variables. We have to duplicate all the code of the subroutine even for nested subroutines. We give hereafter an example of such an elimination. Of course we have to pay a particular attention to the exception table and all the conditional jumps.

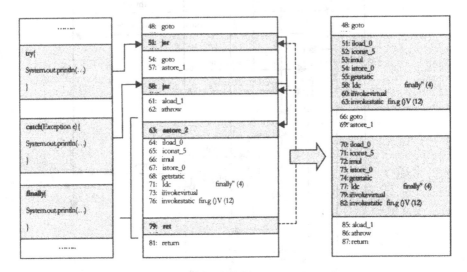

Fig. 5. Subroutine elimination

Implicit Dependency

Dependency can be explicit or implicit. For example, if in a branch statement, one raises systematically an exception, it is possible when catching the exception to infer the value of the conditional. This can be a means to illegally transfer information. For this purpose we have to adjust the level of the state variables to the level of the conditional. When information can be inferred (when both branch join) we have to release the previous level of the state variables. But computing the endif (the join point) can be very difficult. According to [15], it is possible to find structural 2-way conditional and to determine easily the `endif`. A problem arises with unstructured conditionals having abnormal entry or abnormal exit. Abnormal exit occurs when a break or a continue is inserted in one path. In this case we choose a conservative solution by never reducing the level. Of course this can lead to non existing illegal flow detection. When compound conditions (at the Java level) are used this leads to an abnormal entry at the byte code level. In this case, we have to duplicate the code and store the value of the system variables into a stack. For example, in the following Java program it seems obvious that the system variables must be restored before t2. The compound condition (a or not b) is made of two conditionals that are overlapped. It is more difficult at the byte code level to define exactly the end of the compound condition. The solution proposed by [15] uses code duplication and provides only one join point where the system variables have to be restored.

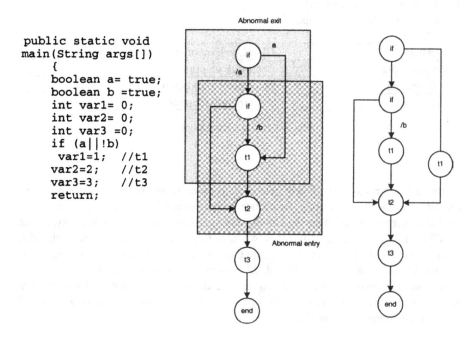

Fig. 6. Compound condition and code duplication

Exception Treatment

The exception mechanism modifies control flow and thus can be a means to illegally transmit information. We have to translate into SMV the possibility that byte code can generate new control paths. Two kinds of exception will not be taken into account here: `OutOfMemoryException` and `StackOverflowError`. For those exceptions, the virtual machine sends back an APDU with an error code and reinitializes the frame. Some byte code can generate one or more exceptions as shown in the following figure.

Byte code Java	Exception
Aaload, baload, bastore, sastore	NullPointerException, SecurityException, ArrayIndexOutofBoundException
Aastore	NullPointerException, ArrayIndexOutofBoundException, ArrayStoreException, SecurityException
Anewarray	NegativeArraySizeException
Arraylength, athrow, getfield-<t>, getfield_<t>_this, getfield_<t>_w, invokeinterface, invokevirtual, putfield_<t>, putfield_<t>_this, putfield_<t>_w	NullPointerException, SecurityException
Checkcast	ClassCastException, SecurityException
Instanceof, putstatic_<t>	SecurityException
Invokespecial	NullPointerException
Sdiv, srem	ArithmeticException

Fig. 7. Byte code exceptions

We translate the possibility of each byte code to generate an exception, by using a non deterministic choice of the next byte code to be executed. For the virtual machine, when an exception is raised during a byte code interpretation, the state of the system is not affected by the byte code. For this, we have to provide to all incoming paths of a given instruction the possibility to execute this instruction or to raise exceptions. Then we have to model the modification of the control flow which is local to the method (exception handler or exception propagation) and in the call graph to indicate how exceptions are raised to the caller. Hereafter, we describe how exceptions are treated locally in the model of the method.

```
case{((active & exeI=NoException) : {
    (next (pc),bc) := switch (pc) {
        -1 : (-1,nop);
         0 :  ({pc+1,4},load);
             1  : (pc+1,invokeSpecial_108);
             2  : (pc+1,load);
             3  : (-1,ret);
             4  : (4,athrow_NullPointerException); };}
    (active & exeI=SecurityException) : {
    (next (pc),bc) := switch (pc) {
         5 : (5,athrow_SecurityException);
```

```
   default : (5,nop);};}
(active & exeI=ArithmeticException) : {
   (next (pc),bc) := switch (pc) {
      6 : (7,load);
      7 : (-1,ret);
   default : (6,nop); };}
(~active) : {next(pc) := pc; bc:= skip;}
```

Fig. 8. Model of the exception mechanism in SMV

In this example, after the first instruction it is possible to execute the
invokeSpecial instruction or to raise a NullPointerException. The
method 108, called with invokeSpecial_108 can raise a
SecurityException or an Arithmetic Exception. This is modelled
with the incoming exception variable exeI. The first one is raised while the second is
locally handeled. Using these variables allows the exceptions to be transferred from a
method to the caller.

4. Results

The PACAP Case Study

The key point of such a tool is its ability to deal with real smart card applications. To
verify the scalability of the prototype we have developed a set of communicating applets. They provide all the functionalities of smart card applets. They have the administrative commands to initialize and personalize the applet. We paid a particular attention to key administration. The three applets have been written in Java, and they have
been compiled and converted into cap file in order to be downloaded into Java cards.
The size of the purse cap file is around 30 ko which represents a big application for
smart cards. By analyzing some methods of the loyalty package, we obtain for the
average size of the methods 58 byte codes, for the maximum 281 byte codes and for
the minimum 4. This provides an idea of the size and complexity of the PACAP application. The following picture presents the applet and their shareable interfaces. For
example, the Loyalty applet will generate four SMV models one for each method of
the interface and the ProcessAPDU command of the Loyalty applet. This command
represents the calls from the terminal.

The ProcessAPDU command can be split into several call graphs. This command is
a dispatcher (a huge switch case) that only transmits the parameters to the *ad hoc*
method and sends back the result of the method. We obtain 52 SMV models for the
Loyalty application. The next table shows information about the size of four of the 52
generated SMV models for the package Loyalty.

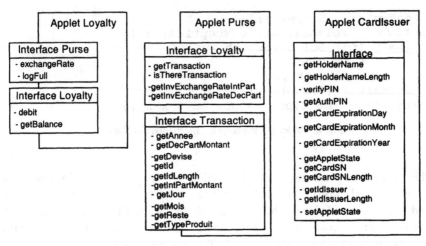

Fig. 9. The PACAP Case study

We have compared this set of applets with applets developed by Gemplus for customers. The size of the PACAP applet is more important and certain structures (*e.g.*: subroutines) have never been encountered. Such applet set is representative of current developments.

	Number of methods	Number of SMV lines	Number of properties
Debit	5	1033	2
Logfull	9	1900	12
ExchangeRate	10	2144	13
getBalance	2	339	1

Fig. 10. Characteristics of some models

Model Analysis

The interaction analysis of the applet set generates 132 SMV models and 421 properties. The Purse generates 66 models and 233 properties, the Loyalty 52 models and 174 properties and the Card Issuer 14 models and 14 properties.

A fourth of the properties are verified within 5 seconds and 90% are verified with less than 10 minutes. One of the property required 23 minutes to be checked on a Sun Ultra 80. The previous picture show the distribution of the time required to verify the

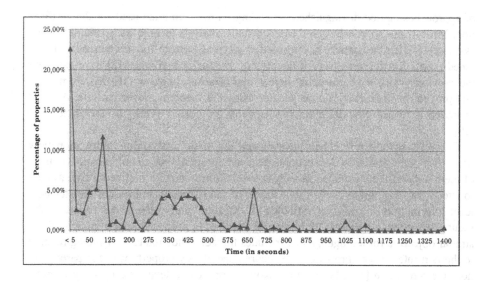

Fig. 11. Time needed to check the properties

properties. Some properties are not verified. For example, in the `logfull` call graph, the following property does not hold :

invoke_isThereTransaction: assert G (bc = invoke_isThereTransaction -> (lpc | stck[stckP + 2] | stck[stckP + 1] -> method[0]))

It corresponds in the `getTransactions` method to the verification of the two parameters of the called method `isThereTransaction`. Those parameters are on top of the stack and their level must not exceed the level of the shared interface purse loyalty.

The detected flow is not really illegal. This is due to the policy used to assign levels to the variables. All the variables of an applet have the level of the applet. Unfortunately such a policy must be more accurately tuned. All the variables that are transferred to an interface method must be declassified to the interface level. But this declassification must be checked for each data. After modifying the levels, all the properties hold.

The next step consists in developing hostile applets and verifying that illegal flow are correctly detected by the PACAP prototype.

5. State of the Art

A lot of work has been going on about the analysis of security properties of Java byte code. The major part of this work is concerned with properties verified by SUN byte code verifier like correct typing, no stack overflow, *etc*. Among this work, two kinds of approaches can be distinguished depending on the technique used for the verification. Most of the approaches are based on static analysis techniques, particularly type systems. In [12], the authors have proposed a typing system for subroutines and provided proofs for the soundness of the system. Freund and Mitchell [2] have extended the previous work by considering object initialization. Nipkow [16] has formalized and proved an abstract byte code verifier using the theorem prover Isabelle. Another approach is to use a model checker to specify the correct typing of Java byte code [10].

Recently, several researchers investigated the static analysis of information flow properties quite similar to our secure dependency property but, to our knowledge, none of them applied their work on Java byte-code. Girard et al. [3] defined a type system to check that a program written in a subset of the C language does not transfer high level information in low level variables. In [3], the typing relation was related to the secure dependency property. Volpano and Smith [11] proposed a type system with a similar objective for a language that includes threads. They relate their typing relation to the non-interference property. The secure dependency property was compared with non-interference in [1]. Myers and Liskov [9] propose a technique to analyze information flows of imperative programs annotated with labels that aggregate the sensitivity levels associated with various information providers. One of the interesting feature is the declassify operation that allows providers to modify labels. They propose a linear algorithm to verify that labels satisfy all the constraints.

In [7] the authors propose a formal program model and specification language for verifying global security properties of code that may contain local security checks. They model security properties related to the control flow in the program. This can model various Java security architectures, such as sand boxing, resource protection, and stack inspection. Verification is automatic based on static program analysis and checking.

The work described in [8] focuses on integrity property by controlling exclusively write operations to locations of references of sensitive objects such as files or network connections.

6. Conclusion

In this paper, we have presented an approach for the certification of applets that have to be loaded on a Java card. The security checks we propose are complementary to the security functions already implemented on the card. The applet firewall controls the interaction between two applets, while our analysis has a more global view and is able to detect illicit information flow between several applets.

Automation of the production of models is thus mandatory for the approach to be practicable. Such an automation is relatively straightforward providing that preliminary treatments are made to prepare the model construction, such as construction of the call graph, method name resolution, etc.

We have demonstrated the ability of the tool to verify real life models and to check non trivial properties. But it seems difficult to obtain a fully automated tool. In fact, when a counterexample is given by SMV it is difficult to isolate the illegal flow and to identify in the source code the origin of the problem. We expect in a close future to provide a more friendly user interface with enough annotations in the SMV model to track the flow in the source code.

As a conclusion, it is clear that the Java Card is a powerful framework to develop and to deploy applications. But the security mechanisms are not sufficient to prevent some kind of attacks of the system as presented here. We believe that abstract interpretation and verification through a model checker is an efficient means to guarantee that a given security policy is correctly implemented by applications.

References

[1]   P. Bieber and F. Cuppens. *A Logical View of Secure Dependencies*. Journal of Computer Security, 1(1):pp.99-129, 1992.

[2]   S. N. Freund and J. C. Mitchell. *A type system for object initialization in the Java byte code language*. In ACM Proceedings of OOPSLA 98, pp. 310-328, 1998.

[3]   P. Girard. *Formalisation et mise en œuvre d'une analyse statique de code en vue de la vérification d'applications sécurisées*. Ph.D. thesis, ENSAE, 1996.

[4]   P. Girard. *Which security policy for multi application smart cards?* In USENIX workshop on smart card technology, 1999.

[5]   P. Girard, J.-L. Lanet. *New Security Issues raised by Open Cards*. In Information Security Technical Report, Vol4, N°2, pp.: 19-27, 1999.

[6]   C. O'Halloran J. Cazin, P. Girard and C. T. Sennett. *Formal Validation of Software for Secure Systems*. In Anglo-French workshop on formal methods, modeling and simulation for system engineering, 1995.

[7]   T. Jensen, D. Le Metayer, and T. Thorn. *Verification of control flow based security policies*. In Proceedings of the 20th IEEE Security and Privacy Symposium, 1999.

[8]   X. Leroy and F. Rouaix. *Security properties of typed applets*. In Proceedings of POPL, 1998.

[9]   A.C. Myers and B. Liskov. *A decentralized model for information flow control*. In Proceedings of the 16th ACM symposium on operating systems principles, 1997.

[10]   J. Posegga and H. Vogt. *Off line verification for Java byte code using a model checker*. In Proceedings of ESORICS, number 1485 in LNCS. Springer, 1998.

[11]   G. Smith and D.M. Volpano. *Secure information flow in a multi-threaded imperative language*. In Proceedings of POPL, 1998.

[12]   R. Stata and M. Abadi. *A type system for Java byte code subroutines*. In Proceeding of 25th Symposium on Principles of Programming Languages, 1998.

[13]   P.Bieber, J. Cazin, P. Girard, J.-L. Lanet, V. Wiels, G. Zanon. *Checking Secure Interactions of Smart Card Applets*, ESORICS 2000, Toulouse, September 2000.

[14]   P. Bieber, J. Cazin, V. Wiels, G. Zanon, P.Girard, J.-L. Lanet. *Electronic Purse Applet Certification* in Workshops on Secure Architectures and Information Flow, London, December 1999. http://www.elsevier.nl/gej-ng/31/29/23/57/show/Products/notes/cover.htt

[15]   C. Cifuentes, *Reverse Compilation Techniques*, Ph.D. Thesis, Queensland University of Technology, 1994.

[16]   T. Nipkow, *Verified byte code verifier*, T.U. München, http://www4.in.tum.de/~nipkow//pubs/fossacs01.html

CardKt: Automated Multi-modal Deduction on Java Cards for Multi-application Security

Rajeev Goré* and Lan Duy Nguyen**

Automated Reasoning Group
Computer Sciences Laboratory
Res. Sch. of Inf. Sci. and Eng.
Institute of Advanced Studies

Formal Methods Group
Dept. of Computer Science
Fac. of Eng. and Inf. Tech.
The Faculties

Australian National University

rpg@arp.anu.edu.au
arp.anu.edu.au/~rpg

ndlan2k@yahoo.com
www.cse.unsw.edu.au/~ndlan

Abstract. We describe an implementation of a Java program to perform automated deduction in propositional multi-modal logics on a Java smart card. The tight space limits of Java smart cards make the implementation non-trivial. A potential application is to ensure that applets down-loaded off the internet conform to personalised security permissions stored on the Java card using a security policy encoded in multi-modal logic. In particular, modal logic may be useful to ensure that previously checked "trust" relationships between pre-existing multiple applets on a Java card are not broken by the addition of a new applet. That is, by using multi-modal logic to express notions of permissions and obligations, we can turn the security check into an on-board theorem proving task. Our theorem prover itself could be down-loaded "just in time" to perform the check, and then deleted to free up space on the card once the check has been completed. Our work is thus a "proof of principle" for the application of formal logic to the security of multi-application Java cards.

Keywords: security of multi-application smart cards, applications of logics of knowledge and belief, modal theorem proving, tense logics.

1 Introduction and Motivation: Java Cards and Security

Smart cards [Pet99] are plastic credit-card sized cards that contain a small on-board computer in a tamper proof plastic casing. Current smart cards contain a few KBytes of RAM and 32KBytes of "disk" space (EEPROM). The card must be inserted into a reading device which provides power. The reading device is typically connected to a host computer connected to the Internet.

Java smart cards [Pet99] are smart cards that contain an on-board Java Virtual Machine (JVM) allowing them to run Java programs (byte-code) [Mic00].

* Supported by a Queen Elizabeth II Fellowship from the Australian Research Council.
** Supported by an RSISE Summer ResearchScholarship.

I. Attali and T. Jensen (Eds.): Java Card 2000, LNCS 2041, pp. 38–51, 2001.
© Springer-Verlag Berlin Heidelberg 2001

The JVM is put onto the card by the manufacturer either in software or in dedicated hardware. When such a Java card is inserted into a card reader with Internet access, it is possible to down-load Java applets onto the Java card on demand, and to run these applets on the card. The Java card we worked with contained 512 bytes of RAM and contained a 32KByte EEPROM.

Java cards are about to revolutionise the way we spend money by incorporating multiple different functions into one smart card [Pet99]: electronic purse, credit card, driver's licence, passport, loyalty programmes, and many more. Such cards would allow a bank customer to down-load extra electronic cash onto the electronic purse by accessing the world wide web pages of the bank. Indeed, it is even possible to insert smart cards into mobile phones and use the mobile phone to connect to the Internet by dialing a phone number [Inc99].

Current Java cards are preprogrammed to contain applets by the manufacturer for the card vendor, typically a bank (for credit and debit cards), or an airline (for frequent flyer cards). But if Java cards are to succeed then a card carrier must be able to down-load new applets onto an existing card "just in time", or even merge existing cards into one card. This would mean that multiple applets from different vendors would reside on the same card.

The single biggest problem with this scenario is that of security. How can we guarantee that a simple query to the drivers licence section of the card for identification purposes (say) will not steal money from the card's electronic purse? If new applets are to be down-loaded then how can the vendor of applet A ensure that a competing vendor's applet will not be down-loaded at a later stage and steal information from applet A? Alternatively, applets A and B may trust each other to some extent, and therefore share some information. But if applets B and C enjoy a similar trust relationship, how can A be sure that B will not tell C information which it has obtained from A [Gir99,PB00] ?

Many methodologies for guaranteeing such security have been investigated, but almost all of them involve a trusted "third" party. For example, the bank applet may be signed using a digital signature obtained from the government that certifies that the applet really did originate from the bank in question. The digital certificate is decoded by the card's on-board digital signature chip and the applet is allowed to access the card's electronic purse. But the need for a certification agency and a certification procedure makes this avenue cumbersome.

An alternative methodology that involves no third parties is for card owners to implement a personal security policy using some international standard "language for security". The electronic purse applet installed on the card may come with such a built in security policy which the user is prompted to tailor to his or her needs. Another applet which wishes to access the electronic purse must now pass a challenge determined by the level of security chosen by the card user.

As new applets are added to the card, they are slotted into this set up either explicitly by the card user, or by some implicit default method. The simplest method is to use some form of access control list as is done by the Smart Card for Windows system (http://www.microsoft.com.smartcard), which uses simple propositional logic in its access control lists. A more sophisticated approach is to use a hierarchy with the "public" applets at the bottom, the "private" applets at the top, and the others in between these two extremes in some partial order [Gir99,PB00]. But this work does not address the problem of the dynamics of this partial order when a new applet is down-loaded. In particular, how can we be sure that all the previously checked "shared secrecy" conditions are satisfied by the new hierarchy ?

One way to define such a security policy is to use formal mathematical logic and to ensure that the permission granted to down-loaded applications meet certain rigorously defined security criteria expressed as formulae of logic. For example, notions like "agent i trusts agent j" are easily encoded as statements of multi-modal propositional logics, which are now well-established in artificial intelligence research as bases for defeasible reasoning [Shv90], logics of agents [RG93], and logics of authentication [MBN90,Mat97]. Multi-modal logics like Propositional Dynamic Logic [Gol87] have also been used to model the changing states of a program. Finally, propositional bi-modal tense logics give a very simple and elegant model of the flow of time [HC96].

Checking that a down-loaded applet meets the security criteria is now reduced to proving, **on-board**, that an appropriate formula is a theorem of the logic used to code the criteria, since this is the only computer that the customer should trust. Multi-modal logics are particularly well-suited to this task as most of them are decidable. Consequently, the ability to perform automated multi-modal deduction on Java smart cards may be of use in electronic commerce.

But surely multi-modal deduction is simply too difficult to perform on a smart card with extremely limited resources ? After all, even classical propositional logic is NP-complete, and most multi-modal logics are actually PSPACE-complete! Here we describe a program that performs automated deduction in bi-modal tense logics on a Java smart card. It is reasonably straightforward to extend this work to other multi-modal logics, and hence to logics of knowledge and belief, or to logics of authentication and security. Thus our work is "proof of principle" that a logic-based security policy could be implemented on current Java cards. As the resources and speed of Java cards skyrocket, the task will only become simpler.

The paper is set out as follows. Section 2 describes the basics of multi-modal theorem proving. Section 3 explains the design of our prover CardKt. Section 4 presents test results while Section 5 presents conclusions.

ACKNOWLEDGEMENTS: We are grateful to Didier Tollé of Gemplus Australia for donating the Java card hardware necessary to carry out this project.

2   Multi-modal Logics, Logic of Security and Tense Logics

Propositional multi-modal logics are classical modal logics [HC96] and were used as the basis for the well-known BAN logic of authentication [MBN90]. Since then, a plethora of such logics have been invented [Mat97], and most are based upon multi-modal propositional logic because these logics provide sufficient expres-

$$
\begin{array}{llll}
w \models \mathbf{t} & \text{for every } w \in W & w \models \mathbf{f} & \text{for no } w \in W \\
w \models p & \text{if } w \in V(p) & w \models \neg A & \text{if } w \not\models A \\
w \models A \wedge B & \text{if } w \models A \text{ and } w \models B \quad & w \models A \vee B & \text{if } w \models A \text{ or } w \models B \\
w \models A \rightarrow B & \text{if } w \not\models A \text{ or } w \models B \\
w \models \Diamond_i A & \text{if } (\exists v \in R_i(w))(v \models A) & w \models \Box_i A & \text{if } (\forall v \in R_i(w))(v \models A)
\end{array}
$$

Fig. 1. Kripke semantics for **Kt**

siveness to encode the desired properties while remaining tractable: nevertheless the decision problem is typically at least NP-complete, and is thus non-trivial.

The **formulae** of multi-modal logic $\mathbf{K_n}$ are built from a set of primitive propositions $\text{PRP} = \{p_0, p_1, p_2, \cdots\}$ plus the verum and falsum constants $\mathbf{t}$ and $\mathbf{f}$ using the classical connectives $\wedge, \vee, \rightarrow, \neg$ and the modal connectives $\Box_1, \cdots, \Box_n$ and $\Diamond_1, \cdots, \Diamond_n$ as follows: every primitive proposition is a formula, the constants $\mathbf{t}$ and $\mathbf{f}$ are formulae, and if A and B are formulae, then so are each of $A \wedge B$, $A \vee B$, $\neg A$, $\Diamond_1 A, \cdots, \Diamond_n A$, $\Box_1 A, \cdots, \Box_n A$.

The semantics of $\mathbf{K_n}$ is given in terms of Kripke frames [HC96] as follows. A Kripke **frame** is a pair $\langle W, (R_1, \cdots, R_n) \rangle$, $1 \leq i \leq n$, where W is a non-empty set (of possible worlds) and each R_i is a binary relation over W. A Kripke **model** is a triple $\langle W, (R_1, \cdots, R_n)), V \rangle$ where $\langle W, (R_1, \cdots, R_n) \rangle$ is a Kripke frame and V is a mapping from $\text{PRP} \cup \{\mathbf{t}, \mathbf{f}\}$ to the set of all subsets of W. Intuitively, $V(p)$ is the set of worlds where p is true. Let $R_i(w) := \{v \in W \mid wR_iv\}$ and let $R_i^{-1}(w) := \{v \in W \mid vR_iw\}$. If $w \in W$ is in $V(p)$ then w **satisfies** p, written as $w \models p$. We extend the satisfaction relation to complex formulae as shown in Figure 1. A formula is **satisfiable** iff it is true at some world in some Kripke model. A formula is **valid** iff it is true at every world in every Kripke model.

Multi-modal logics for authentication like the BAN logic [MBN90] try to capture the essentials of guaranteeing security in message passing systems. Formulae are built from a given set of primitives using logical connectives with particular intended meanings, some of which are shown below [Mat97]:

$P \models X$ means "agent P believes X"
$P \lhd X$ means "agent P sees X"
$P \mapsto X$ means "P is trusted on the truth of X"

Such logics have been used to reason about security protocols and extended and modified to reason about secure mobile code [MAP93].

If we now specialise $\mathbf{Kn}$ so that there is only one reachability relation R and put $R_1 = R$ and $R_2 = R^{-1}$ then we obtain two pairs of modalities $\Diamond_1/\Box_1$ and $\Diamond_2/\Box_2$. The obtained logic is a notational variant of a very simple multi-modal logic called $\mathbf{Kt}$ whose modalities are traditionally written as $\Diamond/\Box$ and $\blacklozenge/\blacksquare$. The logic $\mathbf{Kt}$ is of interest in its own right as it is often used to model the flow of time, branching in a "forwards" and "backwards" direction. Thus we are interested in $\mathbf{Kt}$ mainly as a case study for multi-modal theorem proving.

A labelled sequent calculus $\texttt{KtSeq}$ for $\mathbf{Kt}$ can be found in [BG98]. The proof rules of this calculus are sound and complete with respect to the Kripke semantics outlined above. Consequently, we can use this calculus to decide whether or not a formula A is valid in tense logic **Kt**. The calculus KtSeq has been implemented in C [BG99]. However, the C code cannot be run on a Java card since Java cards only run Java byte code, and current C to Java compilers produce code which simply does not fit onto current cards. In the next section we describe a new implementation of KtSeq designed to run on Java smart cards.

3   CardKt

The details of the sequent system KtSeq cannot be given here due to space limitations so we refer the reader to [BG98] for detailed definitions of concepts such as labelled formula, labelled sequent, deduction tree, forward positions, backward positions *etc.* which are also used in this paper.

For each input formula, the theorem proving problem can be seen as: search for a completed non-axiom node in the deduction tree of the formula. If one is found, the formula is not a theorem of **Kt** and is called a counterexample, otherwise the deduction tree is a proof that the formula is a theorem of **Kt**.

Obviously, it is better to search for a completed non-axiom node while constructing the deduction tree. That means, after creating a new node, CardKt checks whether it is a completed non-axiom node.

The available memory on our Java card was so small that we had to design a special algorithm to construct/search the deduction tree, and design clever, extremely space efficient data structures for the deduction tree. To more intuitively show how that can be done, we will try to illustrate our ideas by examples.

As with KtSeq all formulae are assumed to be in negated normal form (NNF) so that negations symbols appear only in front of primitive propositions. This is not a serious restriction as each formula has a logically equivalent formulae in NNF, with at most a linear increase in size.

3.1   Overall Algorithm

To save memory we use depth first search. The obvious way to construct/search the deduction tree is by recursion, as in [BG99]. But recursion is extremely memory-consuming because stack space for local variables and arguments is allocated for every recursive call. So we used an iterative method.

One extremely useful feature of the deduction tree, as indicated from the set of KtSeq inference rules [BG98] is that each node has no more than two children since the ($\wedge$) rule is the only rule that causes (binary) branching. Furthermore, all the rules are invertible, hence there is no backtracking. These facts mean CardKt can forget any one-child node after processing it and needs to store only the second child of a two-child node in the search-stack. As shown in Figure 2, at the time it is checking node 3, only node 4 is in the stack.

At any time, the consumed memory is therefore just for the current node and for a search-stack to store the first nodes of the next branches which are yet to be searched. After encountering an axiomatic (leaf) node, the program pops

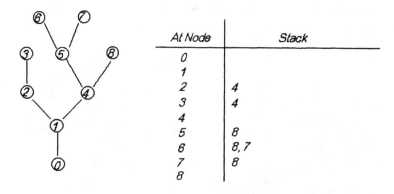

At Node	Stack
0	
1	
2	4
3	4
4	
5	8
6	8, 7
7	8
8	

Fig. 2. Iterative stack base algorithm for constructing/searching the deduction tree

a node out of the search-stack and applies the unique KtSeq inference rule that is applicable to this sequent (node) to construct/search that branch; Figure 2.

3.2   Data Structures

As described in each node of the deduction tree is a labelled sequent, which consists of a label set and three lists of labelled formulae: Λ, Δ and Γ. Each labelled formula contains a label and a formula.

The C data structures in [BG99] have object-oriented features and can be translated to Java classes. Although inheritance and object-referencing (like pointers in C) can be used to save memory, both are still expensive. Each object requires 4 bytes to store its address, an insignificant amount in a modern computer, but significant in a Java card with only 512 bytes of RAM. So, new data structures that minimise spaced were needed, as described next.

Parse Tree of Formula: As is generally known, a formula can be parsed into a tree (notice that this parse tree is different from the deduction tree above). The sub-formula property of the KtSeq inference rules guarantees that every formula that appears in the deduction tree is just a sub-formula of the original NNF formula to be tested (*i.e.* a sub-tree of the original parse tree). So, CardKt just needs to keep the parse tree of the original NNF formula and each formula mentioned in the deduction tree can be represented by a node in that parse tree (as the root node of that formula).

In CardKt the parse tree is encoded into a byte firstNode and six arrays of bytes disjArr, conjArr, allFutureArr, someFutureArr, allPastArr, somePastArr; see Figure 3 where we have used * for ∧ and + for ∨. Thus, each node is encoded as an integer between 0 and 255, thereby using one byte. The f constant is encoded as the integer 0, and the t constant as 1.

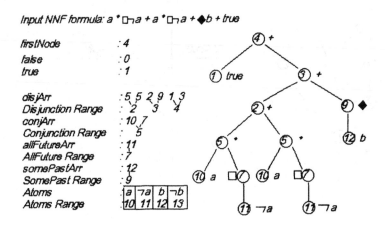

Fig. 3. Array representation of the parse tree

CardKt first reads the given NNF formula A and counts the number of occurrences of each connective. If a connective appears n times, then n consecutive nodes are allocated to this type of connective. The connectives are allocated nodes in the following order: $\vee$, $\wedge$, $\square$, $\lozenge$, $\blacksquare$, $\blacklozenge$, atoms. The example contains three occurrences of $\vee$ so node numbers 2, 3, and 4 are allocated to disjunctive nodes (as 0 is for f and 1 is for t). Similarly, there are two conjunctions so nodes 5 and 6 are conjunctive nodes. The cases for the other connectives are similar and the final node allocated to a connective in this example is node number 9. The rest are allocated to the atoms: nodes 10-255.

At the end of the first pass we know the required lengths of the six arrays since we know the number of occurrences of each connective. We also know the range of node values for each type of connective. For example, we know that disjunctive nodes are in the range 2-4, while conjunctive nodes are in the range 5-6. We refer to these local variables as DisjRange, ConjRange, *etc.* although their values are computable from the sizes of the six arrays we keep.

We now need to make another (bottom-up) pass of the given NNF formula A to fill in the six arrays which represent the parse tree. For example, the first atomic formula a is allocated to the first non-connective node 10, and its negation is immediately allocated to node 11. So although the formula in Figure 3 does not contain an occurrence of $\neg b$, the parse tree contains an entry for $\neg b$. Parsing continues in a bottom-up manner until a disjunctive or conjunctive node is parsed. The two values of the child nodes of a disjunctive [conjunctive] node are stored at two consecutive positions in the DisjArr [ConjArr]. Continuing in this way, we will eventually parse the root. Since the root node is the last one to be parsed, it is usually the last element of some connective's range. In the example, 4 is the root, the last element of DisjRange.

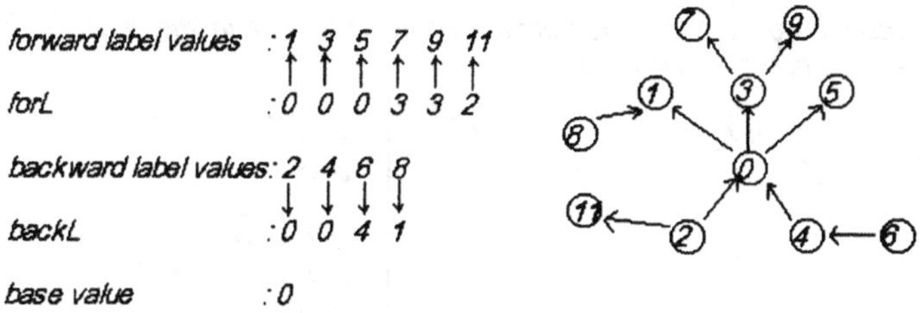

forward label values : *1 3 5 7 9 11*

forL   :*0 0 0 3 3 2*

backward label values: *2 4 6 8*

backL   :*0 0 4 1*

base value   : *0*

Fig. 4. Array representation of the label set

During execution, the most typical task is "find the sub-formulae of node n". The array indices for the children can be calculated from n by its offset in the appropriate Range. For example, to find the sub-formula of node 3 (say), we proceed as follows. The value 3 is between 2 (base of DisjRange) and 5 (base of ConjRange), so 3 is a disjunctive node. The value 3 is the second element of DisjRange 2-4, so its 2 children are the second pair of elements of disjArr, *i.e.* nodes 2 and 9. Repeating this procedure on nodes 2 and 9, we can reconstruct the sub-formula rooted at node 3. AllFuture, SomeFuture, AllPast and SomePast nodes are handled analogously except that these have only one child.

Thus each node or each sub-tree can be referred to by one byte. firstNode refers to the value of the root node of the parse tree. To save more memory, we can even use the same value for repeated subtrees. In Figure 3, the value 5 is used for the repeated sub-formula $a * \Box \neg a$, which is why there is no node 6. Similarly for nodes 7 and 8.

Label Set: The label set is really a label tree, a tree of possible worlds; see Figure 4. We use a similar encoding for the label tree as used for the parse tree. Each label is encoded as an integer between 0 and 255, thereby using one byte. The base label has value 0, forward labels have odd values, and backward labels have even values (except for 0). So two arrays, forL and backL, of bytes are needed. Each label (except for the base label) possesses a position in one of these arrays, depending on whether it is a forward label or a backward label.

A difference between the label tree and the parse tree is that any one node of the label tree can have many children whereas any one node of the parse tree can have only one or two children. Therefore, at a node's position in the label arrays, rather than storing its children's node values as for the parse tree, CardKt stores its parent's node value. Now, each label can be referred to by one byte. This can be seen more clearly in Figure 4. For example, the single one-byte integer 11 represents the label $0.\lfloor 2 \rfloor . \lceil 11 \rceil$ as follows. The value 11 is odd, so we know that it is a forward label, hence the arrow points into node 11, and we must look in the array forL. We compute $(11/2) + 1 = 6$ and look in the 6th element of array

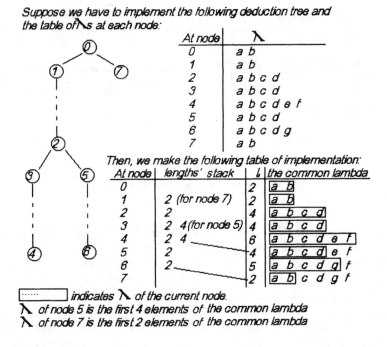

Fig. 5. Stack representation of Λ of all labelled sequents in the deduction tree

forL. There we find its parent label 2, which is even. We therefore know that it is a backward label, hence the arrow points away from node 2, and we must look in the array backL. We compute $(2/2) = 1$ and look in the 1st element of backL to find its parent label 0. Since 0 is the base label we have constructed the whole label $0.\lfloor 2 \rfloor.\lceil 11 \rceil$ from just 11.

In summary, each labelled formula can be referred to by two bytes, one for the label and one for the formula.

Stack of Λ, Δ and Label Set: As mentioned in the algorithm description, a stack of labelled sequents is needed. In CardKt , this stack consists of four stacks, one each for Γ, Λ, Δ and the label set.

It can be seen that the KtSeq inference rules only add more elements into and never remove elements from Λ, Δ and the label set of a principle formula to create a new side formula. Moreover, in the ($\wedge$) rule, the only rule which pushes a new node onto the search-stack, the Λ, Δ and the label sets of the side formulae are the same as that of the principal formula.

This can help to save stack space. For instance, we just need one common list lambda (in CardKt , it is composed of two arrays of bytes, lambdaL of labels and lambdaF of formulae) and a length 1 of Λ of the current node. The list **lambda** represents the Λs of all nodes of the deduction tree simultaneously. Instead of putting the Λ of a new node onto the stack, we put the length of its Λ onto the length-stack. Later on, when the node is popped out of the search-stack, the length of its Λ is popped out of the length-stack into l. Thereby, the first l elements of the common lambda constitute the node's Λ. This is illustrated in Figure 5 where a symbol similar to λ is used to stand for Λ.

For example, when processing node 4, the search-stack contains nodes 7 and 5, lambda contains $a\ b\ c\ d\ e\ f$ and l is 6. Thus, the Λ of node 4 is $a\ b\ c\ d\ e\ f$. The length-stack entries for the "At Node 4" row are 2 and 4. Thus, the Λ for node 7 is $a\ b$ and the Λ for node 5 is $a\ b\ c\ d$. After completing node 4 we pop the search-stack to process node 5 next. At the same time, we pop the length-stack and find the entry 4 which is the length of the Λ of node 5 in lambda. Eventually we will reach node 6, with Λ containing $a\ b\ c\ d\ g\ f$ and l containing 5. This means the Λ of node 6 is the first 5 elements of lambda, i.e $a\ b\ c\ d\ g$. After finishing node 6, we will pop the length-stack to reveal 2, which tells us that the Λ of the next node 7 is $a\ b$.

A similar representation is used for Δ and for the label set. For the label set, two common lists are needed, one each for forward and backward labels.

3.3   General Comments

CardKt has two parsers (generated by Java Cup Parser Generator), one for converting a formula into its NNF equivalent, and the other for converting this NNF formula into the six arrays of bytes.

The fact that we use only one byte for every node in the parse tree means that it can contain at most $(2^8) = 256$ nodes. Consequently, CardKt can accept any formula in tense logic which, when parsed, requires at most 256 nodes in the parse tree. Since repeated subexpressions are stored using only one node, the size of the accepted formulae can potentially be greater than 256 symbols, but this "garbage collection" has not been implemented yet. As the memory on Java cards increases, by replacing arrays of bytes by arrays of shorts, CardKt will be able to accept significantly larger input formulae.

4   Results and Related Work

CardKt was tested on a range of randomly generated formulae; shown in Figure 6 and Figure 7. Each formula was parsed off-card on a host computer into the six arrays, and these were passed to CardKt. Hence the times are for proof search only. The times were the average of three runs as measured using the host computer.

The results show some shortcomings of our rather rough method for measuring times: the simple non-theorem n1 takes 550 ms but the more complex non-theorem n2 takes only 270 ms. Hence we clearly need to refine our method for measuring times. Alternatively, this might just be a manifestation of inherent but unpredictable overheads in the program.

Name	Formula	ms
	Non-Theorems	
n1	a	550
n2	$\blacklozenge(\blacksquare f \wedge d)$	270
n3	$\blacksquare\neg(\Diamond(\blacklozenge(e \wedge f) \vee (\blacksquare a \to \blacklozenge a) \to \blacklozenge\blacksquare e \to f) \wedge \Box(b \wedge \blacklozenge\Diamond\blacklozenge f) \to$	
	$\Diamond((\Box(a \wedge f \to c \wedge d) \to \neg\blacksquare\blacksquare c) \vee (\Diamond((e \leftrightarrow f) \to f) \to$	
	$\Diamond\blacksquare b \vee \Diamond(b \vee d)))) \to b$	880
n4	$\Diamond\blacksquare\Diamond\neg(\Diamond(t \to a) \vee (\blacksquare\neg\neg(c \leftrightarrow t) \leftrightarrow \Box\Box\blacklozenge\blacklozenge d))$	330
n5	$\blacksquare c$	990
n6	$(a \leftrightarrow \neg\Box\neg\Diamond(\Box\neg(f \leftrightarrow b) \leftrightarrow e)) \vee \Box\neg\blacksquare b$	8270
n7	$\Box a$	880
n8	$\blacksquare\neg(b \to \blacklozenge((\Diamond(e \vee d \to \blacklozenge c) \leftrightarrow \blacksquare\neg(e \to c)) \vee \blacksquare\blacklozenge\blacksquare\blacksquare d)) \leftrightarrow \neg c$	2310
n9	$\blacklozenge b$	230
n10	$b \to \neg\neg(e \wedge \neg t \wedge (\neg\blacklozenge\Diamond t \to \neg\neg(b \to b \leftrightarrow \neg b)) \leftrightarrow \blacksquare b)$	5510
n11	$\neg e \vee (\blacklozenge\Diamond\blacksquare\blacklozenge\blacksquare((e \leftrightarrow b \leftrightarrow f \leftrightarrow e) \wedge (\Diamond b \to \Diamond e)) \to$	
	$\Box\blacksquare\blacklozenge\Box(\Box\blacklozenge c \wedge d \vee \Diamond\Box(b \wedge t)))$	7470
n12	$\blacklozenge\Diamond(t \to a \to (\blacksquare d \leftrightarrow \blacksquare\Diamond\Diamond t \leftrightarrow \neg t)) \to \blacksquare d$	5710
n13	$e \wedge \blacksquare\blacksquare\blacksquare\Box\Box((\blacksquare e \to \Diamond(d \to t)) \wedge \blacksquare\Diamond(e \to b))$	940
n14	$\Diamond\blacksquare\neg\blacksquare e$	380

Fig. 6. Times to test non-theorems of the tense logic $\mathbf{K}_t$

Note that CardKt does not get fooled by trivial theorems like t7 (t $\vee \varphi$) and t18 ($\neg\neg(\varphi \to$ t). Another feature is the approximate order of magnitude increase in the times between non-theorems and (non-trivial) theorems. This is to be expected since non-theorems require CardKt to find *one* open branch (the first), whereas the theorems require CardKt to close *every* branch.

The times shown indicate that moderately complex formulae of tense logic Kt can be run effectively on CardKt.

Our work is a continuation of our earlier work in labelled sequent systems for multi-modal logics [BG98], their fast implementations in C[BG99] and theorem proving on Java cards[SGPV98]. We know of no other similar work although work on checking type safety on-card does exist [GLV99].

5   Conclusions and Further Work

We have successfully implemented an automated theorem prover for (multi-modal) tense logic **Kt** that runs on a Java smart card. Trivial modifications yield a proof checker in keeping with the ideas of proof carrying code [Nec97]. An oft-quoted disadvantage of proof carrying code is the size of the proofs. Surely, a Java card cannot possibly store the proof before checking it ? In KtSeq, a proof is simply a sequence of rule names which need to be applied to the given end-sequent to be proved. Thus CardKt can be sent the end-sequent, and a simple sequence of rule names, which it will apply to simulate the proof on-board. Thus

Name	Formula	ms
	Theorems	
t1	$\Box(a \to b) \to (\Box a \to \Box b)$	4500
t2	$\blacksquare(a \to b) \to (\blacksquare a \to \blacksquare b)$	4340
t3	$\Diamond(a \vee b) \to \Diamond a \vee \Diamond b$	7360
t4	$\blacklozenge(a \vee b) \to \blacklozenge a \vee \blacklozenge b$	7850
t5	$a \to \Box\blacklozenge a$	3020
t6	$a \to \blacksquare\Diamond a$	2790
t7	$t \vee \Box\blacklozenge e \wedge (\Diamond(d \vee \blacksquare\blacklozenge\Box(\Diamond c \wedge \Diamond b)) \leftrightarrow \blacklozenge\neg((\blacklozenge(e \wedge a \wedge \blacksquare d) \to (\blacklozenge a \to b \vee c) \to \blacksquare b) \wedge \neg d))$	220
t8	$\Box\blacklozenge d \wedge f \to \Box\blacksquare\blacksquare\Box(e \to (((t \to e) \vee (t \to b)) \wedge (\neg e \vee (d \to c)) \leftrightarrow \blacklozenge(b \leftrightarrow b) \wedge \Diamond(e \leftrightarrow a)))$	880
t9	$\Box\neg\blacklozenge\neg(\Box(\blacksquare(c \to c \leftrightarrow b \to f) \vee (\blacklozenge\blacklozenge f \to \blacksquare d)) \vee \Box\Diamond((a \vee t \to \blacksquare c) \wedge (\neg a \wedge (b \vee d))))$	12640
t10	$\Box\blacksquare(\neg(\Box\Box\neg\neg\Box t \vee (\Diamond\blacklozenge\Diamond c \vee \Diamond\neg(c \to a)) \wedge \Box(\Diamond b \wedge (b \leftrightarrow f) \leftrightarrow \neg\Diamond t)) \to \Diamond\blacklozenge(\blacklozenge\blacksquare(\Diamond t \wedge a) \vee (\neg\Box(b \leftrightarrow d) \vee (d \to b))))$	8520
t11	$\Box t$	2090
t12	$t \vee \blacklozenge(\blacklozenge(((\Diamond c \leftrightarrow \Diamond b) \wedge \Diamond(a \to e) \to \neg(d \wedge t \vee (b \to a))) \to \blacklozenge\Diamond\blacksquare(c \wedge a)) \wedge (\Box\Box(a \vee (c \to c) \leftrightarrow \Diamond\blacksquare a) \to \blacklozenge\blacklozenge\Box\Diamond e)) \wedge d$	660
t13	$e \to e$	870
t14	$\Box t \vee \blacklozenge\blacksquare\blacklozenge a$	1980
t15	$\neg\neg t$	170
t16	$\neg\Diamond f \vee \Diamond(\neg\Diamond\blacksquare f \leftrightarrow \Diamond b)$	2590
t17	$e \wedge \Diamond\blacksquare\blacksquare(\neg\Diamond(f \wedge a \wedge (d \wedge c)) \wedge (((a \leftrightarrow f) \to \blacklozenge e \vee \blacksquare a) \wedge ((e \to (c \leftrightarrow a)) \to \Box\Diamond d))) \to e$	1320
t18	$\neg\neg(\Box(\Box\Diamond((e \leftrightarrow f) \wedge \blacklozenge c \wedge \blacklozenge\blacklozenge b) \wedge (\Box(a \leftrightarrow \blacksquare(d \leftrightarrow e)) \wedge (\neg((d \to e) \wedge \blacksquare a) \to \blacklozenge(c \wedge d) \vee t \wedge (t \vee d)))) \to t$	660
t19	$\Box(\blacksquare\Box\blacklozenge\Diamond\Box(b \vee \neg b \vee \neg(e \leftrightarrow b)) \vee \blacklozenge\blacklozenge(\Diamond\Diamond(d \to (\Diamond d \leftrightarrow f \vee b)) \vee (\blacksquare(\blacklozenge\blacksquare e \wedge \blacksquare\Box b) \vee \Box e)))$	10380
t20	$\Box(b \leftrightarrow b)$	7860
t21	$\blacksquare\Box(\Box\neg(\neg\blacksquare(t \vee d) \to \blacksquare\Box\Diamond c) \vee \neg\Box\Diamond\neg(c \to t \vee a) \vee \Diamond\neg\Box(\Diamond\Diamond(c \wedge c) \leftrightarrow \neg\neg(c \to e)))$	11720
t22	$\blacksquare\neg f$	1970
t23	$c \vee \Box\blacklozenge t$	3520
t24	$\blacksquare\blacksquare\Diamond\Box(((\neg e \vee (a \wedge e \to \Diamond c) \to \Box(\blacklozenge b \vee (e \vee a))) \to (a \leftrightarrow (\Box a \leftrightarrow \blacklozenge e) \vee \neg\blacklozenge f)) \vee t)$	7200
t25	$t \vee f$	610

Fig. 7. Times to test theorems of the tense logic $\mathbf{K}_t$

there is never any need to store the whole proof on the card. Indeed, CardKt can be down-loaded "just in time" and then discarded afterwards.

The biggest disadvantage of KtSeq is its worst-case behaviour, which can take exponential space when polynomial space would suffice. But other sequent calculi for multi-modal logics without this deficiency are well-known [Gor99] but are harder to implement. We intend to investigate their implementation on **Java** cards as further work. Proof checking as described above can still be done one rule at a time, without storing the whole proof.

Further theoretical work is now needed to design a security policy for handling the dynamics of the security requirements of multi-application Java cards. A promising approach would be to use multi-modal logics with nominals [Bla93] which contain an extra set of atomic formulae $\text{NOM} := \{i_0, i_1, \cdots\}$ in addition to atomic formulae PRP. Each member of NOM takes a valuation $V(i) = \{w\}$ for some unique singleton subset of W, hence i "names" world w. Each applet would be given a unique name from NOM and various binary relations like "trusts" and "communicates with" give rise to their own modalities like $\langle\text{trusts}\rangle$, $\langle\text{communicates-with}\rangle$. The formula $i_1 \to \langle\text{trusts}\rangle i_2$ then states that applet "i_1 trusts applet i_2".

A finite collection of such statements gives a set of formulae Th, describing the current set-up of applets, and their inter-relationships. The formula $\hat{Th} \to A$ asks whether some property expressed as formula A follows logically from the set-up Th, where $\hat{Th}$ is just the conjunction of the members of Th. If the set-up changes from Th to $Th' := \{C_1, C_2, \cdots, C_n\}$ by the addition of new applets, and their inter-relationships, the query $\hat{Th}' \to A$ asks whether the old property A still follows logically from the *new* set-up. If it does not, then a version of **CardKt** tailored to handle nominal tense logics would deliver an explicit counter-example to show how the property A can be broken by the new set up Th'.

References

[BG98]   N Bonnette and R Goré. A labelled sequent system for tense logic Kt. In *AI98: Proceedings of the Australian Joint Conference on Artificial Intelligence*, LNAI 1502:71-82. Springer, 1998.

[BG99]   V Boyapati and R Goré. System description: KtSeqC. In N. Murray, editor, *Proc. International Conference on Theorem Proving with Analytic Tableau*, volume LNCS 1617: 29-31. Springer, 1999.

[Bla93]   P Blackburn. Nominal tense logic. *Notre Dame Journal of Formal Logic*, 34(1):56–83, 1993.

[Gir99]   P Girard. Which security policy for multiapplication smart cards. In *Proceedings USENIX Workshop on Smartcard Technology*, pages 21–28, Chicago, USA, 1999.

[GLV99]   G Grimaud, J-L Lanet, and J-J Vandewalle. FACADE: a typed intermediate language dedicated to smart cards. Technical report, Gemplus Research, http://www.gemplus.com/smart/r_d/publications/index.html, 1999.

[Gol87]   R. I. Goldblatt. *Logics of Time and Computation*. CSLI Lecture Notes No. 7, Center for the Study of Language and Information, Stanford, 1987.

[Gor99]   R Goré. Chapter 6: Tableau methods for modal and temporal logics. In M D'Agostino, D Gabbay, R Hänle, J Posegga, editor, *Handbook of Tableau Methods*, pages 297–396. Kluwer Academic Publishers, 1999.

[HC96]   G. E. Hughes and M. J. Cresswell. *A New Introduction To Modal Logic*. Routledge, 1996.

[Inc99]   Funge Inc. http://www.funge.net/, 1999.

[MAP93]   B Lampson M Abadi, M Burrows and G Plotkin. A calculus for access control in distributed systems. *AM Transactions on Programming Languages and Systems*, 15(3):1–29, 1993.

[Mat97]   A Mathuria. *Contributions to Authentication Logics and Analysis of Authentication Protocols*. PhD thesis, School of Information Technology and Computer Science, University of Wollongong, Australia, 1997.

[MBN90]   M Abadi M Burrows and R Needham. A logic of authentication. *ACM Transactions on Computer Systems*, 8:18–36, 1990.

[Mic00]   Sun Microsystems. Sun's java web site. http://java.sun.com, 2000.

[Nec97]   G Necula. Proof-carrying code. In *Proc. of 24th Annual Symposium on Principles Of Programming Languages*, 1997.

[PB00]   P Girard J-L Lanet V Wiels G Zanon P Bieber, J Cazin. Checking secure interactions of smart card applets. Technical report, Gemplus R&D Centre, 2000. http://www.gemplus.com/smart/r_d/projects/pacap.htm.

[Pet99]   C C Peter. http://cctpwww.cityu.edu.hk/computer/c3_smartcard.htm.

[RG93]   A Rao and M Georgeff. A model-theoretic approach to the verification of situated reasoning systems. In *Proceedings of the Thirteenth International Joint Conference on Artificial Intelligence (IJCAI-93)*, pages 318–324. Morgan-Kauffman, 1993.

[SGPV98]   A Slater, R Goré, J Posegga, and H Vogt. CardTAP: Automated theorem proving on a smart card. In *AI98: Proceedings of the Australian Joint Conference on Artificial Intelligence*, LNAI 1502:239-248. Springer, 1998.

[Shv90]   G F. Shvarts. Autoepistemic modal logics. In Rohit Parikh, editor, *Theoretical Aspects About Reasoning About Knowledge*, pages 97–109, 1990.

A Programming and a Modelling Perspective on the Evaluation of Java Card Implementations

Pieter H. Hartel[1,2] and Eduard de Jong[3]

[1] Dept. of Computer Science, Univ. of Twente, The Netherlands.
pieter@cs.utwente.nl
[2] Dept. of Electronics and Computer Science, Univ. of Southampton, UK.
phh@ecs.soton.ac.uk
[3] Sun Microsystems, Inc. Palo Alto, CA 94043 USA.
Eduard.deJong@Sun.COM

Abstract. Java Card Technology has provided a huge step forward in programming smart cards: from assembler to using a high level Object Oriented language. However, the authors have found some differences between the current Java Card version (2.1) and main stream Java that may restrict the benefits of using Java achievable in smartcard programming. In particular, efforts towards evaluating Java Card implementations at a high level of assurance may be hampered by the presence of these differences as well as by the complexity of the Java Card VM and API. The goal of the present paper is to detail the differences from a programming and a modelling point of view.[1]

1 Introduction

With Java[2] Card Technology smart cards can be programmed in Java enjoying the benefits of object orientation. Both the card operating system as well as more application specific programming can be done in Java. Allowing a clearer distinction between the service and application layers in card software than previously possible. The second major advance of the Java Card VM is therefore the support for card applets. These applets take care of all application specific processing in a structured, efficient and secure manner. Moreover, card applets are downloadable and provide the opportunity to dynamically manage the services provided by a card. Thirdly, the Java Card API offers a model for controlled object sharing between applets. Finally, there is a special Java Card run-time library API, designed specifically for smart cards. It includes support for basic cryptographic routines (DES and RSA). There is no need to support say a windowing system on a smart card.

To reflect the limited computing resources inherent to smart cards, the Java Card VM and API impose restrictions. For example, there is no support for

---

[1] This work was supported by Sun Microsystems Inc.
[2] Java and all Java-based trademarks and logos are trademarks or registered trademarks of Sun Microsystems, Inc. in the U.S. or other countries, and are used under license.

I. Attali and T. Jensen (Eds.): Java Card 2000, LNCS 2041, pp. 52–72, 2001.
© Springer-Verlag Berlin Heidelberg 2001

threads, garbage collection, or real numbers. While the standard word size for Java is 32 bits, for the Java Card VM this is 16 bits. Instead of relying on middle ware products, the Java Card API includes a simple transaction facility built in the VM. It also includes an interface to the ISO 7816-4 standard for the format of communication between smart card and terminal. Using this rather low-level protocol in Java is somewhat cumbersome, but Java Card applications are fully compatible with legacy terminals. Without this compatibility, an evolutionary approach for introducing Java Card technology into the market place would not work. Finally, Java Card implementations do not provide generic auditing facilities, which makes it difficult to evaluate the effectiveness of the Java card security mechanisms. Instead, it is left to the Java Card application programmers to ensure that appropriate logging information is maintained.

The already wide adoption of Java Card technology has shown that it has much to offer to the smart card community. Using Java makes it possible to deploy up-to-date software engineering techniques, ranging from object oriented design to formal methods. Gaining experience while deploying Java Cards has revealed the inevitable flaws in a first generation technology; and enhancements and additional features are being proposed by the user community. This paper evaluates the current specification of the Java Card technology to support its further development as the programming environment of choice for smart cards.

Offering programming facilities for smart cards, and adding new ones, places responsibilities on the implementors and users of Java Card systems, to maintain appropriate levels of trust. Responsibilities not common to the world of programmers at large. The goal of this paper is to explore possible avenues of bringing these two worlds closer, with an emphasis on programming patterns and formal modelling.

2   Related Work

A number of reports in the open literature provide evaluations of the Java Card specification.

Oestreicher [14] discusses the Java Card Transaction mechanism and proposes a number of improvements. Montgomery and Krishna [11] expose a potential security problem in the Java Card model for object sharing, and give guidance on how to avoid the problem. Oestreicher and Krishna [15] suggest how the Java Card persistence model may be improved. Rose and Rose [19] comment on the lack of on-card byte code verification and propose a solution. We list and evaluate these and other issues.

Formal modelling of Java Card aspects has been considered by: Denny and Jensen [3], Lanet and Requet [10], Motré [12], Posegga and Vogt [17], and Reid and Looi [18]. For a comprehensive discussion of these papers please refer to our earlier paper [8].

3 Methodology

The Common Criteria for IT Security Evaluation [16] require the presentation of formal models of IT systems for evaluation at the highest assurance level. It is possible to develop such formal models after the fact. However this is not ideal since the modelling activity is sure to uncover hitherto unknown problems in the design and implementation of the actual IT system. A good example is provided by Bertelsen's work on the specification of the JVM [1], and the resulting list of errata to the official Sun documentation.

A more profitable approach to evaluation at the highest assurance levels is to consider formal modelling as an integrated part of the software development process. This would ensure that the system under development can actually be formalised effectively. By effective we mean that the models are sufficiently clear and concise to make them useful for reasoning, whilst assuring that the models are a sufficiently accurate abstraction of the IT system. In an ideal world one would use formal methods throughout the design and implementation process. In practice this may not achievable for reasons of costs, increased production times, or simply lack of skills on the part of the engineering team. However, if the stakes are sufficiently high, such as in the safety critical software industry, the use of formal methods is the norm.

As a compromise we favour a structured interaction between the engineering team and a team of formal methods specialists. Both teams would be in a continued dialogue, with proposals made by one team being reviewed by the other. This would ensure that implementation considerations and modelling issues are both addressed right from the start.

For those critical of formal methods, we should like to point out that the issues most likely to cause problems to modelling and reasoning are precisely the same issues that would be troublesome to the engineering team. Examples include issues that make a system difficult to understand, that cause complex interactions between supposedly independent components, or that make testing a nightmare. Using formal methods is a good way to identify the important issues early in the software life cycle.

To build a formal model of a system is the same as to express the system in a different, more abstract and mathematical way. A particular concept in a system may be represented incorrectly in the model, or may not be found easy to understand. Either case may mean that the concept is complex and difficult to explain, and therefore likely also difficult to implement correctly. Programming, even in a high level language, is still a relatively low-level activity, requiring the programmer to keep an eye on a considerable amount of, often dispersed, details. By contrast, modelling is a high level activity, working with reasonable abstractions within a limited scope. For example in most models it is reasonable to assume that an unlimited amount of memory is available. The programmer might also make this assumption but would then additionally have to build a garbage collector to support it.

To make matters more concrete we focus on a number of aspects of Java Card implementations. A smart card is not a PC; resource constraints and security considerations require special attention. In the current version of the Java Card 2.1 specification this has lead to a significant number of changes and/or additions to the Java language and the API. We reflect on these changes and additions in Section 6, with a view to reduce their number. A specific problem we have encountered is that often a design/implementation seems to require a particular feature to achieve one objective and a different feature to achieve another. However, on further study it may appear that both objectives may be achieved via the addition of a single, somewhat different, feature, thus reducing the complexity of the system. Our recommendations for the process of additions and changes are:

- stimulate reflection on a proposal (additions, changes etc);
- encourage generalisation of the proposal, perhaps at the expense of some efficiency;
- require capitalisation on the "investment" as much as possible, i.e. consider how a feature might be used to achieve other objectives as well;
- assess all the potential interactions between the newly proposed feature and existing features;
- ask for a second opinion, i.e. find ways of viewing the proposal from alternate angles, for which formal modelling is appropriate.

In the context of Java language and API changes or extensions we can make these recommendations more practical. A useful course of action is to investigate whether a desired feature can be expressed in some way in terms of features already provided. For example one could try to write a transaction facility in Java, to discover what is the essence of what is missing in order to make it work. This would focus on the missing essential feature. In a parallel modelling activity one might try to capture the semantics of the missing feature and add it to the semantic model of the existing system. We will give an example of this approach in our modelling case study of Section 5.

Java Card programmers might be less concerned with the principles of language and API addition or extension mechanisms rather than with the practice. Therefore, we also present a case study illustrating some of our observations on a simple example. This is the subject of the next section.

4   Programming Case Study

To illustrate the issues in programming a Java Card applet consider as an example the code fragment of Figure 1. This is taken verbatim from the Java Card 2.1 Application Programming Interface [20, Page 40]. The line numbers have been added for ease of reference.

4.1   APDU Based Communication

Communication between the card and the terminal must be expressed in terms of byte oriented APDU commands. This problem arises merely because the Java

```
1   // The purpose of this example is to show most of the methods
2   // in use and not to depict any particular APDU processing
3
4   public void process(APDU apdu){
5    // ...
6    byte[] buffer = apdu.getBuffer();
7    byte cla = buffer[ISO7816.OFFSET_CLA];
8    byte ins = buffer[ISO7816.OFFSET_INS];
9     ...
10  // assume this command has incoming data
11  // Lc tells us the incoming apdu command length
12  short bytesLeft = (short) (buffer[ISO7816.OFFSET_LC] & 0x00FF);
13  if (bytesLeft < (short)55) ISOException.throwIt( ISO7816.SW_WRONG_LENGTH );
14
15  short readCount = apdu.setIncomingAndReceive();
16  while ( bytesLeft > 0){
17      // process bytes in buffer[5] to buffer[readCount+4];
18      bytesLeft -= readCount;
19      readCount = apdu.receiveBytes ( ISO7816.OFFSET_CDATA );
20      }
21  //
22  //...
23  //
24  // Note that for a short response as in the case illustrated here
25  // the three APDU method calls shown :
26  // setOutgoing(),setOutgoingLength() & sendBytes()
27  // could be replaced by one APDU method call : setOutgoingAndSend().
28  // construct the reply APDU
29  short le = apdu.setOutgoing();
30  if (le < (short)2) ISOException.throwIt( ISO7816.SW_WRONG_LENGTH );
31  apdu.setOutgoingLength( (short)3 );
32
33  // build response data in apdu.buffer[ 0.. outCount-1 ];
34  buffer[0] = (byte)1; buffer[1] = (byte)2; buffer[3] = (byte)3;
35  apdu.sendBytes ( (short)0 , (short)3 );
36  // return good complete status 90 00
37  }
```

Fig. 1. The main method of a prototypical Java Card applet.

Card framework addresses the specific problem of using Java to write smart card applications. Card applications are fundamentally small server programs that rely on communication with an inherently limited bandwidth and a severely restricted packet size. The usual programming abstraction of communication as an unlimited stream is hard to maintain in the card API in its full generality. The Open Card framework [2] addresses the complementary problem for terminals. The two frameworks use the standardized APDU communication format as an interface. The code fragment shows typical in card processing for this format.

The `process` method receives an APDU object to discover which command to process (line 4). However, the actual command information is not available in the APDU object, but needs to be acquired by the `apdu.getBuffer()` method call (line 6). This method returns a reference to a global buffer with the actual command data. Regardless of the requirements of the actual command, the data is offered as a raw array of bytes. This leaves the application programmer with the unenviable task of manually unmarshalling application data. For example the `class` byte is obtained by an array access (line 7). In keeping with the object oriented philosophy one would have preferred to write `apdu.cla`, or `apdu.cla()`, or in accordance with the Java style recommendations `apdu.getClassByte()`.

A second example of the difficulty in manually unmarshalling data is found at line 12. Here the byte at offset `ISO7816.OFFSET_LC` is an *unsigned* value. The masking operation, and the fact that in Java intermediate results of a computation are integers ensures that bytes in the range -128 .. -1 are mapped onto shorts in the range 128 .. 255. This level of detail is not something that one would like to burden the programmer with.

A third example of how tricky low level programming is can be found at line 34, where obviously by a cut and paste error, an assignment is made to `buffer[3]` instead of `buffer[2]`.

Not obvious from the coding example is the fact that sending and receiving APDU commands has some degree of protocol dependency: T=0 and T=1 do not always have the same view on the number of bytes sent or received.

A solution would be to create an all embracing framework that abstracts away from APDU commands, perhaps using a lightweight RMI style interface. Full RMI would be too expensive to implement on a smart card, it is too powerful and general purpose for smart cards, and RMI does not offer the security that is required. Work is in progress on a number of other solutions, for example the GemPlus Direct Method Invocation (DMI).

4.2   Type Casts

Java is based on 32-bit words; the Java Card VM uses a mixture of 8, 16 and 32-bit semantics. The APDU communication is based on byte arrays. The stack contains 16 bit items. There is optional support for 32 bit integers. Since intermediate results from 8 or 16-bit calculations may require 32-bits, the Java language requires the programmer to state explicitly (by inserting appropriate type casts) where data may be lost.

Type casts are notoriously difficult to get right. Consider as an example the code at lines 13 and 16. One of the comparisons uses a type cast, and the other does not. The type cast is redundant here, because the intermediate result of the comparisons is of type int. By contrast the type cast in line 12 is required by the Java semantics, as the result of the expression on the right hand side is automatically an integer. Programmer action is required to explicitly cast an integer result into a short. This is a standard feature of Java. However, the problem arises because Java Card support for the int type is optional. Some Java Card implementations therefore would not be able to cope with the example if the short had been replaced by int.

It is probably more a matter of months than years before smart cards are sufficiently powerful to sustain full 32-bit applications. This would solve this problem.

4.3   Memory Management

Java Card programmers cannot rely on the services of a garbage collector. Instead they are required to pre-allocate all storage, both in RAM and EEPROM. Reusing space is fully under control of the programmer. This creates similar memory allocation problems to what one would find in C programs, such as premature re-use of space, or space leaks.

The advantage of pre-allocation is that applets always have the required heap space available. However, they might still run out of stack frames.

Preallocation has two disadvantages. Firstly, it does not cope with transient data. Therefore the Java Card API provides a feature to make sure that pre-allocated RAM data is cleared appropriately.

Secondly, since all applets pre-allocate their store, it is not possible that one applet temporarily uses more than its share. Such scenarios might arise in particular when applets call upon other applets for some service. Over commitment has been a standard technique used in operating systems for many years, and it could have been used here with success.

With a garbage-collected heap, neither pre-allocation nor explicitly transient objects would be necessary. One argument has been raised claiming that transient objects in RAM are useful to maintain cryptographic session keys. However, from a security perspective, it is probably easier to spy out data in RAM than it is to spy out EEPROM. The relative strength of the memory technologies seems irrelevant as the more precious master keys are stored in EEPROM, from which the session keys are derived.

Potential solutions to the pre-allocation problem include using transacted memory [9], or using a moving garbage collector that migrates long-lived data from RAM to EEPROM.

The Java Card VM does not support finalizers, because it does not support garbage collection. However, not having finalizers is generally considered an advantage, because the presence of finalizers makes the meaning of Java programs dependent on the, asynchronous, behaviour of the garbage collector. Without finalizers there is no such dependency.

While a space conscious system, the current Java Card specification seems to have paid less attention to stack space requirements. First it has 16-bit words; secondly there is no limit on stack growth, since Java Card applets can be recursive. With recursion banned, which is certainly feasible for programs with the scope of a Java card applet, a tool could work out the maximum number of stack frames needed by an applet, which coupled with a maximum heap size as required by the programmer could yield a true deadlock free applet at least in terms of space requirements.

Exceptions in Java are objects, and in the JCRE (the Java Card Runtime Environment) an object has been preallocated for every exception that could be raised by a Java Card applet. Such exceptions are accessed via an index in a table, and they are raised using the throwIt() method, as illustrated at line 13 and 30 of the code fragment of Figure 1.

This mechanism is considered redundant, at least in its exposure to the card application programmer. Similar savings could have been achieved by allowing the VM storage allocator to cache the objects created for exceptions. Assuming that most applets throw far fewer exceptions than there are defined by the Java Card specification, this represents a significant saving. An implementation based on caching could be entirely transparent to the programmer, thus obviating the need to redefine that part of the API that deals with exceptions.

4.4   Concurrency

The innocent looking method call on line 35 represents an interesting problem because the sendBytes call may be asynchronous. This means that the data stored in the shared buffer must not be altered until the send operation has completed. There is no way for an applet of finding out whether the operation has actually completed. This is the only aspect of the Java Card specification that permits concurrency, as threads are not supported. Programming concurrent systems is harder than programming sequential systems, and not surprisingly modelling work on concurrent systems is harder than modelling sequential systems.

We believe that the small optimisation that may be present in some Java Card implementations by allowing an asynchronous send does not outweigh the disadvantage of having to cope with concurrency, and the possibility of differing semantics of an applet on different implementations of the VM.

5   Modelling Case Study

In this section we model an environmental constraint pertinent to smart cards known as "card tear", which is the sudden removal of power from the processor. We study how it might interact with the normal operation and persistence in a Java Card implementation. Our model makes some simplifying assumptions, making it possible to learn about card tear in an abstract setting that is not cluttered by detail. One would have to check of course that the lessons learned also apply to a real system. This is future work.

Nielson and Nielson [13] provide an excellent introduction to the methods and notation used. LETOS has been used to typecheck and execute our specifications [7].

Every Java thread has a method `uncaughtException`, which is called when the thread raises an exception that is not caught [4, Section 20.21.31]. In contrast, the Java Card VM takes the view than an uncaught exception is handled in an implementation defined way [22, Section 2.3.3.1]. This difference may be relevant for review, but is not considered here.

Most Java exceptions are synchronous, which means that they are raised as a result of the current computation. Exceptions are also precise [4, Section 11.3.1] in the sense that they are raised immediately a semantic constraint is violated. Java also has two asynchronous exceptions: `ThreadDeath` and `InternalError`, which may be raised at any time. As the Java Card specification does not allow threads, it does not allow `ThreadDeath`. The Java Card specification does permit raising `InternalError`, but leaves it up to the implementation to decide how to handle it [22, Section 2.3.3.1]. The intention is that Java Errors can only be caught if the situation is deemed recoverable. For now we will assume that an `InternalError` cannot be caught, and that it renders the card muted to avoid security problems. This effectively removes all asynchronous exceptions from the Java Card specification.

Standard Java does not provide persistence. Therefore a Java applet does not expect objects to be preserved between to runs of the applet. In contrast, the Java Card API does support persistence. Java Card applets retain some of their objects (those stored in EEPROM), but loose others (stored in RAM). To acknowledge this, the life time of the Java Card VM is deemed to be the same as the life time of the smart card on which it runs [21, Chapter 2]. The Java Card VM detects whether an applet has been interrupted by a power failure, and ensures that the persistent objects of the applet are in a consistent state upon restart of the applet.

This raises the question of how to model power failure and recovery. The most appropriate way of doing so seems to be to introduce an asynchronous exception `PowerFailure`. In the model, the Java object store is represented by a RAM, and an EEPROM which shadows the RAM. The programmer is responsible for choosing the moment at which to save RAM contents into EEPROM. Java programs are modelled by a small subset covering the essence of an applet, saving and storing RAM contents and the handling of exceptions. This is the subject of the following sections.

5.1 Syntax

Consider the smallest fragment of Java as shown below, which permits throwing and handling exceptions. The fragment offers just four statements: `throw` to raise an exception, `try ... catch` to bind a statement to its exception handler, the increment statement ($v + +$, where v represents a program variable), and the method calls `save()`, and `restore()`. The (first) semicolon represents statement composition, ϵ represents an empty statement sequence.

$s \equiv$ throw x | try{s}catch(x){s} | v ++ | save() | restore() | s ; s | ϵ;

Also define two exceptions (ArithmeticException, and PowerFailure), and an out-of-band value (normal) that indicates normal processing.

$x \equiv$ ArithmeticException | PowerFailure | normal;

5.2 Transition Relation

A machine to execute the statements (s) would also need the state of the RAM (r), and the state of the EEPROM (e). The RAM is modelled as a mapping from variables to numbers (data). The EEPROM is modelled as a copy of saved RAM contents.

$$r \equiv \{\langle v \mapsto \mathbb{N}\rangle\};$$
$$e \equiv r;$$

The transition relation ($\rightarrow$) giving the natural semantics of the Java fragment has the type:

$$\rightarrow :: \langle s, \ r, \ e\rangle \leftrightarrow \langle r, \ e, \ x\rangle;$$

An increment statement stores a new value in RAM. The **save** operation stores the contents of the RAM in the EEPROM, and the **restore** operation recovers the RAM contents.

[++] $\langle v\ ++, \ r, \ e\rangle \rightarrow \langle r \oplus \{v \mapsto r(v) + 1\}, \ e, \ \text{normal}\rangle;$

[save] $\langle$save(), r, _$\rangle \rightarrow \langle r, \ r, \ \text{normal}\rangle;$

[restore] $\langle$restore(), _, e$\rangle \rightarrow \langle e, \ e, \ \text{normal}\rangle;$

Raising an exception is modelled by recording the exception in the third component of the result state.

[throw^1] $\langle$throw x, r, e$\rangle \rightarrow \langle r, \ e, \ x\rangle,$
        if $x \neq$ PowerFailure;

A power failure additionally wipes out the RAM. This models the fact that the RAM contents is actually lost when the power fails, and not when the power is restored. We could have decided to leave the RAM in an undefined state, which probably models real hardware more accurately, but this would represent a security risk. Memory remanence [6] might make it possible with some memory technology for some of the old contents to reappear when power is restored.

$$[\mathtt{throw}^2] \; \langle\mathtt{throw}\; x, \; r, \; e\rangle \rightarrow \langle\{\langle v \mapsto 0\rangle \mid v \in domain(r)\}, \; e, \; x\rangle,$$
$$\text{if } x = \mathtt{PowerFailure};$$

The **try**...**catch** statement can be executed in different ways, depending on whether an exception is raised, or whether the **try** clause has completely normally. The first possibility below applies when the **try** clause completes without raising an exception.

$$[\mathtt{try}^1] \; \frac{\langle s_t, \; r, \; e\rangle \rightarrow \langle r', \; e', \; x_t\rangle}{\langle\mathtt{try}\{s_t\}\mathtt{catch}(x)\{s_c\}, \; r, \; e\rangle \rightarrow \langle r', \; e', \; \mathtt{normal}\rangle,}$$
$$\text{if } x_t = \mathtt{normal};$$

If the **try** clause has caused an exception and the current **catch** clause can handle it, the statements of the **catch** clause are executed.

$$[\mathtt{try}^2] \; \frac{\langle s_t, \; r, \; e\rangle \rightarrow \langle r', \; e', \; x_t\rangle,\quad \langle s_c, \; r', \; e'\rangle \rightarrow \langle r'', \; e'', \; x_c\rangle}{\langle\mathtt{try}\{s_t\}\mathtt{catch}(x)\{s_c\}, \; r, \; e\rangle \rightarrow \langle r'', \; e'', \; x_c\rangle,}$$
$$\text{if } x_t \neq \mathtt{normal} \wedge x_t = x;$$

If the **try** clause has caused an exception and the current **catch** clause cannot handle it, the exception will be propagated to another, embracing handler.

$$[\mathtt{try}^3] \; \frac{\langle s_t, \; r, \; e\rangle \rightarrow \langle r', \; e', \; x_t\rangle}{\langle\mathtt{try}\{s_t\}\mathtt{catch}(x)\{s_c\}, \; r, \; e\rangle \rightarrow \langle r', \; e', \; x_t\rangle,}$$
$$\text{if } x_t \neq \mathtt{normal} \wedge x_t \neq x;$$

Statement composition is handled in a similar way as described above. The execution proceeds differently, depending on whether the first statement causes an exception to be raised, or whether it completes normally.

$$[;^1] \; \frac{\langle s_1, \; r, \; e\rangle \rightarrow \langle r', \; e', \; x_1\rangle,\quad \langle s_2, \; r', \; e'\rangle \rightarrow \langle r'', \; e'', \; x_2\rangle}{\langle s_1 \; ; \; s_2, \; r, \; e\rangle \rightarrow \langle r'', \; e'', \; x_2\rangle,}$$
$$\text{if } x_1 = \mathtt{normal};$$

$$[;^2] \; \frac{\langle s_1, \; r, \; e\rangle \rightarrow \langle r', \; e', \; x_1\rangle}{\langle s_1 \; ; \; s_2, \; r, \; e\rangle \rightarrow \langle r', \; e', \; x_1\rangle,}$$
$$\text{if } x_1 \neq \mathtt{normal};$$

Finally, a statement may not be able to complete due to power failure. This is modelled by the rule below.

$$[\mathtt{power}] \; \langle \_, \; r, \; e\rangle \rightarrow \langle\{\langle v \mapsto 0\rangle \mid v \in domain(r)\}, \; e, \; \mathtt{PowerFailure}\rangle;$$

The power axiom duplicates the object of the throw² axiom. The rule is applicable whenever any of the other 10 rules are applicable. The semantics has thus become non-deterministic. From the programmers point of view this means that any statement can be replaced by throw PowerFailure. This can be done any number of times.

The current draft of the SCSUG Smart Card Protection Profile [5, Section 3.2] specifies the same assumption as we have made here: "Power and Clock come from the terminal. These are not considered reliable sources". Interpreting unreliable as 'can happen at any time' translates directly into the use of non-determinism in our semantics.

5.3   Operational Semantics

We are now able to put all the pieces together in a function S (below), which gives the semantics of an applet j.

An applet can never handle a power failure. Therefore, we require that there are no occurrences of try{...}catch(PowerFailure){...} in j. All other exceptions are required to be handled by the applet j itself, as is the case in standard Java.

Almost paradoxically, to allow the applet j to complete normally, we will try to execute it repeatedly. Each time a power failure occurs, execution is interrupted and then restarted, until finally j completes normally. This coincides with the view that the Java Card VM lives as long as the carrier smart card is operational. The repeated execution is modelled by wrapping applet j in a try statement as shown by the local definition of w in the semantic function S below.

The recursive definition of the wrapper w ensures that when the applet j is aborted by a power failure, the catch clause causes the whole process to be started again. If the applet j runs to completion, the catch clause is ignored and the wrapper w terminates.

Each run of j begins by restoring the RAM contents from the EEPROM, and ends either with a PowerFailure, or normal termination. The initial EEPROM and RAM map all addresses to zero.

$$S[j] = \langle w, r, r \rangle \rightarrow$$
$$\textbf{where}$$
$$w = try\{restore()\ j\}catch(PowerFailure)\{w\}$$
$$r = \{\langle a \mapsto 0 \rangle \mid a \in [0..]\};$$

5.4   Example Applet

We can now use the semantic function to trace the execution of a applet, for example the following applet j_1:

$$j_1 = a\ ++\ ;\ save();\ b\ ++;$$

The applet j_1 is not intended to do something useful, but it happens to count the power failures witnessed when trying to execute the b + + statement. The number will be reflected in the final state of the RAM and the EEPROM, which therefore may assume any final state as shown below:

$$S[\![j_1]\!] \in \{ \langle \{ \langle a \mapsto n \rangle, \langle b \mapsto 1 \rangle \}, \{ \langle a \mapsto n \rangle, \langle b \mapsto 0 \rangle \}, normal \rangle \mid n \in [1..] \};$$

Here is another, simpler example:

$$j_2 = a\ ++\ ;\ b\ ++;$$

As compared to j_1, this applet lacks the **save**. Therefore its behaviour is characterised by one of two possible outcomes:

$$S[\![j_2]\!] \in \{ \langle \{ \langle a \mapsto 1 \rangle, \langle b \mapsto 0 \rangle \}, \{ \langle a \mapsto 1 \rangle, \langle b \mapsto 0 \rangle \}, normal \rangle,$$
$$\langle \{ \langle a \mapsto 1 \rangle, \langle b \mapsto 1 \rangle \}, \{ \langle a \mapsto 1 \rangle, \langle b \mapsto 0 \rangle \}, normal \rangle \};$$

Both assertions are can be proved by induction on the number of times PowerFailure is raised.

5.5 Properties

There are several useful properties that one might study for the given semantics. Of particular interest is the influence of the wrapper on the semantics of the applets j.

Preservation of termination. Firstly it would be desirable to prove that the wrapper preserves termination of applets.

The set of rules is compositional, so any derivation tree is finite, and thus all applets j terminate. Assume that there are $n \geq 0$ power failures during the life time of the applet j. We now sketch a proof by induction on n that the wrapper preserves termination.

In the base case ($n = 0$) and by our requirement that all exceptions (except PowerFailure of course) are handled by j itself we have by rules [**restore**], [$;^1$] and [**try**^{1}]:

$$\frac{\langle \textbf{restore}(), r, e \rangle \rightarrow \langle r', e', normal \rangle, \quad \langle j, r', e' \rangle \rightarrow \langle r'', e'', normal \rangle}{[] \ \langle \textbf{try}\{\textbf{restore}(); j\}\textbf{catch}(\textbf{PowerFailure})\{w\}, r, e \rangle \rightarrow \langle r'', e'', normal \rangle};$$

In the general case assume that there are $n > 0$ power failures during the life time of the applet. Then unfolding the recursive definition of the wrapper w by n times would give us the inductive case.

Here we have glossed over one issue: the **power** rule is always applicable. Therefore even in the base case the following derivation is valid:

$$[] \ \langle \textbf{try}\{\textbf{restore}(); j\}\textbf{catch}(\textbf{PowerFailure})\{w\}, r, e \rangle \rightarrow$$
$$\langle \{ \langle v \mapsto 0 \rangle \mid v \in domain(r) \}, e, \textbf{PowerFailure} \rangle;$$

To remedy this shortcoming of our model we make a fairness assumption, which states that a derivation may not begin with an application of the power rule, and which also rules out an application of the power rule immediately after the previous.

EEPROM preservation. A second property would establish that whatever is written to the EEPROM can eventually be read back. Ideally one would like to prove this preservation of information property in the deterministic setting, i.e without the rule power present. However, the proof would not carry over to the extended semantics, because the extension is not operationally conservative. Therefore one would have to re-prove the preservation property in the extended setting. This represents the cost of adding a feature (i.e. modelling power failure).

5.6 Modelling in Java

A natural question to ask is: What could have been achieved by attempting to model power failure in Java itself? To answer this we implemented the formal model by way of a Java 'simulator', a fragment of which is shown below. The fragment corresponds to a single unfolding of the wrapper w, with the sample applet j_1 from Section 5.4.

The tear() method simulates the non-deterministic choice of whether card tear should trigger the PowerFailure exception.

```
class PowerFailure extends Exception {
    PowerFailure() { super( ); }
}
```

The power() method actually raises the exception, after clearing the RAM. The result is that any statement of our sample applet j_1 is either executed or aborted, as required by the formal model.

```
try {
    if( tear() ) power() else restore() ;
    if( tear() ) power() else a++ ;
    if( tear() ) power() else save() ;
    if( tear() ) power() else b++ ;
} catch( PowerFailure e1 ) {
    try {
        if( tear() ) power() else restore() ;
        if( tear() ) power() else a++ ;
        if( tear() ) power() else save() ;
        if( tear() ) power() else b++ ;
    } catch( PowerFailure e2 ) {
        . . .
    }
}
```

The simulator has been validated by using it to execute a number of rather trivial example applets, and by comparing the resulting states to those obtained by a proof from the formal model.

To return to the question raised at the beginning of this section, we believe to have shown that a lot can be achieved by modelling in Java. However some of the concepts required are not particularly obvious from a programmer's perspective, such as the recursive wrapper, or the non-deterministic choice. Some mathematical training is essential to apply these ideas. On the other hand, using an exception to model power failure, and clearing the RAM to enhance security could be ideas natural to the programmer.

The main difference between formal modelling and simulation in Java is that the latter activity does not support proofs. We believe that engineering and modelling skills should be present in an engineering team to achieve best results.

6   Comparison of the Java and Java Card Specifications

Having presented two detailed case studies, we now give a comprehensive overview of the differences between the Java and Java Card specifications. This section is best read with the relevant Java Card documentation [20,22,21] available.

The Java Card specification is based on a subset of Java and its APIs. The subset was chosen primarily to cope with resource constraints. However, it is also an extension of the subset, with the extensions to provide additional smart card specific functionality. Table 1 lists the exclusions by the subset and the additions by the extension. The table is provided by way of summary, we will not discuss it entry by entry. Instead we will discuss the issues in an appropriate context.

6.1   Software Engineering Aspects

Some aspects of using the programming environment we believe need to be improved in future specifications:

- Some of the limitations and exclusions imposed in the Java Card specification (i.e. memory size) cannot be enforced statically. This makes it more difficult for the programmer to test and debug Java Card applets, because they may not hit the restriction or limitation on any development environment.
- The Java Card specification encourages a low level programming style that that does not sit comfortably with mainstream object oriented analysis and design.
- Java and Java Card documentation sometimes express high-level concepts in low-level terms. For example the Java 2 security model talks about stack inspection, and the Java Card security model discusses which byte codes access objects. Java programmers should be able to understand security in Java terms.

Table 1. A summary of the differences between the Java and Java Card specifications.

subset	[20]	superset of the subset
no class files	1.2	cap + export files
no dynamic class loading	2.2.1.1	applet installer
no security manager	2.2.1.1, 3.4	contexts
no garbage collection	2.2.1.1	
no finalization	2.2.1.1	
no threads	2.2.1.1	asynchronous writes using APDU buffer
no cloning	2.2.1.1	
no native code in applets	2.2.1.2	
subset of Java visibility rules	2.2.1.1, 5.4.1	two kinds packages: library and applet, with different visibility rules
no multidimensional arrays	2.2.1.3	
no char, double, float, or long types	2.2.1.3	
only a small part of the Java API	2.2.1.4	Java Card API
no reflection, no class Class	2.2.1.4	
type int is optionally supported	2.2.3.1	
limited number of numbers of classes, interfaces, methods, fields, array elements, and cases.	2.2.4.1	
only initialisation of static fields that are of primitive type or array of primitive type	2.2.4.5	
no long, float, double, and monitor byte codes, 73 in total	2.3.2.1	All different byte codes
no checked exceptions, only some runtime exceptions and errors	2.3.3	SystemException with reason codes
	4.2	Application Identifier (AID)
no name based linkage	4.3.6	token based linkage
no class based linking and loading	4.4	loading is package based
no primitive final fields in the constant pool	4.4	primitive final fields are inlined
binary compatibility not fully supported by the off-card byte code verifier, extra restrictions	4.4,4.5	major and minor version numbers
	5.4.1	sharable interfaces, global arrays
no 32 bit stack	7.4	16 bit stack

- Java Card vendors have considerable freedom in extending/revising their Java Card versions. This may hamper portability at the level of CAP and Export files (not at the level of class files).

Also, the consequences of the language specification as a superset of a subset of Java we have recognized as:

- Java API's or applets cannot be ported easily to Java Card implementations, and, vice versa, Java Card applets cannot be developed easily using a generic Java IDE.
- As a naturally evolving programming environment new features will be added and old features will disappear; addressing the inherent legacy problem will be harder.
- Main-stream Java programmers, in addition to learning the card application framework API, will have to be specially trained to use the card specific extensions.

Summarising, there is less portability between Java and Java Card implementations, in terms of software engineering techniques, than the authors consider desirable.

6.2   Object Life Times

The Java Card specification takes the useful view that the life time of applets spans terminal sessions. This means that the objects held on to by the applets may also live forever. Therefore, objects are by default persistent, as is indeed required in smart cards. An applet itself is an object, which is created by the static `install` method of the applets defining class. The JCRE implementation arranges for a context switch when calling the `install` method to satisfy the ownership relation.

An applet may communicate with the terminal only when it is selected. Only one applet is selected at any one time. An applet may call on another applet for some service. This causes a context switch, but not a deselect of the caller. There are thus two notions of an applet being 'current': "current context" and "currently selected".

An applet is automatically deselected when the terminal selects another applet. An applet is not deselected upon power failure. This arrangement makes it hard for the applet to perform a proper cleanup [21, Section 3.5].

There is a notion of a default applet, which is implicitly selected after a card reset. It is unclear how such an applet may know whether it has been selected by default, or explicitly [21, Section 4.1], or, if indeed this is relevant.

6.3   Linking and Loading

Linking and loading of Java Card code has a number of aspects that Java does not have:

- Linking and loading is package based, rather than class based.
- The linking and loading process creates the additional in-card generic object attribute of ownership. This attribute is essential to the Java Card security model. However, it does not exist in Java and its relationship to the package as unit of linking and loading seems arbitrary.
- Visibility rules differ between library packages and packages that contain applets.
- The information from a class file is represented in two different files (the cap file and the export file), thus making it possible for the files to get out of synchronisation, while it is harder for a class file to become internally inconsistent.
- Version control is only supported with a major and minor version number, and not with byte code verification (on the card).
- Binary compatibility in the Java Card specification is a based on a subset of Java's binary compatibility rules, e.g. changing final static fields of primitive types is a binary compatible change according to Java, but not so according to the Java Card specification.
- Cap files contain considerable redundant information to optimize the loading, linking and applet installation, as well as the efficient lookup of methods etc, making this code representation less robust. Particular examples include the ordering of virtual methods in the appropriate table, the inclusion of the entire class hierarchy in the export file, and the separation of name spaces for public and private virtual methods [20, Section 4.3.7.6].

A further investigation into the interaction of these issues would be worth while.

6.4   Security

The Java Card API offers a protocol which applets have to go through to obtain an object shared with another applet. This has two problems: First, the protocol is quite involved, and secondly the mechanism is not fully object based. Let us consider some of the important aspects of the sharing model.

A context is a trusted domain, which acts as a principal. All applets defined in the same package share a context. A context is called a group context if it contains more than one applet. Only applets and the run-time environment create objects. The run-time environment is represented by a 'pseudo' context. The context of the applet that creates an object is the owning context of that object. An applet is an object, it is owned by its context; however, a context is not an object.

Objects created by applets in the same context may be shared freely. Objects from different contexts can only be shared if a special protocol is followed [20, 6.2.4.2]. Ownership is thus a relation between contexts and objects. In an object oriented world it would be more natural and flexible to define this relation between objects.

There are two relevant relationships: ownership and access. An applet may grant another applet access, subject to following the 'shared interface protocol'. An owner may invoke methods, read and write fields etc. An applet with only access may only invoke methods on the shared object.

A context is a static concept. There is a current context, maintained by the run-time environment. The current context is switched by calls to (instance) methods and returns from those calls, in LIFO order. Contexts are also switched by exceptions. Invoking a method and throwing an exception may cause a security exception, when the context switch is not permitted. For symmetry reasons, returning from a method should be able to also generate a security exception. Static methods and fields are transparent for context switches. The run-time environment knows which context and object belongs to from the object header.

The ownership scheme has two problems: Firstly, it does not allow for server applets to create objects on behalf of other applets, because ownership is not transferable [20, Section 6.1.3]. Secondly, the ownership scheme does not allow an applet to manage a group of other applets, because applets are owned by a context, not by an object.

The JCRE owns a number of global arrays, and a number of entry point objects. All fields, methods and components of these are accessible to all applets. References to temporary entry point objects and global arrays can only be manipulated in certain ways, subject to fairly involved rules [20, Section 6.2].

Summarizing, there are three notions of sharing: entry point objects, global arrays, and sharable interface objects. Ideally there should be just one. Unfortunately, none of the sharing mechanisms address cryptographic security. Perhaps a more logical notion of sharing would use the same mechanisms that are now used to share information between the terminal and the card. In this case, APDUs (or the high level equivalent) could be shared between either the terminal and the cards or between different applets on the card.

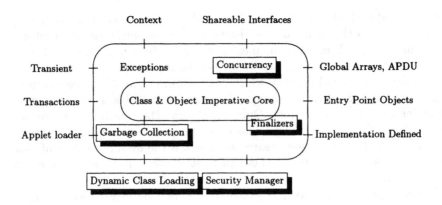

Fig. 2. Interactions between features of the Java and Java Card specifications.

7 Conclusion

Figure 2 summarises our findings graphically. The innermost area consist of Java's imperative core and the object oriented features. The next layer adds exceptions, concurrency, garbage collection and finalizers. Each of these added features interacts with the object orientation and the imperative core, potentially requiring the programmer to understand, and the modeller to study many separate interactions. Java also adds a security manager and dynamic class loading requiring further interactions to be considered for regular Java. The Java Card specification does not offer the grayed features, but has a variety of features of its own. In addition the Java Card specification leaves some issues open to the implementation (e.g. whether to support int, which exceptions are recoverable). We believe that this gives rise to rather too many interactions to be considered easily in formal analysis and recommend simplification.

We have presented two case studies. The first discusses the programmer's view on the somewhat low level feel to Java Card programming. The second case study presents a formal model of card tear, that is shown to be consistent with the Draft SCSUG Smart Card Protection Profile. We have translated the formal model back into a simulator written in Java to show that modelling provides practical information to the Java design level.

From both case studies we conclude that Java Card specifications can be improved by simplification. In fact we give a number of concrete suggestions for such simplifications.

References

1. P. Bertelsen. Semantics of Java byte code. Technical report, Technical Univ. of Denmark, Mar 1997. www.dina.kvl.dk/ ~pmb/.
2. OpenCard Consortium. *OpenCard Framework – General Information Web Document*. IBM Deutschland Entwicklung GmbH, Böblingen, Germany, second edition, Oct 1998. www.opencard.org.
3. E. Denney and Th. Jensen. Correctness of Java card method lookup via logical relations. In E. Smolka, editor, *9th European Symp. on programming (ESOP)*, *LNCS 1782*, pages 104–118, Berlin, West Germany, Mar 2000. Springer-Verlag, Berlin.
4. J. Gosling, B. Joy, and G. Steele. *The Java Language Specification*. Addison Wesley, Reading, Massachusetts, 1996.
5. Smart Card Security User Group. *Smart Card Protection Profile*. U. S. Dept. of Commerce, National Bureau of Standards and Technology, May 2000. http://csrc.nist.gov/ cc/.
6. P. Gutmann. Secure deletion of data from magnetic and Solid-State memory. In *6th Int. USENIX Security Symp. Focusing on Applications of Cryptography*, pages 77–89, San Jose, California, Jul 1996. Usenix Association, Berkely, California.
7. P. H. Hartel. LETOS – a lightweight execution tool for operational semantics. *Software—practice and experience*, 29(15):1379–1416, Sep 1999. www.ecs.soton.ac.uk/ ~phh/ letos.html.

8. P. H. Hartel. Formalising Java safety – an overview. In J. Domingo-Ferrer, D. Chan, and A. Watson, editors, *4th Int. IFIP wg 8.8 Conf. Smart card research and advanced application (CARDIS)*, pages 115–134, Bristol, UK, Sep 2000. Kluwer Academic Publishers, Boston.

9. P. H. Hartel, M. J. Butler, E. de Jong, and M. Longley. Transacted memory for smart cards. In *10th Formal Methods for Increasing Software Productivity (FME), LNCS*, page to appear, Berlin, Germany, Mar 2001. Springer-Verlag, Berlin. www.dsse.ecs.soton.ac.uk/ techreports/ 2000-9.html.

10. J.-L. Lanet and A. Requet. Formal proof of smart card applets correctness. In J.-J. Quisquater and B. Schneier, editors, *3rd Int. Conf. Smart card research and advanced application (CARDIS 1998 preproceedings)*, Louvain la Neuve, Belgium, Sep 1998. Univ. Catholique de Louvain la Neuve.

11. M. Montgomery and K. Krishna. Secure object sharing in Java card. In *USENIX Workshop on Smartcard Technology (Smartcard '99)*, pages 119–127, Chicago, Illinois, 1999. USENIX Assoc, Berkeley, California.

12. S. Motré. Formal model and implementation of the Java card dynamic security policy. In *Approches Formelles dans l'Assistance au Développement de Logiciels - AFADL'2000*, Grenoble, France, Jan 2000. http:// www-lsr.imag.fr/ afadl.

13. H. R. Nielson and F. Nielson. *Semantics with applications: A formal introduction*. John Wiley & Sons, Chichester, UK, 1991.

14. M. Oestreicher. Transactions in Java card. In *15th Annual Computer Security Applications Conference (ACSAC)*, pages 291–298, Phoenix, Arizona, Dec 1999. IEEE Comput. Soc, Los Alamitos, California. www.acsac.org/ 1999/ abstracts/ thu-b-1500-marcus.html.

15. M. Oestreicher and K. Krishna. Object lifetimes in Java card. In *USENIX Workshop on Smartcard Technology (Smartcard '99)*, pages 129–37, Chicago, Illinois, 1999. USENIX Assoc, Berkeley, California.

16. National Institute of Standards and Technology. *Common Criteria for Information Technology Security Evaluation*. U. S. Dept. of Commerce, National Bureau of Standards and Technology, Aug 1999. http:// csrc.nist.gov/ cc/.

17. J. Posegga and H. Vogt. Byte code verification for Java smart cards based on model checking. In J.-J. Quisquater, Y. Deswarte, C. Meadows, and D. Gollmann, editors, *European Symposium on Research in Computer Security (ESORICS), LNCS 1485*, pages 175–190, Louvain-la-Neuve, Belgium, Sep 1998. Springer-Verlag, Berlin.

18. J. Reid and M. Looi. Making sense of smart card security certifications. In J. Domingo-Ferrer, D. Chan, and A. Watson, editors, *4th Int. IFIP wg 8.8 Conf. Smart card research and advanced application (CARDIS)*, pages 225–240, Bristol, UK, Sep 2000. Kluwer Academic Publishers, Boston.

19. E. Rose and K. H. Rose. Lightweight bytecode verification. In *OOPSLA'98 Workshop on Formal Underpinnings of Java (FUJ)*, Vancouver, Canada, Nov 1998. www-dse.doc.ic.ac.uk/ ˜sue/ oopsla/ cfp.html.

20. Sun. *Java Card 2.1 Applications Programming Interface*. Sun Micro systems Inc, Palo Alto, California, Jun 1999. http:// java.sun.com/ products/ javacard/.

21. Sun. *Java Card 2.1 Runtime Environment (JCRE) Specification*. Sun Micro systems Inc, Palo Alto, California, Jun 1999. http:// java.sun.com/ products/ javacard/.

22. Sun. *Java Card 2.1 Virtual Machine Specification*. Sun Micro systems Inc, Palo Alto, California, Mar 1999. http:// java.sun.com/ products/ javacard/.

Secure Internet Smartcards

Naomaru Itoi, Tomoko Fukuzawa, and Peter Honeyman

Program in Smartcard Technology
Center for Information Technology Integration
University of Michigan
Ann Arbor
http://www.citi.umich.edu/projects/smartcard/

Abstract. Smartcards have traditionally been isolated from computer networks, communicating exclusively with the host computers to which they are attached. As a result, users can only use smartcards on local hosts. This can be disturbing in typical office environments, where a user has multiple workstations, or uses remote workstations as well as local ones. The most straightforward way of addressing this problem would be a remote smartcard access mechanism that allows users to use remote smartcards as if they are local. However, there are two issues that are incurred by going remote, i.e., security and naming. Communication between an application and a smartcard goes through the Internet, and can be sniffed. Also, if a smartcard is identified by the name of the host, the smartcard's name changes every time it moves from a host to another.

In this paper, we describe middleware that solves these problems. Our work extends the Internet infrastructure for smartcards, which has recently been developed by Guthery et al. [9] and Rees et al. [20]. It addresses the security problem by encrypting communication with the session key established by the *Simple Password Exponential Key Exchange* (SPEKE). As a result, it is secure against off-line dictionary attack and man-in-the-middle attack. It also provides convenient naming by embracing the domain name service.

We have implemented two applications, Kerberos and SSH, on this infrastructure to illustrate its usability. Thanks to the object oriented programming mechanisms of Java Card and the UDP based interface of the infrastructure, it is straightforward to implement such applications. The performance of this system is less than ideal, as it takes more than 10 seconds to complete an authentication session.

1   Introduction

Smartcards are well known for their three major advantages in protecting secrets, bypassing the security problems of passwords, and improving convenience of applications. For example, smartcards are used in the Kerberos / smartcard integration to provide a secure storage for user keys, and to replace passwords with random keys, thus countering dictionary attacks [13]. As smartcard device

I. Attali and T. Jensen (Eds.): Java Card 2000, LNCS 2041, pp. 73–89, 2001.

drivers and development environments are maturing, and major operating system vendors such as Microsoft and Sun Microsystems are starting to support smartcards, we foresee a widespread use of smartcards in the near future.

Although smartcards are becoming popular, the current technology limits smartcards to local use, namely, they can only be accessed through serial ports from the workstations they are attached to. Smartcard applications, as in authentication [1,13] and payment systems [6,15], generally assume that smartcards are on the same workstation. The fact that smartcards cannot be used remotely poses a severe limitation as the following scenarios illustrate. First, consider a typical office, in which a user has several workstations providing diverse services. If smartcards are used to enhance the security of services, the user is forced to install smartcard readers on all computers and move the cards around as the tasks demand. Second, consider a scenario in which the user logs into a remote workstation that is physically out of her reach, and wants to use a local smartcard. She simply cannot do so without a remote smartcard access mechanism.

A solution to this problem has been developed in PC/SC-Lite framework [3]. It is among the more sophisticated card managers, in that it allows applications to access card readers on remote hosts. However, there are a few problems with PC/SC-Lite. First, it does not encrypt data in transit between the smartcard and the remote host, and thus exposes potentially sensitive communication to Internet eavesdroppers. Second, PC/SC-Lite does not provide a location independent name for a smartcard: a smartcard is identified by the host's domain name and a serial port on that host. If a card moves from one host to another or if the reader is moved to a different port, the smartcard's name becomes invalid.

To solve these problems, we have developed a smartcard remote access mechanism which provides a location independent name, and protects the information transmitted. Our work pursues the approach developed by Guthery et al. [9] and Rees et al. [20], which use Internet protocol for smartcards. We adapted the smartcard web server developed at CITI [20] by adding UDP support and a protocol for secure, authenticated remote communication.

The building blocks of our system are listed below.

- A smartcard is given a long-lived domain name.
- A UDP/IP stack is implemented as a JavaCard applet.
- The *Simple Password Exponential Key Exchange* protocol (SPEKE) [14] is used to establish a session key between the smartcard and the remote workstation. Subsequent communication is encrypted with the session key.
- Kerberos and SSH clients, which have previously been modified to accommodate smartcards [13], are further modified to take advantage of this system for remote smartcard access.

Our middleware and sample applications demonstrate the convenience of our system and offer a development infrastructure for similar applications.

We assume that readers have a certain amount of knowledge about smartcards. Those who are not familiar with smartcard terminology are advised to consult the book by Guthery and Jurgensen [10].

2 Design

In this section, we describe the goals of our system and the decisions we made to achieve the goals.

2.1 Location Independent Naming

One of a smartcard's essential features is mobility. A smartcard owner can carry it around and use it at different locations. For maximum convenience, the name of the smartcard should not change when the smartcard moves; otherwise, the owner has to assign and remember multiple names. This can be a significant burden for the owner. Identifying a smartcard with DNS solves this problem by providing a smartcard with a location-independent name.

We assign a unique, durable, Internet domain name [18] to each card. The Internet domain name service (DNS) maps the domain name to an IP address. This assumes deployment of a secure, dynamic DNS [22] or mobile IP [19].

By way of an example, the smartcard used in developing this project is always called `aya.citi.umich.edu`, no matter which workstation it is attached to.

2.2 Transport Layer

Because an IP stack for Java Card has been developed already in our lab [20], it is natural for us to choose UDP or TCP for data transmission. TCP has many advantages over UDP, namely: reliability and error correction. Nonetheless, we elected to implement UDP because it is much simpler than TCP and has a smaller "footprint", essential for the limited hardware resources available on a smartcard. These limited resources force CITI's TCP implementation to be less than complete, e.g., it does not retransmit dropped packets because smartcards lack an internal timer. The simplicity of UDP allows a more complete, standards-compliant implementation.

2.3 Security

Smartcard-based systems usually assume that the connection between a host and a smartcard reader is secure. This assumption is reasonable when the smartcard is attached to the local host over a serial line, which is hard to snoop or other-wise tamper with. The assumption no longer holds when part of the connection between a smartcard and a user's host is the Internet, which is generally an inse-cure medium. Consequently, our security goals require establishment of a secure channel between a host and a remote smartcard.

A secure channel has the following three properties: authenticity, secrecy, and integrity [4]. Our system achieves the first two properties by employing SPEKE, a secure key exchange protocol [14]. SPEKE establishes a session key for channel encryption while at the same time authenticating both parties with a shared secret.

We did not implement cryptographically secure integrity checking, or even UDP checksum in this implementation; at this time we find checksum calculation to be too time consuming for our applications. Our experience so far indicates that the lack of integrity checking does not have a detrimental impact on reliable communication. Implementing integrity checking would address one type of denial-of-service attack, but many others remain available to a powerful adversary in control of network traffic.

2.4   Alternatives to SPEKE

There are several alternatives to SPEKE, each with significant disadvantages.

- No encryption
  All messages are transmitted in the clear. This allows an adversary to eavesdrop and obtain all communication between the user and her smartcard.
- Sending a PIN
  The user sends a cleartext PIN to the Internet-attached smartcard and the card verifies it. This achieves authenticity, but allows an adversary to eavesdrop and steal the PIN.
- Encrypt with PIN
  A PIN can be used as a session key to encrypt the messages between the smartcard and the user's host. This achieves both authenticity and secrecy because it requires the parties to know the secret PIN. However, this is vulnerable to off-line guessing attacks: when a message contains identifiable strings, such as ASCII text or IP headers, an adversary can obtain the ciphertext and try all possible (exhaustive search) or likely (dictionary attack) PINs to decrypt the encrypted message. If a meaningful sequence of plaintext characters is uncovered, the PIN is revealed.
- Diffie-Hellman
  Diffie-Hellman key exchange (DH) can establish a session key between two parties [5]. However, it does not achieve authenticity, and is vulnerable to man-in-the-middle attack [21].
- Encrypted Key Exchange
  Encrypted Key Exchange (EKE) [2] achieves both authenticity and secrecy and blunts the DH man-in-the-middle attacks by cleverly using a shared secret, even one that is susceptible to off-line attacks.
  EKE's patent holders did not not offer us permission to use the protocol.
- Open Key Exchange
  Open Key Exchange (OKE) [16] achieves the same goals as EKE and is not patented. Moreover, OKE is accompanied by a rigorous mathematical proof of its security properties. However, the protocol is fairly complicated and expensive, requiring modular multiplication, modular division, and three different hash functions; none of these is supported in the Schlumberger Cyberflex Access smartcard that we use.

S	a secret shared between Alice and Bob
p	a prime number used as DH modulus
$f(S)$	a function that converts S into a suitable DH base
R_A, R_B	random numbers chosen by Alice and Bob
C_A, C_B	random challenges chosen by Alice and Bob
K	a session key generated as a result of SPEKE
$h(x)$	a one-way hash function, such as SHA1
$A \to B$: x	Alice sends x to Bob

DH Stage

Step 1.   Alice computes $Q_A = f(S)^{R_A} \bmod p$ $A \to B$: Q_A
Step 2.   Bob computes $Q_B = f(S)^{R_B} \bmod p$ $B \to A$: Q_B
Step 3.   Alice computes $K = h(Q_B^{R_A} \bmod p)$
Step 4.   Bob computes $K = h(Q_A^{R_B} \bmod p)$

Verification (optional)

Step 5.   Alice picks random number C_A $A \to B$: $E_K(C_A)$
Step 6.   Bob picks random number C_B $B \to A$: $E_K(C_A, C_B)$
Step 7.   Alice verifies C_A $A \to B$: $E_K(C_B)$
Step 8.   Bob verifies C_B

Fig. 1. SPEKE protocol

2.5   SPEKE Protocol

We settled on SPEKE, which achieves the same goals as EKE and OKE and can be implemented with resources available on smartcards. David Jablon generously permitted us to use SPEKE for non-commercial purposes.

SPEKE is a key exchange protocol based on Diffie-Hellman. SPEKE differs from DH mainly by using a shared secret to derive the base, instead of publishing the base in the initial exchange. This feature defeats the well-known man-in-the-middle attack on DH by forcing both parties to prove knowledge of a shared secret.

SPEKE computes the DH base by mapping the PIN to a base of prime order that is exponentiated by a random element. Without knowledge of the random exponent, an adversary is forced to compute the discrete log in order to gain information about the base; this is believed to be computationally prohibitive.

Because SPEKE does not use the shared secret to encrypt messages, it also avoids exposing plaintext/ciphertext pairs to off-line guessing attacks. SPEKE thus offers the essential properties we need to establish a secure channel.

The existence of a shared secret is reasonable for a system using smartcards: it is common practice to protect data in a smartcard with a personal identification number (PIN), which is a shared secret between the user and the smartcard. We return to this issue in Section 5.2.

Figure 1 summarizes the SPEKE protocol. The first stage of SPEKE uses the shared secret and DH to establish a session key. The session key may optionally be verified in the second stage by exchanging random challenges. Kerberos and SSH are self-authenticating, so we omit consideration of this step in the remainder of this paper.

Figure 2 illustrates our design. $f(S)$ is precomputed and stored on the card. The host and the smartcard exchange two request/reply pairs, initiated by a connection request from the host. This signals the smartcard to generate its first message while a user is entering her PIN, possibly achieving some overlap.

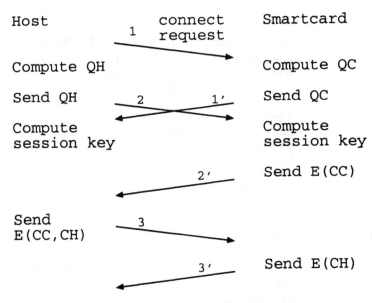

Fig. 2. SPEKE implemented with smartcard

3   Implementation

3.1   Overview

Figure 3 illustrates the overview of our system. "Application" is a Kerberos or SSH client in our implementation. We modified off-the-shelf implementations of Kerberos and SSH to move their key management and cryptographic needs to a remote smartcard.

The Kerberos client uses the remote smartcard to unseal a DES-encrypted ticket granting ticket (TGT). The SSH client uses the remote smartcard to digitally sign a challenge presented by an SSH server. Viewed from a high level, these applications have similar needs, although they use different base technologies.

The Kerberos or SSH client first establishes a session key with the remote smartcard using SPEKE, then exchanges messages with the smartcard to use its

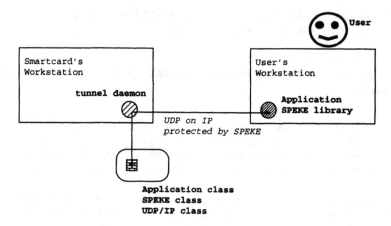

Fig. 3. Implementation Overview

services. The messages are encrypted with the session key generated by SPEKE and are transmitted by UDP/IP.

A daemon on the smartcard's host receives IP packets destined for the smartcard and forwards them to the smartcard through a "tunnel", which encapsulates IP payloads in ISO 7816 Application Protocol Data Units (APDUs) [8].

Upon arrival of a message, the smartcard's UDP/IP class strips off the IP and UDP headers, and passes the datagram to the application class, which handles the request. The smartcard also has a SPEKE class, which plays the smartcard's part in session key establishment and message encryption.

We use DES for message encryption. The length of the modulus p is 1024-bit. The size of exponents R_A and R_B is 128-bit. Smaller exponents were tested, but did not significantly affect performance. Larger exponents would not improve security, given that we are using DES. The (public) modulus is a safe prime that is hard-coded on both ends. The base, derived from the shared secret, is precomputed and stored on the card. Exponents and challenges are randomly generated in every session.

The host-side program was developed on Sun OS 5.6, and has been ported to Linux 2.2. The tunneling host runs OpenBSD 2.7 and has a Todos card reader attached. The card-side applet is written for the Schlumberger Cyberflex Access JavaCard. The Kerberos client is based on MIT distribution version 5-1.0.5, and SSH is based on SSH-1.2.27.

3.2   Component Details

The system is divided into five components: host-side application, host-side SPEKE library, tunnel daemon, card-side application and card-side SPEKE library. This section details each component.

```
#define MAXDATASIZE 220   /* 248 - IP & UDP header length */
#define SPEKE_HDR_SIZE 3*sizeof(unsigned char)

typedef struct speke_t {
  unsigned char ver, msgid, len, data[MAXDATASIZE - SPEKE_HDR_SIZE];
} speke_t;
```

ver stores a constant (0x10) indicating the SPEKE protocol.

msgid identifies the type of a message. Possible values of msgid are MSG_CONNECT, MSG_QB, MSG_QA, MSG_CHALLENGE_A, MSG_CHALLENGE_AB, MSG_CHALLENGE_B, MSG_REQUEST and MSG_REPLY.

len is the length of data contained in the packet. Cyberflex DES methods require the data length to be a multiple of 8 bytes so the data may need to be padded. len indicates the logical length of the data.

data is the data to be transmitted

Fig. 4. SPEKE data structure

Host-Side Application. The host-side application is a program that provides service to a smartcard user. Our demonstration applications are Kerberos and SSH clients. In the remainder of this section, we describe the Kerberos implementation; SSH has the same basic issues.

The Kerberos client is a modified kinit program, which carries out user authentication with the Kerberos Key Distribution Center (KDC) using a user's key stored in a smartcard. This kinit is similar to the one developed at CITI for Kerberos/smartcard integration using a local smartcard [13], except that it uses UDP/IP to communicate with a smartcard on a remote host instead of communicating conventional APDUs over a serial port to a locally-attached reader. Where the earlier smartcard-enabled kinit uses CITI's sc7816 communication library [20], the implementation described here uses our SPEKE library.

The Kerberos client follows three steps to receive the service from the smartcard: (1) establish a session key, (2) get a principal name × key number table from the smartcard, and (3) use the smartcard to decrypt the reply from the KDC. The first step is accomplished by calling speke_connect(). The others use speke_send() and speke_recv().

Here is an example of calls to the SPEKE library. speke is a data structure that stores the context of a SPEKE session. sockfd is a socket descriptor used to communicate with a smartcard.

```
/* key establishment */
speke_open (&speke, sockfd, hostname,
  SERV_PORT);
```

```
/* send 2 bytes to card */
n = speke_send (&speke, sockfd, bufr, 2);

/* receive up to 256 bytes from card */
n = speke_recv (&speke, sockfd, bufr, 256);
```

SPEKE Library. This host-side library implements the SPEKE key exchange protocol and exports procedures for connection establishment, connection destruction, and data transmission. The roles of these functions are summarized below.

speke_open asks the user for a PIN and establishes a session key using SPEKE
speke_send encrypts and sends data to the card
speke_recv receives and decrypts data from the card
speke_close destroys the session key

The SPEKE library uses UDP/IP for data transport. All the SPEKE packets sent and received by the SPEKE library are UDP datagrams, with the format depicted in Figure 4.

SPEKE uses several cryptographic operations, such as DES, modular exponentiation, and SHA1. The host-side SPEKE library includes three libraries to enable these operations: a DES library (libdes-4.01) by Eric Young [23], the GNU Multiple Precision Arithmetic Library [7], and the CTC library [17].

Tunnel Daemon. The tunnel daemon is the only component that runs on the smartcard's host computer. The job of the tunnel daemon is to encapsulate IP packets into APDUs, which smartcards understand. The routing table of the smartcard's host is configured so that the tunnel daemon receives packets directed to the smartcard's IP address.

When the tunnel daemon receives an IP packet, it prepends a 5-byte APDU header to it, and sends the APDU to the smartcard using CITI's sc7816 library. If a reply packet is available from the smartcard, the tunnel daemon issues a get-response APDU to the smartcard.

After receiving a response packet from the card, the tunnel daemon strips the APDU header and transmits the payload to the address specified in the IP header. Beyond this, tunnel daemon operation does not depend on the IP payload; it merely attaches and strips APDU headers and routes IP packets between the network and a serial device.

Card-Side Application. The remaining three components run on the smartcard. The highest level component among them is a card-side application program that provides application-specific services. For example, the Kerberos application decrypts a message that is encrypted with a user's symmetric key; the SSH application encrypts a random challenge with a private RSA key.

Thanks to the object oriented style of programming supported by JavaCards and to the SPEKE class taking care of the details of key exchange and message secrecy, all an application class has to do for communication is to inherit the SPEKE class and issue send() and recv() methods. An example follows:

```
public class KrbSpeke extends UdpSpeke {
  public void process(APDU apdu) {
    short len = recv(apdu);
    if (len >= 0) {
      len = kerberos_process (apdu, len);
      send (apdu, len);
    }
  }
}
```

SPEKE Class. The next layer on the smartcard is the SPEKE class. Similar to the host-side SPEKE library, the SPEKE class implements the SPEKE key exchange protocol and exports methods for data transmission. The API consists of two methods, send() and recv():

recv parses a packet. If the packet contains a message for key exchange, this method creates an appropriate packet and sends it out. Otherwise (i.e., if the packet carries data), it decrypts the data and passes it to the application class.
send encrypts a message and sends it.

The SPEKE class inherits the UDP class.

```
public class UdpSpeke extends Udp7816 {
  void send (APDU apdu, short len);
  short recv (APDU apdu);
}
```

UDP/IP Class. The last component is the UDP/IP class, which processes UDP/IP datagrams. This is built on CITI's smartcard IP stack. For incoming packets, the recv() method strips off UDP and IP headers and hands the data to the upper layer, in our case, the SPEKE class. Packets transmitted in the other direction are handled by the send() method, which adds UDP and IP headers to a message and sends it out of the smartcard.

4   Performance

In this section, we discuss performance. This system is not fast. Therefore, we focus on highlighting system bottlenecks, and discuss how performance can be improved.

Performance evaluation was carried out on two workstations in our LAN. The user's workstation is Linux 2.2 on a 400 MHz Pentium, and the smartcard's workstation is OpenBSD 2.7 on a 400 MHz Pentium. The smartcard is attached to the workstation with a Litronic PC-3 reader communicating at 115 Kbps.

4.1 Execution Time

The table shows the execution time of Kerberos and SSH client programs using our SPEKE library. The performance results of clients that use local smartcards and the sc7816 library are shown for comparison. All times are reported in seconds and are the average of five time trials. Variance is negligible.

	remote (s)	local (s)
Kerberos	12.8	3.33
SSH	12.6	3.43

The remote versions are much slower than the local ones. The difference is due largely to two factors: setting up SPEKE and the cost of encrypting and decrypting payloads. The next section focuses on these two factors.

4.2 Details

In this section, we discuss execution of the Kerberos client. Our observations also apply to the SSH client.

The events in the Kerberos client are listed below in chronological order. All times are reported in seconds and are the average of five time trials. Variance is negligible.

time (s)	events
0.00	kinit start
0.02	SPEKE connect start
0.03	Host send SPEKE1 (connect request)
0.03	Host send SPEKE2 (Q_A)
2.07	Host recv SPEKE1 (Q_B)
3.56	Host recv SPEKE2 (connect ok)
3.56	get_key_num start
5.88	get_key_num finish
5.88	decrypt ticket start
9.93	decrypt ticket finish
9.93	decrypt ticket start
12.80	decrypt ticket finish
12.80	kinit end

Data to be decrypted is divided into two blocks and sent separately because, at 224 bytes, a Kerberos ticket is too large for a smartcard to decrypt at once.

Within the total 12.80 seconds, time for using smartcard dominates, taking 12.78 seconds. This is not surprising: it takes 2 – 4 seconds to exchange a pair of request-reply packets, and there are five such pairs:

request type	time (s)
SPEKE1 ($\rightarrow$ connect request, $\leftarrow Q_B$)	2.04
SPEKE2 ($\rightarrow Q_A$, $\leftarrow$ connect ok)	1.49
get_key_num request ($\leftarrow$ princ table)	2.33
decrypt block 1 ($\rightarrow$ data, $\leftarrow$ data)	4.06
decrypt block 2 ($\rightarrow$ data, $\leftarrow$ data)	2.87

S a secret shared between Alice and Bob
P a public key generated by Alice
K a session key generated as a result of EKE
$A \rightarrow B$: x Alice sends x to Bob

Step 1. Alice generates P, encrypts it with S $A \rightarrow B$: $E_S(P)$
Step 2. Bob obtains P, generates K, computes $E_S(E_P(K))$ $B \rightarrow A$: $E_S(E_P(K))$

Fig. 5. EKE protocol key exchange. The optional verification step is not shown.

Now we analyze the message exchange bottleneck. Processing a request is divided into five phases.

- time spent in the smartcard
- IP communication between the user's host and the smartcard's host
- overhead of the tunnel daemon
- sc7816 library overhead
- communication between the smartcard and the smartcard's host. (This includes time for `get-response` APDU.)

Using the first message, SPEKE1, as a sample, we measure the following events. All times are reported in seconds and are the average of five time trials. Variance is negligible.

event	time (s)
IP + tunnel + sc7816	0.00
in-the-card	1.83
card communication	0.21
Total	2.04

Execution time in the smartcard dominates the other parts with a ratio of 9:1. Cryptographic operations, such as modular exponentiation by an RSA method, DES, and random number generation, are the main reasons that it takes so much time in the smartcard. Significant improvement in performance of our system is impossible without a faster smartcard or a protocol that is less computationally demanding.

Card communication time can be reduced with the T=1 protocol instead of T=0. With T=0, a get-response APDU is necessary to obtain data returned from a smartcard in addition to a service request APDU. With T=1, the smartcard returns data immediately after a request is made, eliminating the overhead of the get-response APDU. The Cyberflex Access smartcards we use do not support T=1.

4.3 EKE Measurement

Although we cannot use it in our projects because of a patent issue, we implemented and measured EKE to satisfy our curiosity. EKE is a simple and well-known protocol. The EKE protocol, described in Figure 5, is implemented with one pair of messages and optional verification. Like our SPEKE implementation, we initiate EKE with a connection request, which allows the smartcard to overlap its random number generation with the host's key pair generation and PIN input. The first message, EKE1, requests connection. The smartcard starts generating random numbers after receiving it. The second message, EKE2, implements steps 1 and 2.

A chronological event list is shown below. EKE takes 4.47 seconds to complete connection establishment, compared to 3.56 seconds for SPEKE.

time (s)	events
0.00	EKE connect start
0.01	Host send EKE1 (connect request)
1.43	Host send EKE2 ($E_S(P)$)
4.45	Host recv EKE2 ($E_S(E_P(K))$)
4.47	EKE connect ok

Time taken for each message pair is as follows.

request type	time
EKE1 ($\rightarrow$ connect request, $\leftarrow$ NULL)	0.83
EKE2 ($\rightarrow E_S(P)$, $\leftarrow E_S(E_P(K))$)	2.95

Although EKE is simpler than SPEKE, the time required to generate a key pair on the host (approximately 1.5 sec) hurts performance. Moore's law influences key generation time, but this is moderated by the fact that faster computers demand longer keys, which take longer to generate. On the whole, though, we expect key generation time to improve with new generations of microprocessors.

5 Discussion

In this section, we summarize the advantages of using Internet-attached smart-cards and discuss the security of our system.

5.1 Summary

The following four aspects highlight the value of this work.

Useful and necessary. Two year ago, we implemented and deployed our sc7816 version of the smartcard-integrated Kerberos to staff at CITI, who frequently use a lot of different workstations. It quickly became clear that accessing a smartcard remotely would extend the benefit of smartcard-enabled Kerberos to all our computers while saving us from having to install a reader on each of them.

The first application of smartcard IP for personal usage. We find smart-cards very effective when used as personal security devices connected to the Internet. Our work is the first implementation of such a system (that we know of).

Standard API. Our protocols are built on UDP and IP, universally accepted communication standards. We hope to positively influence today's smartcard API woe: many smartcard APIs are proposed, but none has established domi-nance, forcing developers to learn API after API.

Development framework. Our system enables developers to implement IP-based smartcard applications easily. Our source code is freely available on the CITI smartcard web page.

5.2 Security Considerations

In this section, we consider three potential vulnerabilities that could compromise the security of Internet smartcard: host compromise, off-line dictionary attack, and on-line attack.

Host compromise. Host compromise may yield the PIN entered by a user, by either finding it in memory, or obtaining it through a Trojan horse. The lack of trusted path from the keyboard to applications on most workstations make PIN / password typing dangerous. The adversary, with the PIN in hand, can convince the smartcard that he is the legitimate user, and receive services from the smartcard.

However, losing the PIN is not as bad as losing the password. In a smart-card protected system, the adversary must obtain the PIN and must access the smartcard to impersonate the user. In contrast, in a password protected system, the adversary can impersonate the user only by obtaining the password.

In addition, one can enhance the security of the system by taking advantage smartcard properties: physical isolation and trustworthiness. First, communication with a smartcard always goes through the smartcard reader and the serial port. These devices can indicate ongoing communication, for example, by a LED blinking on data transmission. The user can tell that the adversary is using the smartcard, if data are transmitted without the user's direction. Second, because a smartcard is a trustworthy device, one can implement a logging system in the smartcard that reports a fraud usage.

Off-line dictionary attack. An off-line dictionary attack does not pose a critical threat to our system. The adversary may mount this attack on the PIN using the messages transmitted in the SPEKE session establishment. However, because the PIN is only used to generate a key, and the key is only used to encrypt random numbers, the adversary cannot distinguish the right PIN from the wrong ones.

Jablon suggests a number of methods that can be used to prevent information leakage in SPEKE (and EKE) [14]; although we have not implemented all of these, we would find it prudent to do so before fully deploying the system. Following Jablon's suggestions, we feel confident that SPEKE can effectively blunt this attack.

On-line attack. An on-line attack is a potent threat. This attack would proceed as follows. An adversary tries each candidate PIN to establish a secure channel with the smartcard. Subsequent use of the channel either reveals a cleartext Kerberos TGT (or properly signed SSH nonce) or random garbage. Eventually, the adversary will try the correct PIN and defeat the PIN-based security of the system.

If four-digit PINs are used (which users may prefer because they are often used in banking cards), this attack is feasible. If we assume that a session can be completed in five seconds, then the entire space of potential PINs can be tested by an on-line adversary in 50,000 seconds, less than a day if the card is kept online.

The best way of solving this problem is to always pull off the card from the reader after using it. However, the user may want to leave the smartcard in her office and access it remotely. In that case, she cannot pull it off the reader.

To solve this problem, we suggest a counter on the card that keeps track of failed attempts to complete a Kerberos or SSH session. When the counter reaches a certain limit (e.g., 5 failures), the card blocks itself. However, this presents a denial-of-service attack, in which the adversary tries random PINs, quickly blocking the card. We are considering adding an administrative interface that uses a strong key to allow the counter to be reset remotely.

Alternatively, the PIN space could be expanded; a seven-digit PIN would require over a year of continuous testing to search the entire space. The S/KEY one-time password system [11,12] represents random keys by selecting short phrases made up of taken from a 2,048 word dictionary, e.g., "WAIT POD LIMA." Each word contributes 11 bits to the size of the search space; a three-word phrase would require centuries to search the entire space.

6   Conclusion

We designed and implemented an Internet-standards compliant middleware infrastructure that provides secure access to remote smartcards, and built two demonstration applications on it. The performance of the system reflects the performance realities of today's smartcards. Yet, we find the infrastructure useful, and anticipate that it will enable many new types of smartcard applications.

Acknowledgment. This work extends Jim Rees' pioneering implementation of Internet protocols on a smartcard. We thank Dug Song, Niels Provos, Wolfgang Ley, Gasper Carson, and Angelos Keromytis for valuable discussions. David Jablon kindly allowed us to use the SPEKE protocol.

This work was partially supported by a research grant from Schlumberger, Inc.

References

1. Bastiaan Bakker. Mutual authentication with smart cards. In *Proceedings of USENIX Workshop on Smartcard Technology*, May 1999.
2. Steven M. Bellovin and Michael Merritt. Encrypted key exchange: Password-based protocols secure against dictionary attacks. In *Proceedings IEEE Computer Society Symposium on Research in Security and Privacy*, pages 72–84, Oakland, CA, May 1992.
3. David Cocoran. Movement for the use of smart cards in a linux environment. http:// www.linuxnet.com/.
4. Dorothy Denning. *Cryptography and Data Security*. Addison-Wesley, 1983.
5. W. Diffie and M. E. Hellman. New directions in cryptography. In *IEEE Trans. Inform. Theory*, volume IT-22, Nov 1976.
6. Europay, MasterCard, and Visa. Emv'96: Integrated circuit card application specification for payment systems, June 1996. http://www.mastercard.com/ emv/emvspecs02.html.
7. The gnu multiple precision arithmetic library. http:// www.swox.com/ gmp/.
8. S. Guthery, Y. Baudoin, J. Posegga, and J. Rees. IP and ARP over ISO 7816-3 (Internet Draft), February 2000.
9. Scott Guthery. How to turn a gsm sim into a web server. In *CARDIS 2000*, Bristol, UK, September 2000.
10. Scott B. Guthery and Timothy M. Jurgensen. *Smart Card Developer's Kit*. MacMillan Technical Publishing, Indianapolis, Indiana, December 1997.
11. N. Haller. The s/key one-time password system, RFC 1760, Feb. 1995.
12. N. Haller and C. Metz. A one-time password system, RFC 1938, May 1996.
13. Naomaru Itoi and Peter Honeyman. Smartcard integration with Kerberos V5. In *Proceedings of USENIX Workshop on Smartcard Technology*, Chicago, May 1999.

14. David P. Jablon. Strong password-only authenticated key exchange. *ACM Computer Communications Review*, October 1996.

15. SET Secure Electronic Transaction LLC. Set standard technical specifications, 1999. http:// www.setco.org/.

16. Stephan Lucks. Open key exchange: How to defeat dictionary attacks without encrypting public keys. In *The Security Protocol Workshop '97*, Ecole Normale Superieure, April 1997.

17. Ian Miller and Mr. Tines. Ctc library. http:// www.bifroest.demon.co.uk/ ctc/ manuals/ ctclib.htm.

18. Paul Mockapetris. Domain names - concepts and facilities, STD 13, RFC 1034, Nov. 1987.

19. C. Perkins. Ip mobility support. Network Working Group Request for Comments: 2002, October 1996.

20. Jim Rees and Peter Honeyman. Webcard: A Java Card web server. In *CARDIS 2000*, Bristol, UK, September 2000.

21. Bruce Schneier. *Applied Cryptography*. John Wiley & Sons, Inc., 2 edition, 1996.

22. P. Vixie, S. Thomson, Y. Rekhter, and J. Bound. Dynamic updates in the domain name system (dns update). Network Working Group Request for Comments: 2136, April 1997.

23. Eric Young. libdes des library. ftp:// ftp.psy.uq.oz.au/ pub/ Crypto/ DES/.

Issues in Smartcard Middleware

Roger Kehr[1], Michael Rohs[2], and Harald Vogt[2]

[1] T-Nova Research Labs, Deutsche Telekom AG
Darmstadt, Germany
`roger.kehr@telekom.de`
[2] Institute of Information Systems, ETH Zurich
8092 Zurich, Switzerland
{`rohs, vogt`}`@inf.ethz.ch`

Abstract. Integration of smartcards in distributed computing environments still suffers from the lack of connectivity and processing power available on smartcards. A natural solution is the use of service proxies to mediate between network clients and smartcards. Main requirements to such architectures are spontaneous and transparent service integration, remote access, and usage security. We discuss these requirements using the JiniCard system as an example which provides seamless integration of smartcard services within a spontaneous networking environment.

1 Introduction

One of the main obstacles to the unification of smartcard usage is the specialization of applications and protocols used between the card and the terminals. Even with Java cards this will not change, since there is no standardized way of exhibiting a smartcard's interface to the outside world. Smartcards communicate by exchanging byte sequences, APDUs, which are only weakly structured. For the ease of parsing, this is often done by using TLV encodings, but in general, each card type defines its own formats.

Traditionally, these formats are standardized by large institutional bodies. However, standardization efforts suffer from their high cost and the rapid change of market needs. Practical interoperability therefore cannot be achieved by standardizing card application interfaces.

Smartcards heavily depend on the environment they are used in. Since these systems are generally equipped with more computing resources than smartcards, the key to interoperability could lie within more sophisticated, generally applicable techniques that help to discover card services and grant access to them. These techniques should support the following issues:

- **Spontaneous integration of cards.** There should be minimal effort required to make an existing system work with new cards. Vice versa, it should be easy to set up a new system using existing cards.
- **Transparent usage of card services.** The system should not have to care about any details regarding the communication to the services that rest on the card.

I. Attali and T. Jensen (Eds.): Java Card 2000, LNCS 2041, pp. 90–97, 2001.

- **Remote access.** Card services should be available within a distributed environment. For example, the same card, but different services, could be used for terminal login and accounting phone calls.
- **Security.** Only the legal owner of the card must be able to initiate the use of card services. Transactions have to be authorized by the card owner.

This paper shortly describes the JiniCard framework which was developed to enable the seamless integration of smartcards in distributed environments. We give an overview of the system and discuss some security issues in more detail. The system's implementation is available at [4].

2   The JiniCard Framework

In this section, we give a short overview of the system design and show how the requirements are tackled. A more detailed description of the framework can be found in [5]. Security issues are discussed in the next section.

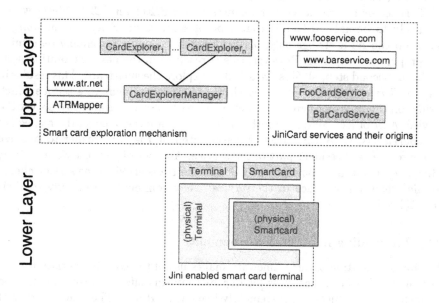

Fig. 1. Components of the JiniCard framework

2.1   Design Overview

The JiniCard system is comprised of two major parts. One part consists of a component that directly controls the card reader, while the other part lies within the "net". The core of the card terminal component is the *CardExplorerManager* (CEM). The task of this component is to manage the exploration process of the card. The network part supports the CEM by providing card and service specific components.

Figure 1 shows the components of the system. The lower layer offers basic operations to access card reader functions remotely. Its software parts and the CEM are physically located on the card terminal. All other components reside on remote locations and are requested for code objects only when needed.

2.2 Functional Description

The main idea of the JiniCard framework is to keep all functionality that is required to interact with a specific card service remotely on the net. It is loaded only when the respective card is actually inserted into the reader. There needs to be a mapping between the card and the location where the required code can be found. This mapping is established in two steps.

In the first step, the CEM reads the ATR (or multiple ATRs, if the card issues more than one) of the card and compiles a (HTTP) request which is sent to a server at a well-known address, e.g. *www.atr.net*.

This server returns a set of references to *CardExplorer* (CE) objects which are likely to be able to handle that type of smartcards. Since the mapping is based on the ATR strings only, it might not be possible to reliably determine the proper card explorer. However, this is resolved in the next exploration step

In the second step, all CEs are asked to explore the smartcard. This results in a set of *ServiceInfo* (SI) objects. Each SI object corresponds to a service which resides on the smartcard and for which a CE exists which was able to discover the service. A SI object contains another reference to a piece of code, the respective *CardService* (CS). A CS object is instantiated at the card reader to manage access to the card resident part of the service. Another object, the *ServiceProxy* (SP), can be obtained through the CS. SPs are transferred to the service clients to offer them an interface to the service. They communicate directly to their peer CS objects.

2.3 Embedding in a Jini Environment

The implementation of our framework makes use of the code instantiation facilities offered by Java. The class loading mechanisms offer a convenient method for instantiating objects from (remotely loaded) JAR files. The central server at *www.atr.net* keeps a set of these files, each containing the classes needed by a card explorer.

The CSs are also stored in JAR files and are instantiated through a special class loader which implements further optimizations such as caching of already known card services.

Jini [7] comes into play when card services are to be announced in a distributed environment. Jini offers methods for clients to look up whether needed services are available and also supports many of the administrative tasks linked with the use of remote services (such as timeouts when clients crash or services become unavailable).

The central component of Jini, the Lookup Service, is used to store service proxy objects which implement interfaces to their respective services. Clients send queries to the Lookup Service, asking for proxies which implement a certain service interface. A suitable proxy is downloaded to the client which can use this object to establish a communication to the actual service, which resides on the smartcard.

We assume that the card terminal has sufficient resources to participate in a Jini federation. This requires a relatively large amount of computing and storage capabilities. But since Jini is used only for the announcement of card services, the requirements imposed on terminals could be weakened in more static environments where components are equipped with knowledge about each other.

However, we regard the flexibility of dynamic code loading as crucial in achieving a high degree of interoperability between a wide variety of applications and smartcards. The responsibility of implementing service proxies is shifted to the service implementors who gain freedom in the design of their services. Anyway, the problem of standardized service interfaces remains, but on a much higher level, i.e. on the level of Java interfaces.

2.4 Discussion

The only information that can be reliably used for identification of smartcards lies within the ATR. We use the ATR to roughly determine which card explorers could be suitable for further investigation of the card. Since card explorers are not stored in the card terminal itself but kept remotely on the network, it is easily possible to introduce new cards by providing a new card explorer; no local intervention is necessary.

Transparent usage of card services is provided by service proxies. All details of the protocols used by the smartcard are encapsulated within the proxy. From an application's point of view, the service is represented by a Java object.

Conventional smartcard services are designed to work with a single client. Interleaving card sessions are normally not allowed. As with Java cards, this restriction is eased to some degree.

Within our framework, it is possible for multiple clients to download proxies that talk to a single smartcard. Problems arise when these proxies try to talk to the card concurrently. This happens, when a proxy initiates a conversation with some card applet and sends an APDU to the card, and another proxy does the same right afterwards. The card is then likely to produce no meaningful answer; it is even possible that data will get lost.

To avoid this, we introduced the possibility for proxies to gain exclusive access to a smartcard by acquiring a lock. The card terminal guarantees that no other proxy's APDUs are sent to the smartcard until the lock is released.

A typical interaction with a JavaCard is somewhat different. An applet is selected, then a sequence of APDUs is exchanged. Since there is no (card-) global state information stored within an applet, it poses no problem to deselect an applet at any time and reselect it again to continue the conversation. This enables concurrent usage of different applets on a single card. To handle this transparently to the clients, there exists a convenience method named `setSelectAPDU` in the `SmartCard` interface which is used to define an APDU for re-selecting the applet.

3   Secure Remote Smartcard Access

In the previous section we have outlined an architecture that allows a smartcard to offer services in a network by means of a proactive exploration mechanism initiated by the card terminal. Clients access these card services through Jini service proxies that use the basic interface methods of the card terminal to communicate with the card-resident portion of the service. The most obvious problem with such an approach is the secure access from remote clients to the card, and the problem of the card holder verification procedure (CHV).

3.1   Card Holder Verification

In traditional smartcard scenarios readers are attached to terminals with which the card holder performs CHV to unlock the card for security-sensitive operations. This can be the PIN typed into an ATM, or the PIN entered into a GSM handset to activate the network authentication procedure.

The underlying assumption with this approach is that the communication link between the pinpad or keyboard and the smartcard is secure and cannot be eavesdropped or tampered with. For most of the practical application scenarios smartcards are used in, this assumption sounds quite reasonable. In the scenarios described in our service architecture though, the link between the client and the smartcard must potentially be considered as untrusted and insecure, and special precautions have to be taken.

3.2   End-to-End Security Approaches

The ultimate solution to this problem would be to completely encrypt all information exchanged between the client and the smartcard. This would imply that the traditional ISO 7816 interface based on APDUs cannot be used anymore since it assumes unencrypted APDUs exchanged with the environment. Mechanisms like *secure messaging* [3] are only suitable to encrypt and authenticate the data part of APDUs, but not the class and instruction bytes. Tampering with header information can be detected by adding a digital signature of the header data to the body of an APDU. But not encrypting header information leaves opportunities for eavesdroppers. If the whole APDU is encrypted, then the structure of the APDU becomes meaningless. Such an APDU could only be interpreted after decryption.

In addition to such a completely new card interface we would run into a key distribution problem in case we use symmetric algorithms for encryption. Either the proxy contains the secret key in its state, which could potentially be observed in some runtime environment and exploited to decrypt future sessions with such a smartcard. A better solution would be to use protocols similar to SSL/TLS [1] that use asymmetric encryption to agree on a shared session key between a client and a server. We are in the process of investigating such an approach by implementing the server-side portion of the SSL protocol on a smartcard.

3.3   Secure Session Management via SSL

If we cannot rely on end-to-end secured communication with a smartcard we can require the card terminal itself to be a secure platform. In this case we could, e.g., require any communication from a network client to be transported over SSL. This could be done, for instance, by tunneling Java RMI invocations on top of SSL for which off-the-shelf solutions are available, e.g. [6]. As a first step, this would offer encrypted communication between the client and the card terminal. Of course we must trust the card terminal not to compromise such an approach. Current practice, e.g. ATM machines, operate with the same trust model. This makes us confident to consider this approach as feasible for many application domains. The main difference between ATM machines and PCs as terminals is that the former are strongly physically secured, whereas the degree of physical protection of PCs is not as high.

Simply encrypting communication to the card terminal is not sufficient, though. It would help to perform a secure remote card holder verification, but leaves the card unlocked for a certain period of time. If an intruder manages to send APDUs to the card via the terminal while the card is unlocked, the system could be compromised.

A solution would be to closely couple operations that require privileged access to the card and SSL sessions. The card terminal that offers access via SSL can uniquely identify peers based on the symmetric session keys used for encrypting and authenticating the communication. When a client performs a card holder verification the card terminal records the peer's identity. Further requests to this card are only allowed from the SSL communication channel that has unlocked the card. This effectively blocks any APDUs sent from other clients until the card is reset again and locked. This is essentially a variant of the semaphore operations beginMutex/endMutex methods offered by the terminal.

4   Related Work

Closely related to our approach of smartcard integration is the OpenCard Framework [2]. Originally, OCF was designed to run within a single Java VM which would block card readers to other applications. Also, it has no support for remote smartcard access. The proxy concept is used to hide the protocol to the service implementation on the smartcard. Similar to our approach is the use of *CardServiceFactory* objects which produce Java objects through which card resident services can be accessed. Anyway, we found the concept insufficient.

OCF uses an "application driven" paradigm. An application, which runs in the same Java VM as OCF itself, asks for a particular card service and waits until a card implementing that card service arrives. The card remains passive and does not get a chance to announce its capabilities and available services. To achieve this goal, a proactive paradigm is needed, in which the card is asked for its services that are then made available to the environment.

Although OCF defines interfaces and classes for application and card management, they are realized only rudimentary. In particular, the mapping from service descriptions to service instances is not defined.

OCF is a statically configured framework, where all available services must be registered in a configuration file. This is in opposition to the requirement of spontaneous integration that we identified as an important issue in smartcard middleware.

5   Conclusion

We have motivated the need for a standard way of exhibiting a smartcard's interface to the outside world. This issue is still not solved with the advent of Java cards, because the Java card approach does not change the basic means of interaction with smartcards, namely through APDUs.

Smartcards depend on their environments to provide useful services and are also inherently portable by their human owners. Given these characteristics we have identified four key areas, which need to be taken into account by middleware that aims for the interoperability of smartcards. These are spontaneous integration into environments, transparent usage of card services, remote access to card services, and security that is effectively controllable and observable by the card's owner.

We have given a brief description of the JiniCard framework, which aims at the seamless integration of smartcard services into distributed environments. JiniCard relies on the dynamic download of code to identify and instantiate the services that are available on a smartcard. It provides a well-defined platform for the execution of card-external parts of card services.

To achieve spontaneous integration into environments we chose Jini as the underlying middleware technology, because Jini's objective expressly is to provide simple mechanisms which enable devices to plug together to form an impromptu community.

Our approach is easily extensible by uploading new card explorers to a well known web server and by providing card service implementations. It also handles mutual exclusion of multiple clients that try to use a card concurrently. The independence of applets on Java cards seems to make a relatively transparent scheduling approach possible.

Accessing smartcards remotely poses new security issues. In particular, the assumption that the communication between clients and card services is secure no longer holds. Communication between clients in the net and smartcard services can potentially be observed (eavesdropping) and even altered (tampering).

Therefore it is considered problematic to completely unlock a card via card holder verification. New approaches have to be investigated to ensure the security of card-to-service communication. One solution that we are currently investigating is to implement the server-side portion of the SSL protocol on a smartcard or on the terminal attached to the smartcard reader. This makes it possible to geographically separate a card from its client.

Acknowledgements. We would like to thank Joachim Posegga for inspiring discussions at the beginning of the JiniCard project.

References

1. T. Dierks and C. Allen. The TLS Protocol Version 1.0. Internet RFC 2246, January 1999.
2. Uwe Hansmann, Thomas Schäck, Frank Seliger, and Martin Scott Nicklous. *Smart Card Application Development Using Java.* Springer-Verlag, 1999. See also www.opencard.org.
3. International Standards Organization. *International Standard ISO/IEC 7816: Identification Cards - Integrated Circuit Cards with contacts*, 1989.
4. JiniCard. http://www.inf.ethz.ch/~rohs/JiniCard/.
5. Roger Kehr, Michael Rohs, and Harald Vogt. Mobile Code as an Enabling Technology for Service-oriented Smartcard Middleware. In *The 2nd International Symposium on Distributed Objects and Applications (DOA)*. IEEE Computer Society Press, 2000.
   http://www.inf.ethz.ch/department/IS/vs/publ/papers/jinicard.pdf.
6. A. Popovici. ITISSL - A Java 2 Implementation of the SSL API based on SSLeay/OpenSSL. http://www-sp.iti.informatik.tu-darmstadt.de/itissl/, 1999.
7. Jim Waldo. The Jini Architecture for Network-centric Computing. *Communications of the ACM*, 42(7):76–82, July 1999.

Open Platform Security

Marc Kekicheff[1], Forough Kashef[1], and David Brewer[2]

[1] Visa International Services Association
Post Office Box 8299
San Francisco, CA 94128-8999
[2] Gamma Secure Systems Limited
Diamond House, 149 Frimley Rd Camberley, Surrey GU15 2PS, UK

Abstract. The Java Card^{TM}2.1.1 Runtime Environment (JCRE) Specification [1] describes a secure virtual machine environment for smart cards that facilitates the post-issuance loading and installation of applets, via an optional "Installer". The Open Platform (OP) Card Specification [2] provides a robust specification for that installer. It identifies the on-card security features necessary to safeguard the various actors that are involved in a smart card system, including card issuers, application providers as well as cardholders.

Such is the nature of information security these days it is necessary to demonstrate the trustworthiness of the OP approach. The Common Criteria (ISO 15408:1999) [3] presents an obvious course of action. A "Protection Profile", termed OP3 [4] has therefore been produced in order to ensure the benefit of Common Criteria evaluation of the OP installer, and by virtue of specifying the security requirements of the underlying operating system and integrated circuitry, of Java Card^{TM} and the chipcard platform itself.

Evaluation will demonstrate that the OP security requirements are correctly implemented and cannot be bypassed, deactivated, corrupted or otherwise circumvented – at least to a given level of confidence (an EAL in Common Criteria terms). This is an amazingly useful first step. However, there are important off-card assets that the smart card does not protect. Common Criteria evaluation does nothing to mitigate the risks to those assets. A Common Criteria evaluation will make assumptions about the environment of the target of evaluation. Evaluation does nothing to validate those assumptions. The assumptions usually concern the compromise of security data held off-card. It therefore makes little sense to rely just on the CC evaluation of just the smart card in order to establish and maintain the security of the overall system. Other steps are necessary.

The paper describes what is being done to progress the Common Criteria evaluation of OP and what else is necessary to ensure confidence in the security of the overall system. Researches indicate that Common Criteria evaluation at a modest level of evaluation (e.g. EAL 4) together with an "Information Security Management System" (ISMS), as specified in BS 7799:1999 Part 2 [5] –particularly to address the off-card security issues– reduces the need for smart card evaluation at higher EALs.

I. Attali and T. Jensen (Eds.): Java Card 2000, LNCS 2041, pp. 98–113, 2001.
© Springer-Verlag Berlin Heidelberg 2001

1   Introduction

The paper examines the security requirements of the Java Card™2.1.1 Runtime
Environment (JCRE) Specification [1] for a reconfigurable smart card installer.
It shows how those requirements have been translated into the language of the
Common Criteria (CC) [3] to produce the first public draft of the *Open Platform
Protection Profile (OP3)* [4]. This is the first installment of an overall program to
establish the trustworthiness of OP technology and project that trustworthiness
to the market place. The paper describes what else is necessary to establish the
trustworthiness of modern smart card technology, and in so doing challenges the
need for very high Common Criteria Evaluation Assurance Levels (EALs).

2   The JCRE and OP Specifications

Java Card™assumes that the life time of the newly installed applet begins
when it is registered with the JCRE and can be "selected" by the card acceptance device (CAD) and finishes when the card is terminated. Thus, for a
multi-application card, the life of all applets expires at the same time. The JCRE
Specification recognizes that the post-issuance installation of applets on smart
cards using Java Card technology is a complex topic. The specification therefore
gives JCRE implementers as much freedom as possible in their implementations, by specifying the minimal installation requirements necessary to achieve
interoperability across a wide range of possible Installer implementations.

The OP Card Specification extends the JCRE specification to define a secure
Installer, including the deletion of applets prior to card termination. It also allows
the Card Issuer to share the application space with other organizations (called
Application Providers), to install and manage their applications on their behalf
or to delegate that responsibility to them. These extensions, coupled with the use
of the Java™programming language provide a broad range of business benefits,
including:

- A significantly shorter "time-to-market", allowing new applications to be rapidly developed, piloted, rolled out in vast quantities and easily upgraded in
  response to market demands.
- The ability to present an enormous appeal to both merchants and consumers
  by allowing several applications to be housed on a single card and take advantage of new Internet and wireless technologies.

Indeed, it is anticipated that the ability to reconfigure the application content
of a smart card during its lifetime will be recognized as one of the greatest
technological contributions to e-business.

These business benefits, however, expose the smart card to new threats, such
as viruses and the ability of an attacker to delete applications and replace them
with others, or install agents with a view to spying on the cardholder or stea-
ling their money. It is also necessary to be mindful of threats more familiarly
associated with smart cards, such as electrical probing and differential power
analysis.

These are not necessarily difficult security problems to solve, but it is nevertheless very necessary to establish the trustworthiness of the Open Platform product and demonstrate that fact to the market.

2.1   The Open Platform Specification

The purpose of OP is simply to manage the loading, installation and deletion of applications. The primary components of the OP architecture (see Figure 1) are the *Card Manager*, the *Security Domains* and the *OP API*. The Card Manager is the on-card representative of the Card Issuer and is the central administrator of the entire card. Security Domains are the on-card representatives of Application Providers and may manage the loading and installation of applications pre-approved by the Card Issuer. The OP shares a runtime environment and hardware neutral API (i.e. the *JCRE API*) with the applications. Beneath this (not shown in the figure) is the runtime environment itself (i.e. Java Card^{TM}) and the integrated circuitry (collectively referred to as the *Card/Chip Operating Environment (COE)*). Applications may invoke the OP services via the OP API and the services of the COE via the JRCE API. The multiplicity of Security Domains allows each Application Provider's security data (such as cryptographic keys) to be kept separate and private from that of other Application Providers and the Card Issuer. The smart card typically takes power from *a Card Acceptance Device (CAD)* once inserted and is powered down when removed. Communication with the card is via the CAD and an on-card *Application Protocol Data Unit (APDU) interface*. The OP authenticates itself to a host computer (e.g. the Card Issuer's card management system) via the CAD and vice versa. The users of OP are the on-card applications and the Card Issuer and Application Providers' host systems. If a Card Issuer offers the cardholder a choice of whether to load an application, the negotiation would be conducted via the CAD and the host system, and not directly between the card and the cardholder. If this results in a request to load an application, the host machine would establish a secure mutually authenticated communication channel (termed the *Secure Channel*) and command OP to load and install the application. OP does not require cardholder authentication. Applications may use the *Secure Channel Protocol* for their own purpose as a means for achieving mutual authentication and preserving the confidentiality and integrity of APDUs. OP also provides an optional cardholder authentication service to applications called the *Global PIN*.

Chip card technology is available today in a range of product and price configurations, based on the capabilities and security of card hardware and software. This is reflected in the OP Specification by a variety of options that allow Card Issuers to choose products that match their business and security requirements. A minimal OP configuration (that omits the Security Domains) restricts the use of the smart card to the Card Issuer. In that configuration, the Card Issuer manages the loading and installation of all applications and therefore acts on behalf of the Application Providers. At the other extreme, a different OP configuration allows Application Providers, with pre-authorization from the Card Issuer, to manage the loading and installation of their own applications.

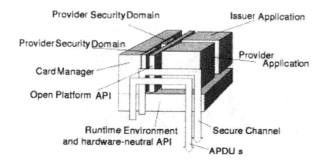

Fig. 1. Architecture of an OP smart card

2.2   Security Requirements

Security Assumptions. The OP-installer is a component of a much larger system that includes people, organizations and other computer systems, as well as the remainder of the Java Card^{TM}smart card and the applets that from time to time will be installed and removed. To determine the security responsibilities of OP it was first necessary to make assumptions about the security that will be provided by these other components. A general property of these assumptions is that their invalidity would expose an exploitable vulnerability that the OP could not possibly protect itself against. The assumptions concern:

- The security characteristics of the COE
- Byte code verification of applications and the absence of native code applications
- Off-card key management, and security in general
- Roles and responsibilities
- The initial state of the card when it is issued to cardholders.

While these assumptions simplify the analyses that are required to demonstrate the trustworthiness of OP (e.g. through Common Criteria evaluation) they imply a specification for other on-card and all off-card entities that must be satisfied.

Threats to Security. Figure 2 shows a categorization of the threats that are endemic to a smart card in general (see SCSUG-SCPP [6], for example) that are dealt with by the COE, and those that are specific to OP. Group I threats concern direct attacks on the chip circuitry using techniques that are usually reserved for testing and debugging chips. Group II threats concern more sophisticated attacks that monitor the external effects of the chip operation, such as power consumption. Group III concerns attacks using cards that have yet to be issued, cards from previous issue generations and clones of current cards. Group IV threats concern the card's usual interface to the outside world via the CAD and deals with problems such as those arising from the premature removal of the card from the CAD. Group V deals with attacks on the JCRE and OP that are made through the card's interface to the CAD. Group VI deals with the threats

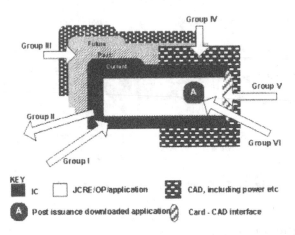

Fig. 2. Attack path analysis for a smart card

concerning the post-issuance loading of applications and their subsequent need to share resources.

OP has an interface to its users. The first point of an attack in Group V would therefore be an attempt to *impersonate an authorized user*. If the attack was successful then OP might be fooled into loading unauthorized applications, divulging security data and making unapproved management commands, such as terminating the card. Alternatively, a bona fide user may read, modify, execute or delete applications, information or other resources without having permission from the authority that owns or is responsible for the application, information or resources. For example, without proper security control, an Application Provider might accidentally delete the Card Issuer's applications. Thus the second type of attack is a user who, even if properly authenticated, *may attempt to do things that are outside of their intended authorization*. The third form is that a user who, even if properly authenticated and authorized, *may systematically experiment with different forms of input in attempt to violate OP security*. This attack is based on the "black box" software engineering technique of establishing the nature of algorithms and predicates ("IF" statements). If carried out exhaustively it could facilitate the reverse engineering of OP as well as the extraction of operational and security related information. A fourth type of attack is that *an attacker might eavesdrop on OP communications with a host*. They might do this as a precursor to masquerading as a Card Issuer or Application Provider, to steal confidential information (including application code) in transit or to record APDU sequences for a subsequent replay attack. The fifth type of attack is the *replay attack* itself. In this case intercepted APDU commands may be replayed, possibly with modification or in a different sequence, to facilitate a successful attack. These five classes of attack are common to all forms of applications.

The first type of a Group VI attack of relevance to OP concerns the *malicious generation of errors in the set-up sequence* prior to card issue. During the stages of card issuance that involve loading the OP with cryptographic keys, li-

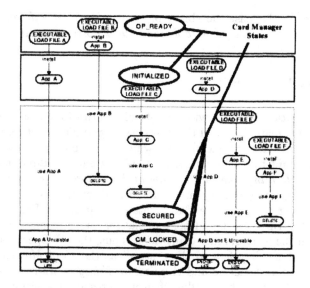

Fig. 3. State transitions enforced by the Card Manager

fecycle states etc, the data itself may be changed from the intended information or may be corrupted. Either event could be an attempt to penetrate the OP security functions or to expose the security in an unauthorized manner. Errors could be generated through simple errors, or through failure of some part of the transfer mechanisms. These errors could occur during loading of programs and/or loading of data. For example, memory usage limits could be exceeded, both at application load and when an application requests data memory. Similar attacks could be attempted when applications are loaded, installed and personalized post issuance. An attacker may utilize *unauthorized applications* to penetrate or modify the OP security functions. Such applications could include copies of authorized applications that had been infected with a virus or a Trojan horse. An attacker might attack an application based on an *analysis of the same application in a different environment,* such as a PC. An attacker might *delete applications without authorization.* Finally, an attacker may *force OP into a non-secure state* through inappropriate termination of selected operations, e.g. through premature termination of transactions or communications between OP and the CAD, insertion of interrupts, or by selecting related applications that may leave files open.

Normally, an adequate trust relationship will exist between the Application Providers and the Card Issuer, which will ensure that Application Providers are confident in the integrity of their applications when the Card Issuer loads them. Application Providers should also have confidence in the effectiveness of the Card Issuer's security systems that would prevent an attacker from modifying the application code prior to loading. Under certain circumstances, these assumptions may be invalid. In this case the ability of an attacker to *modify an Application Provider's application code prior to dynamic load* poses an additional threat.

2.3   Security Functions

The OP Specification details a wide variety of security functions to counter the aforementioned threats. Many of these are cryptographic in nature (see below). There are extensive access control rules, which serve to counter the threat that users might attempt to *delete applications without authorization* and that users *may attempt to do things that are outside of their intended authorization.* Some of these rules are discretionary in nature; the discretion being in the hands of the Card Issuer to approve access rights to Application Providers and applications. Other rules are mandatory in nature and are imposed by the OP Specification in the form of state transitions. Thus, the OP Specification describes a state machine. It refers to those states as the *Card Manager Lifecycle*, *Executable Load File Lifecycle* and *Application Lifecycle* states. A sample card configuration illustrating the possible lifecycle states and transitions of the Card Manager, Executable Load File and applications is illustrated in Figure 3 (see the OP Specification Chapter 5 for details). Note the sequence of Card Manager states, which also reflect the overall state of the card. The sequence starts with the OP_READY state. It is in this state that the OP is ready to accept the Card Issuer's instructions for loading cryptographic keys, and the pre-issuance loading and installation of applications. Applications can be loaded for future installation. The card must only be issued when it is in the SECURED state. These discretionary and mandatory rules and state transitions serve to frustrate an attacker who *may systematically experiment with different forms of input in attempt to violate OP security.* This objective is further enhanced by rules that allow applications to block themselves and, given the right privileges, to even block the card itself. If an attacker finds a weakness in an application, by *analysis of the same application in a different environment,* the offending application can be locked and subsequently replaced when a remedy has been found. Other security functions check the validity of OP security data and provide a form of intrusion detection. In the latter context the OP is empowered to lock applications if it perceives an internal security threat, for example because the application is raising too many runtime exceptions of a particular type. It is also necessary for the OP to de-allocate memory in the event of a power failure while loading an application. This provides a defense against an attacker who uses power failure to *force the OP into a non-secure state.*

Cryptographic Solutions. The remaining threats are addressed by cryptographic means. Mechanisms exist to load cryptographic keys both before and after issuance in a secure manner, to generate session keys and destroy keys. Mechanisms also exist to maintain independent key sets for the Card Manager and each Security Domain. Applications may therefore load their own keys encrypted by their Security Domain's key encrypting key.

The Secure Channel Protocol provides *host-card authentication, key confidentiality, message encryption, message authentication* and *MAC*[1] *chaining* using 3-DES and double length keys. Secure Channel mutual authentication is achieved through session key agreement by deriving a common set of session DES keys from static DES keys and subsequently using the session keys to calculate and to verify authentication data. Message authentication verifies the integrity as well as the authenticity of an APDU command sequence. The integrity of the sequence of commands being transmitted to the card is achieved by using the MAC from the current command as the Initial Chaining Vector (ICV) for the subsequent command. This ensures the card that all commands in a sequence have been received. These security functions counter the threats of *impersonating an authorized user, eavesdropping on OP communications, replay attack* and *malicious generation of errors in the set-up sequence*.

Additional cryptographic functions using RSA with at least 1024 bit keys and the secure hash algorithm, SHA-1, are used to counter the threat of loading *unauthorized applications* when the task of loading and installing applications has been delegated to an Application Provider. There are two functions. In the first, the Card Issuer digitally signs the application and its installation parameters to indicate that it is an authorized application. OP checks the validity of the signature prior to loading and installation. In the second, OP generates cryptographic receipts to say that the application has been loaded and installed (or for that matter deleted) and returns the receipts to the Card Issuer.

Another cryptographic function, which may use RSA/SHA-1 or DES to generate a data authentication pattern, is used to prove that *an Application Provider's application code has not been modified prior to dynamic load*.

3   The Open Platform Protection Profile

Like other protection profiles (e.g. [6, 7]), the Open Platform Protection Profile, OP3 [4] identifies the relationship between the Target of Evaluation (TOE) and its operational environment, the threats, the assets to be protected and the security objectives necessary to counter those threats. It enumerates the security functions necessary to meet those objectives, and the assurance requirements necessary to deliver the desired degree of confidence that the security requirements function as intended and cannot be bypassed. Unlike these other profiles, OP3 is very specific in terms of the security requirements. This difference should not be surprising as OP3 invokes the OP Specification whereas the other profiles do not and therefore have to be generic. The following extract serves as an example. Note the use of the + sign to indicate that the component is iterated.

> The TSF shall perform **delegated management receipt generation** in accordance with a specified cryptographic algorithm **(3-DES)** and cryptographic key **of double key length** that meet the following: **ANSI X9.52, FIPS 46/3 and OP Specification, paragraphs 7.9.2, 7.9.4, 7.9.5, 11.1, 11.1.3, 12.1.2.3, 13.9, 13.9.1, 13.9.2 and 13.9.3.** [FCS_COP.1+7.1]

---

[1] Message Authentication Code

The corresponding statement in [6] is:

> The TSF shall perform *list of cryptographic operations* in accordance with a specified *cryptographic algorithm* and *cryptographic key sizes* that meet the following: *list of standards*.

Another difference is that for OP3 the TOE is just the OP software; it does not include the applications or the COE. Instead, OP3 provides a specification for the COE and the security services that it provides to the applications. This has the benefit that application developers do not have to worry about the underlying security infrastructure. OP3 takes care of that. However this approach does mean that an "Integration" protection profile is required in order to confirm that the COE has the required properties and taken together, the COE and the OP form an effective whole. This is particularly important. The OP software might be an applet as far as the JCRE Specification is concerned but it is a highly privileged applet. Nevertheless there are benefits. The vendor may for example reduce evaluation risk by evaluating against OP3 first and latter against the integration protection profile. The impact of any change to the integration protection profile on OP3 will be reduced.

OP3 deals with the optional requirements in the OP Specification by utilizing the CC concept of a package. The functionality identified in Table 1 was mapped onto four packages: *Basic, Delegated Management, DAP Verification* and *Global PIN* as shown in Table 2. The Basic Package must always be present. Including or excluding the other packages serves to differentiate between the different OP configurations. The bulk of the assumptions, policies, threats, security objectives and TSFs are part of the Basic Package, only the differences belong in the other packages. The ability to iterate a component proved to be a useful feature in implementing these packages. For example, OP3 utilizes three iterations of FDP_IFC.1 [Information flow control policy] and FDP_IFF.1 [Information flow control functions]. Two respectively concern the mandatory rules for state transitions and use of the OP API, and form part of the Basic Package. The third concerns the mandatory rules associated with the Global PIN and belongs to the Global PIN Package.

Table 1. Open Platform Card configurations

Configuration/ Feature Set	OP Functionality				Cryptographic Support	
	Card Manager	Security Domains	Delegated Management	DAP Verification	DES	RSA
Configuration 1a	X				X	
Configuration 1b	X	X			X	
Configuration 1b*	X	X		X	X	
Configuration 2a	X	X	X		X	X
Configuration 2b	X	X	X	X	X	X

Table 2. Functional packages

Configuration	OP Functional Package			
	Basic	Delegated Management	DAP Verification	Global PIN
1a, 1b	✓			optional
1b*	✓		✓	optional
2a	✓	✓		optional
2b	✓	✓	✓	optional

3.1 The *COE* Specification

OP3 summarizes the specification for the COE with the following assertion:

1. It is tamper resistant, making it practically very difficult for an attacker to extract any data directly from the chip by using techniques commonly employed in integrated circuit failure analysis and reverse engineering efforts.
2. It is resistant to differential power analysis and other forms of sophisticated attack.
3. Following power loss or smart card withdrawal prior to completion, it will allow the OP to eventually complete an interrupted operation successfully, or recover to a consistent and secure state.
4. It will handle exceptions raised by applications and report the nature of the exception and the identity of the offending application to the OP.
5. It prevents the OP security functions from being bypassed, deactivated, corrupted or otherwise circumvented.
6. It enforces separation between applications (including OP components) so that one cannot interfere with another or even the COE itself.
7. It prevents the contents of mutable persistent memory from being accessed when that memory is reused (e.g. so that data belonging to a physically deleted application cannot be accessed).

OP3 translates this assertion one-on-one into the security objectives for the COE. In turn, OP3 identifies the security functions necessary for the COE to satisfy these objectives. Finally, it maps these objectives onto the applicable security threats in the SCSUG-SCPP plus three others. First: an attacker may exploit the ability of one application to pass data to another to covertly leak sensitive data. Second: an attacker may exploit the ability of one application to share resources with another to modify the operation of that other application in an undesirable fashion. Third: an attacker may find ways to bypass, deactivate, corrupt or otherwise circumvent any additional levels of security provided by the applications within the COE's Scope of Control. These additional threats highlight the importance of not simply deferring to another protection profile. The applications in the third threat include the OP.

3.2   Applications

Statement 5 of the COE assumption is particularly noteworthy as it implies that applications can have their own security requirements. OP anticipates this by making available its secure communication channel (called the Secure Channel Protocol) to applications on a take it or leave it basis, and a global PIN facility. These are provided via the OP API (see Figure 1) and may be considered as an extension to the JCRE.

From an application perspective the OP forms part of the application's COE and the COE assumption becomes the *OP Assumption*, derived by augmenting the COE Assumption as follows:

- It is impossible to load an application onto an OP smart card without the authorization of the Card Issuer.
- Card Issuers and Application Providers can check the authenticity and integrity of their applications when they are loaded and can ensure confidentiality of application code and data.
- It is only possible to remove applications from an OP smart card with the authority of its owner or of the Card Issuer.

The application protection profile author is then invited to refer directly to OP3 as the means by which the OP Assumption is met, or alternatively use the assumption to generate a Secure Open Platform Specification, using the COE Specification given in the OP3 as a model. The requirement of the OP Specification, and hence OP3, are sufficiently detailed to allow the first of these approaches to work. The second approach facilitates the development of protection profiles for applications intended for use in a variety of environments (e.g. PCs as well as smart cards). In the former case, the OP Assumption (which embraces the COE Assumption defined earlier in this paper) ought to be sufficient to ensure platform independence. In other words, an application need not be evaluated on every platform in combination with every other possible application. The reasoning is as follows. The OP would have been evaluated in conjunction with the COE and the validity of both the COE and the OP Assumptions would have been established. The application is written in a hardware independent language.

In addition to providing a secure environment for applications, the OP offers the services of the Secure Channel Protocol, the Global PIN and the ability to control various state transitions via the OP API. The CC does not provide an elegant way to invoke such services; i.e. there are no CC components that are specifically aimed at defining security APIs. Instead, as currently recommended in OP3, the application author is invited to select those CC components that best describe the interface and use application notes to complete the specification. The OP3 recommends various CC components as a starting point; for example, FIA_UAU (User authentication) should be used to invoke the Global PIN. The OP3 notes that security targets should provide a mapping of the implementation of the TSFs used to invoke the OP services to the appropriate API calls defined in the OP Specification. Until the CC provides a means for defining security APIs, applications will have to follow this same, rather inelegant approach to invoke the RTE API.

4   Establishing Trustworthiness

Evaluation will demonstrate that the OP security requirements are correctly implemented and cannot be bypassed, deactivated, corrupted or otherwise circumvented – at least to a given level of confidence. This is an amazingly useful first step. However, there are off-card assets that the smart card does not protect. Some of these are more valuable than the on-card assets. Common Criteria evaluation does nothing to mitigate the risks to those assets. A Common Criteria evaluation will make assumptions about the environment of the target of evaluation. OP3 makes assumptions about the COE, off-card security, key management, roles, responsibilities and initial card states. Evaluation does nothing to validate these assumptions. It therefore makes little sense to rely on the CC evaluation of just the smart card in order to establish and maintain the security of the overall system. Other steps are therefore necessary.

4.1   Risk Analysis

A quantitative risk analysis of the overall system was carried out to determine what those other steps might be. The analysis was conducted with the use of a risk analysis tool[2] that computes the residual risk in a computer network as a function of *threat × vulnerability × asset value.* In the case of OP the "network" corresponds to the system of smart cards and off-card entities (such as key management and personalization systems). The tool expresses threat in terms of its ability to access the smart card or off-card entity (physically and/or electronically), the capability and motivation of the attacker and the likelihood of an attack. Vulnerability is described in terms of the susceptibility to exploitation, the damage that successful exploitation might cause, the age of the vulnerability and how much information is available, which would explain, for example, how to exploit the vulnerability. Assets are valued in terms of the impact on the business should their confidentiality, integrity or availability were to be compromised. The network is represented as a set of components. Assets and software entities are assigned to those components. The software entities are associated with vulnerabilities. Thus:

$$
\text{risk} = \sum\nolimits_{\text{all components}}
$$
$$
[\sum\nolimits_{\text{all threats}} \mathbf{T}(\text{accessibility, motivation, capability, likelihood}) \times
$$
$$
[\sum\nolimits_{\text{all assets}} \{\mathbf{A}(\text{confidentiality, integrity, availability}):
$$
$$
\textit{provided A is associated with the given component}\} \times
$$
$$
[\sum\nolimits_{\text{all vulnerabilities}} \{\mathbf{V}(\text{susceptibility, damage, information, age}):
$$
$$
\textit{provided V is associated with the given component}
$$
$$
\textit{and can be exploited by the threat}\}]]]
$$

---

[2] L-3 Network Security "Expert" version 3.0.

Safeguards are evaluated in terms of the same parameters. Thus a threat-based safeguard such as a firewall or a locked door will reduce the accessibility of certain threats. A threat-based safeguard such as personnel vetting will reduce the motivation of certain threats. A vulnerability-based safeguard such as a hotfix or service pack will reduce, or possibly even totally remove the vulnerability. However, safeguards are associated with the components that they protect. For example, it is the network components located behind a firewall that benefit by the presence of the firewall, rather than the firewall itself. Safeguards also have a tendency to address a particular class of impact, i.e. confidentiality, integrity or availability, or perhaps some combination of all three.

4.2   Threats

A wide range of threats was defined. They were categorized as being internal, external or natural. Internal threats concern people employed by a card manufacturer, card issuer or application provider, whilst external threats concern everyone else, even the cardholder. In addition internal and external threats were categorized as being hostile or non-hostile in intent, and either structured (e.g. premeditated or planned) or unstructured (e.g. opportunistic or accidental) in nature. Natural threats include tearing, wear and tear, as well as earthquake, fire and flood. Examples are "programmer error", "aggrieved operator", "hacker", "organized crime", "Curious George[3]" and "cardholder error".

4.3   Assets

A wide range of assets was defined. An asset representing the Visa brand was attached to every network component. Assets representing cryptographic keys were divided into two classes. Type 1 affects the whole, or a significant part of the cryptographic system (e.g. the issuer's private key in an asymmetric key system or the root key in a symmetric key system). Type 2, derived from type 1; affect a single card, or maybe just a single transaction. The type 1 keys were assigned only to off-card components. Type 2 keys were assigned to both on-card and off-card components. A distinction was made between data held on-card and copies held off-card. The off-card data, being an aggregate of the on-card data was given a greater asset value. A distinction was also made between personal data and card-content data, particularly to reflect the European Data Protection Legislation. In general the off-card assets were valued higher than the on-card assets.

4.4   Risk Reduction

The question arose, is there anything that can be done to the non-evaluated components that would have a risk reducing effect similar to that of the Com-

---

[3] Someone with access to an OP card, sophisticated technical equipment, time and plenty of curiosity, but non-hostile in intent.

mon Criteria? The answer lies in British Standard (BS) 7799:1999,[4] which is a management standard somewhat akin to ISO 9001:2000. Part 2 of BS 7799 provides a specification for an Information Security Management System (ISMS). The purpose of an ISMS is to provide the *management* of an organization (e.g. the Card Issuer or Application Provider) with the ability to identify, deploy and **ensure the continued effectiveness** of the safeguards needed to protect its information assets from improper disclosure/modification, corruption, destruction or unavailability. The use of BS 7799 is modeled within the risk analysis tool.

The overall quantitative risk analysis resulted in an interesting case where the decrease in risk due to implementing an ISMS was greater than the increase in risk due to evaluating the on-card and associated technology at EAL 4 instead of EAL 7. The precise arguments are of a mathematical nature and may be the subject of another paper in a more appropriate forum.

4.5   Residual Risk

Figure 4 compares the residual risk for the overall system (i.e. including on-card and off-card entities) for different levels of evaluation, with or without the presence of an ISMS. The following were computed:

- the risk in the absence of any safeguard;
- the residual risk resulting from the technical on-card safeguards (i.e. as defined in the OP Specification);
- the residual risk that would then result if some or all of these were to be evaluated at EAL1, EAL4 and EAL7;
- the residual risk that would result by the application of the off-card measures specified in the OP Specification;
- the residual risk that would result from the application of any other safeguards;
- the effect of BS 7799 assessment (i.e. demonstration of an effective ISMS).

The level of acceptable risk in Figure 4 was determined by asserting that there must be some confirmation in practice that the OP3 assumptions are met. The calculations were performed for card population of 100,000. Increasing the card population did not have any significant impact on the results.

4.6   Observations

The risk analysis showed that on-card evaluation of OP/COE at EAL 4 plus an ISMS is more effective than just an EAL 7 evaluation of OP/COE. The observation is predicated on the assertion that an ISMS is a threat-based safeguard. The presence of highly valuable off-card only assets may also have an influence. In addition, the ISMS allows the Card Issuer and Application Providers to monitor the security of their applications, and take appropriate action (e.g. locking

---

[4] British Standard (BS) 7799:1999 is a de facto international standard for information security management. It has been adopted as a national standard in Holland, Norway, Australia, New Zealand, Brazil, to name but a few, and is currently in process of being balloted to become an ISO standard.

and ultimately replacing an application). This is, of course, a necessary security management function in its own right. Maintaining the Common Criteria evaluation at EAL 4, keeps the evaluations within the MRA.

4.7   The Next Steps

Public comments have been invited on OP3. It is the authors' intention to revise OP3 in the light of these comments and the to put OP3 forward for formal Common Criteria evaluation. It is further intended to revise OP3 in the light of experience once two or three product evaluations have been carried out. In the meanwhile, further work is being carried out to investigate more fully the ISMS concept and how it best to apply it in practice.

5   Summary

The paper has described the security requirements of a Java Card^{TM}installer and how those requirements are met by the OP technology. The security requirements are described in terms of the various assumptions that have to be made about the operating environment of the installer, the various threats to security and the security functions necessary to counter them. The Common Criteria is being used to establish the trustworthiness of OP implementations, and to that end a protection profile (OP3) has been written. OP3 is a very detailed protection profile as it is a translation of the OP Specification into the language of the Common Criteria. It deals with the optional components of the OP Specification by using the Common Criteria "package" concept and invokes an Integration PP in order to validate the assumptions that it makes about the Chip/Card Operating Environment (COE). However, a Common Criteria evaluation does not address off-card risks. A risk analysis has been carried out that shows that the decrease in risk due to the deployment of an Information Security Management System (ISMS) more than makes up for the increase in risk that results from using a lower level of evaluation.

Acknowledgments. The authors would like to thank Dr. Ken Ayer for his enthusiastic support and most helpful comments and suggestions.

References

1. Java Card ^{TM}2.1.1 Runtime Environment (JCRE) Specification, Sun Microsystems Inc, May18, 2000, *http://java.sun.com/products/javacard*
2. The Open Platform Specification, Version 2.0.1' issued May 2000, http://www.globalplatform.org
3. The Common Criteria for Information Technology Security Evaluation Version 2.1, August 1999 (ISO 15408:1999)
4. The Open Platform Protection Profile, Version 0.5.0.1 issued May 2000, http://www.visa.com/nt/suppliers/open/protect_form.html
5. British Standard BS 7799:1999 "Information Security Management"

6. The Smart Card Security User Group Smart Card Protection Profile, Draft Version 2.0, 1 May 2000, `http://csrc.nist.gov/cc/sc/sclist.htm`
7. Protection Profile 9806 - Smartcard Integrated Circuit (revision of PP 9704 - Smartcard Integrated Circuit), Protection Profile 9810 - Smartcard Embedded Software, Protection Profile 9911 - Smart Card Integrated Circuit with Embedded Software (supersedes PP9809 - Smart Card Integrated Circuit with Embedded Software), Protection Profile PP0001 – Smart Card IC with Multi-Application Secure Platform `http://www.eurosmart.com` and `http://www.scssi.gouv.fr`

A Simple(r) Interface Distribution Mechanism for Java Card

Ksheerabdhi Krishna and Michael Montgomery

Austin Product Center, Schlumberger, 8311 North FM 620 Rd, Austin,
TX 78726, USA
{kkrishna, mmontgome}@slb.com

Abstract. Conventional interface distributions rely on Interface Description Language (IDL) files. From these IDL files, stubs are automatically generated to allow code to link to the desired interfaces. In contrast, the Java Card interface distributions require both export files (IDL) and class files (stubs). This leads to the possibility of mismatched versions of the export files and class files. Furthermore, the class files distributed are typically generated from the original Java card sources, which allows access to private information contained in the class file. Modifying sources to strip private code is error prone. In order to address these problems, a mechanism is proposed by which the necessary Java class files may be synthesized from the export files, eliminating the need to distribute class files. This mechanism could be extended to other Java platforms as a general-purpose means for interface distribution.

1 Instructions

Java Card technology enables programs written in a subset of the Java programming language to run on smart cards [1]. However, there is a slight modification to the typical Java development cycle. A Java Card developer uses a standard Java development environment augmented with a Java Card converter. The converter transforms the compiled program, typically a set of classes constituting a package, into a loading unit referred to as a CAP (Converted APplet) file, amenable to loading in a smart card. Figure 1 shows the various elements in the augmented Java Card development cycle.

Java Card also uses a different approach from typical Java for binary representation of the card executable. Java executables are distributed as a set of class files to facilitate dynamic loading. Since Java Cards do not support dynamic loading of classes yet, the CAP file is a representation comprised of all the necessary elements needed for on card interpretation. More importantly, Java class files are too big to be loaded on a smart card. Smart card resource constraints dictate that the size of the CAP file be minimized, while being semantically equivalent to the class files it represents. The key enabler for reducing the size of the CAP file was the realization that Java binaries (class files) could be split into a core and an auxiliary piece, the core which will contain the bare essentials needed for execution to be loaded onto the card, and the auxiliary containing information needed by other applications linking against it, which will not be loaded on the card. Together these pieces are comparable to the package of class files they represent.

I. Attali and T. Jensen (Eds.): Java Card 2000, LNCS 2041, pp. 114-120, 2001.

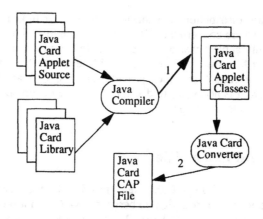

Fig. 1. Jave Card Development

Java Card binaries therefore come in two parts, executable and interface binaries. Executable binaries are known as CAP files, containing the minimal set of information needed to link and interpret applets in the card. A CAP file can contain a user library, or one or more applet definitions. A CAP file consists of a set of components that can vary, depending on whether the file contains a library or an applet exporting a set of interfaces. Interface binaries are known as export files, containing minimal symbolic information extracted from class files augmented with a matching token assignment used by the corresponding executable binary. An export file contains name and link information of packages that are imported by the classes being converted. When a library or an applet (with exportable interfaces) package is converted, the converter must produce an export file for that package, since that package provides services that may be utilized by subsequent client applets. Figure 2 illustrates the Java Card conversion process, the dotted line illustrates that export files are only produced for libraries or applets exporting interfaces.

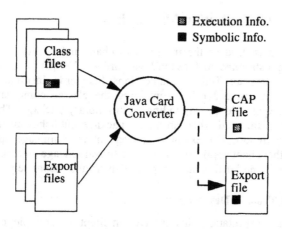

Fig. 2. Running the Jave Card Converter

Hence, Java Card distributions contain up to three inter-linked pieces. Class files are developed, which are converted to CAP files that are loaded onto a card. For class files containing only applets that do not provide any services, it is not necessary to distribute an export file, since a client applet will never need to link against such an applet. However, for class files which provide services, such as libraries or applets exporting interfaces, it is necessary to distribute both the export files and the package class files to client applet developers.

2 The Java Card Export File

Early implementations of Java Card were faced with the need of updating or enhancing card resident libraries. Schlumberger's Java Card introduced the notion of an upload file to address this need [4]. An upload file is a text file containing a mapping from symbolic information (represented as strings in Java) to identifiers (unique integers). This mapping enabled consistent token assignments across libraries and could be used by an oncard linker to resolve tokens to references prior to execution.

In order to realize the "write once run anywhere" concept of Java, Sun Microsystems Inc. and the Java Card Forum [6] engaged in a standardization process that produced a set of specifications for source and binary level interoperability. Just as the Java Virtual Machine Specification [2] defines the Java class file as a standard for binary compatibility for the Java platform, the Java Card 2.1 Virtual Machine Specification [5] defines the CAP and the export file format as a standard for binary compatibility for the Java Card platform.

A Java Card 2.1 export file contains the public interface information for an entire package of classes. An export file produced by a Java Card converter may be used later to convert another package that imports classes from the first converted package. Information in the export file corresponding to the first package is used by the CAP file of the second package to link the contents of the second package to items imported from the first package.

3 The Current Distribution Mechanism

The Jar file format is used as the transport mechanism for CAP files. When card libraries are being distributed such as the Java Card 2.1 API [5] from Sun or the GSM 3.19 API from European Telecommunications Standards Institute [3], they are published in two pieces: a Jar file containing the classes comprising the library package, and an export file corresponding to this library package. This is the same distribution mechanism used when an applet package publishes an interface that a client applet may import. For example, a frequent flyer mileage application may provide services that client applications may use to add mileage credits. An export file can be transported in the Jar file, but is typically distributed separately.

3.1 The Role of Trust in Development

There are different trust relationships involved in client/server applet development. If the developer of the client application is in the same company as the developer of the server, then the client developer could perhaps be trusted with the complete source code of the server application. However, if the client application is being developed by a different company, the trust relationship may be much more limited. In this case, the company developing the server needs to disclose enough information so that the services can be used, but would prefer not to disclose any other information.

The issue of trust in the development scenario just outlined is addressed in Java Card by ensuring that services are accessible only via Shareable interfaces [1]. The issue of privacy is addressed by distributing only the interfaces in the export files. However, in the case of an on card library, the library developer would like to provide class descriptions containing only the public and protected information about the classes needed by the applets, but no private information or code.

3.2 Motivations for Change

There are several reasons why distributing class file packages separately from export files is highly unattractive.

First, it is undesirable to send the original class files due to privacy concerns, since such files contain the full implementation of the classes. This could be of concern to the author of the class, who jeopardizes his intellectual property by revealing the implementation in the class file. Moreover, it is also of concern to the user, who may wish to avoid any connection to the implementation in order to maintain a clean room status for his work. Therefore, it is desirable to strip the implementation from the class file before distribution. But this process is tedious and error prone.

Second, the class files and the export files must be linked. Bundling the class files and export files is error prone as well. Furthermore, even if the distribution is created correctly, the linkage may be broken at the user side, if the user fails to maintain the correlation between the class files and export files. This mismatch may be detected by establishing an authentication scheme for off-card development; however, this is a burden on the issuer and the developer.

Finally, for environments which do not need the card class files because they are already loaded on the card, the distribution is an order of magnitude larger than needed.

4 The Proposed Distribution Mechanism

Conventional interface distributions rely on Interface Description Language (IDL) files. From these IDL files, stubs are automatically generated to allow code to link to the desired interfaces. In contrast, the Java Card interface distributions require both export files (IDL) and class files (stubs). Just as stubs are generated from IDL files, it would be very desirable for the class files to be generated from the export files, so that only the export files need to be distributed.

The crux of the problem behind distributing two related yet separate pieces lies in the redundancy of information. While the redundancy is required by the requisite tools, Java compilers need class files and the Java Card converters need export files, they cause the aforementioned problems. The distribution problems can be overcome if we distribute the richer of the two pieces. From an interface standpoint, the export file is richer than the class file since it contains the unique token assignments required by an on card linker in addition to the symbolic information corresponding to the class files. Class files could be synthesized from the export files via a simple standardized tool. Since only public and protected method and field signatures are needed for off-card compiling and linking, the synthesis of class files from export files would suffice.

However, the export file format prescribed in the Java Card 2.1 Specification lacks a few critical pieces of information that are required for the complete class file synthesis. Specifically, Java Card 2.1 export files do not contain:

- immediate super class information. Each class_info structure contains a list of all the super classes in an unspecified order, making it difficult to determine the immediate super class. The immediate super class is sufficient because Java posits a single inheritance model; the remainder of the class hierarchy is not needed for class synthesis.

- information on overridden methods and fields. Inherited members of a class are indistinguishable from overridden members. All the methods from the super-classes and super-interfaces of a class are included in the class' export file because the class may inherit from a non-exported class not present in the export file, causing the public methods inherited from the non-exported superclass to "show through" the exported subclass. A class file synthesizer needs to know which of these are declared and/or overridden by the class being synthesized so that a compiler can generate correct symbolic information for methods and fields accessed in this class.

- exception information, if any, for each method. Method related exception information can be used to improve the quality of the synthesized class file, but is not strictly required. In Java, the exception information is not part of a method's signature; hence a list of exceptions thrown by a method are kept in a separate Exceptions attribute. Exception declarations are not enforced by the Java virtual machine but by the Java compiler [2].

These missing pieces of information can be added by simple modifications to the export file format of the existing Java Card 2.1 specification.

- Immediate super class information can be provided by simply requiring that the list of super classes begin (or end) with the immediate super class of the class in question. This incurs no extra overhead in the export file.

- Overridden methods and fields can be addressed by addition of a flag to the method_info and field_info structures called ACC_INHERITED. If the ACC_INHERITED flag is set it would indicate that the field or method was inherited, and hence not overridden by the class. Because space for this flag is already available in access_flags, this also incurs no extra overhead.

- Per method exception information may be added as an Exceptions attribute to the method_info structure of the export file. Attributes are defined in the Java Card export file specification. The layout of the Exceptions attribute could be exactly the same as that defined for the Java Virtual Machine Specification. The following structure is presented here for convenience. Refer to Section 4.7.3 of the Java Virtual Machine Specification [2] for the exact details of this structure.

```
Exceptions_attribute {
    u2 attribute_name_index
    u4 attribute_length
    u2 number_of_exceptions
    u2 exception_index_table[number_of_exceptions]
}
```

With the aforementioned updates, the augmented export files along with a class file synthesizer are now sufficient for the purposes of interface distribution. Appendix A outlines an algorithm for synthesizing required class file packages from an augmented export file.

5 Future Work

Mainstream Java distributions could benefit from augmented export files. Java libraries are distributed along with the entire implementation. Apart from increasing the size of the distribution, in those cases where the executable version of the libraries is not needed or desired, this leads to the clean room problem stated earlier. If these libraries were distilled into augmented export files, the augmented export files could be distributed instead, with tools that automatically generate the library classes as needed.

6 Conclusion

In summary, export files present a new opportunity for distributing interfaces for Java Card. We have presented a unique scheme that leverages the export file mechanism to replace class file distribution of interfaces altogether. The proposed interface distribution mechanism has the following advantages:

- On-card libraries and server applets can be distributed simply as their corresponding export file(s).
- Distributions provide all the information needed for client applet development while ensuring maximal privacy.
- Distribution and development problems are reduced due to lower chances of error.
- Version mismatches between class files and export files can be eliminated.
- Emerging Java Card technologies such as Java Card RMI will benefit due to completeness of information for stub generation.

This scheme may be extended to mainstream Java.

References

[1] Chen, Zhiqun, Java Card Technology for Smart Cards: Architecture and Programmer's Guide, Addison-Wesley Publishing, June 2000.

[2] Lindholm, Tim and Yellin, Frank, The Java Virtual Machine Specification, 2nd Edition, Addison-Wesley Publishing, April 1999.

[3] GSM 03.19 V7.0.1, Digital cellular telecommunications system (Phase 2+); SIM API for Java Card, DTS/SMG-090319N, ETSI Secretariat, F-06921 Sophia Antipolis, Cedex - France, //www.etsi.org

[4] Cyberflex™ Pre-Release Developers' Series, Programmer's Guide, Schlumberger, May 1997.

[5] Sun Microsystems Inc., Java Card 2.1 Specification, //java.sun.com/products/JavaCard/ [6] Java Card Forum, //www.javacardforum.org

Appendix A: Algorithm for Synthesizing Classes from Export Files

```
Parse arguments {
    export file path = Set of directories indicating location of export files
    jar file name = Name of jar file to be generated (containing synthesized classes)
    export file name [optional] = Export file from which to synthesize classes/jar file
}
For each Export file to be parsed {
    Parse export file and extract package name
    For each class that belongs to the export file {
        Initialize import list
        Set the super class of the class in accordance with the super class info in the export file
        For each field that belongs to the class whose access_flags does not set ACC_INHERITED {
            Create the field with the right signature and access condition
            Process attributes {
                If the field has a ConstantValue attribute {
                    Read the constant value and store it in the field
                }
            Update import list if field type refers to a class not in this package
        }
        For each method that belongs to the class whose access_flags does not set ACC_INHERITED {
            Create the method header with the right signature and access condition
            If method name begins with an <init> (a constructor method) {
                Set name to correspond to the class name
                Set return type to null
            }
            If the method returns a reference
                Set the return value to null
            Else
                Set the return value to 0 - cast appropriately to match the method's return type
            Process attributes {
                If the method has an Exceptions attribute {
                    Read the fields attribute and store the throws clause(s)
                }
            }
            Update import list if method return or argument type refers to class not in this package
        }
        Synthesize class file {
        Create a source file named <classname>.java in the appropriate directory
        Append package statement
        Append the imports list
        Append the class/interface statement with superclass/superinterface list
        Append field declarations
        Append method stubs
        Compile the generated source
        }
    }
    Place the synthesized class files in a Jar file
}
```

Automatic Test Generation for Java-Card Applets*

Hugues Martin[1] and Lydie du Bousquet[2]

[1] Gemplus Research Labs, BP 100, 13881 Gémenos Cedex, France
[2] Laboratoire LSR-IMAG, BP 72, 38402 Saint Martin d'Hères cedex, France
Hugues.Martin@gemplus.com ,Lydie.du-Bousquet@imag.fr

Abstract. Open-cards have introduced a new life cycle for smart card embedded applications. In the case of Java Card, they have raised the problem of embedded object-oriented applet validation. In this article, we describe a methodology for Java Card applet verification, and its application on a case study. This methodology is based on automatic test generation. We first take benefits of the Java Card platform validation, focusing on application conformity testing. Then, using UML, we model the applet and its probable communication with other embedded elements. In the next step, the resulting model is used to automatically generate test suites, using UMLAUT and TGV tools. The full process is iterative and incremental, in order to conform to an object-oriented approach. Moreover, this incremental process allows integrating priorities on validation, by focusing first on main functions and properties.

1 Introduction

Most of smart cards are, at the present time, dedicated to only one application. In this traditional approach, the embedded application is considered as a whole. Software is burned in the chip, and after delivering, the embedded application cannot evolve anymore.

The Open Card platforms have introduced the possibility to change and/or update applications embedded during the full life cycle. This possibility of loading and executing new applications during the card life has induced new software structure of the card system, and new life cycle for smart card applications. It has also raised new problems for embedded application validation, as developers and testers do not have necessary cards when they develop new applications. However, the quality and security requirements are still the same as for traditional smart cards. Developers and testers need to use methods and techniques that are compliant with a high security level and that fulfil industrial software development constraints such as time to market.

The solution proposed in this article takes benefits of object-oriented software engineering, and is adapted to the Java Card world. In details, we take into

---

* This work is the result of a collaboration between Gemplus Research Labs and IRISA (project PAMPA).

I. Attali and T. Jensen (Eds.): Java Card 2000, LNCS 2041, pp. 121–136, 2001.
© Springer-Verlag Berlin Heidelberg 2001

account the fact that the only permanent elements of the card are the Java Card Virtual Machine (JCVM) and the Operating System (OS), and that most of security requirements are based on them. In order to optimize the application validation process, we integrate the JCVM and OS validity as test hypotheses.

Our main goal is then to verify the application conformity to the specification, and to verify the applet integration with other loaded applets within the card. Our process consists in two steps, first an object-oriented specification elaboration, and then a validation based on conformance testing. This solution is illustrated with a large case study.

In the following, the end of the introduction introduces Java Card and the case study. Section two is dedicated to the Java Card application specification. Section three is dedicated to its validation. Section four details the results of the case study. Finally, section five is devoted to the conclusions and future works.

1.1 Java Card

Many different kinds of validation can be performed on Java Card, at different levels of the application. Indeed, the Java Card is a smart card that is not anymore structured as a monolithic bloc of executable code. The system embedded on the smart card includes the Java Card Runtime Environment (JCRE), the Java Card Application Programmable Interface (API), the interpreter and the OS (Figure 1).

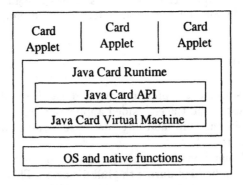

Fig. 1. JCRE architecture

The JCRE has its own security process: the firewall. The firewall is the dynamic security mechanism of the JCVM. This feature is due to a specific requirement: the on-card object access policy. The firewall creates a secure environment, controlling every information access between applets. Every object (class instance or array) on the card is owned by the applet which instantiated it, that is, the applet which was active at the time the object was created. An applet has full rights to access its objects, but the firewall still verifies that an applet does not try to access information illegally. However, the security mechanisms cannot avoid that an embedded malicious applet attacks the other embedded applets. Thus all the security functions must be carefully developed in the applets in order to avoid any latent error that should be used by an attacker. One of the means for fault prevention consists in using formal methods. Then, it can possible to prove that an implementation matches its specification. For this purpose, several algorithms have been formally developed (protocol [Lan98], backup [LS99], firewall [Mot00]).

In our verification process, we only focus on the card applet validation. We can then check that the implementation is conform to the specification, but we do not verify security properties such as those previously described.

Finally, we consider that communication mechanisms are automatically generated, following an approach similar to the one described in [VV99]. As a consequence, we suppose that these communication mechanisms are valid. They are then out of the scope of our validation process.

1.2   Case Study

In order to apply our methodology and the previously described verification techniques, we use a well-known type of smart card applications: a purse. The purse applet we consider provides most common functions to the end user such as debit, credit, and balance. It also provides other administrative functions in order to manage usability constraints. For the purpose of this article, we provide only a very few part of our case study. This part consists in the diagrams concerned by the purse credit function.

In its full version, our case study contains nine operations dedicated to the cardholder and forty operations dedicated to the applet manager. Its compiled size, to be embedded in a Java Card, exceeds 23Ko. Its source code size exceeds 7000 lines of Java code. It uses the Java Card API and the mechanisms of shareable interfaces, to communicate with other embedded Java Card applets.

2   Java Applet Specification

As our methodology has been developed to be used in an industrial process, we have chosen to use a specification language that is well accepted by industrial developers. UML appears to be the best choice, for three main reasons. Firstly, UML takes benefits of most common object-oriented specification languages. Secondly, UML appears to be easy to learn, and at the same time can be used even for complete and unambiguous models. Thirdly, UML models can be used to automatically generate test suites [JLP98].

2.1   Unified Modeling Language (UML)

Booch, Jacobson and Rumbaugh have proposed the Unified Modeling Language (UML) to the OMG, to gather the object-oriented notions into one single language [BJR98a]. It has been standardized by the OMG, and is now more and more widespread, integrating more and more evolutions [UML99].

UML enables to express models from different points of view thanks to several kinds of diagrams. The use case diagrams encapsulate or abstract a coherent unit of services, functionality, or actions to be provided by self-identifiable parts of the system being analyzed. A use case diagram is composed of actors (represented by a stick figure) and ellipses (which are called "use cases"). Decomposing a system into use cases and actors means essentially decomposing a system into service providers and service users. Use case diagrams may be used to capture requirements at different level of abstractions.

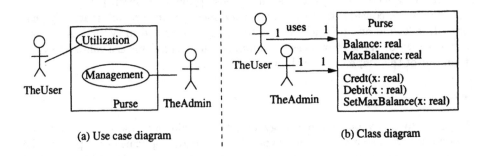

(a) Use case diagram   (b) Class diagram

Fig. 2. Simple UML use case and class diagrams

The use case diagram in figure 2(a) captures the following. The purse is a system that has two different types of clients: a user and an administrator. Both of them are human actors. Two types of operation can be done: management (by the administrator) and use (by the user).

The class diagram shows the type of the objects present in a system and the static relationships among them. The most important relationships are associations. They represent the relationships between the instances of the class. Association ends have cardinality and may be decorated by an arrowhead to express the navigability in a given direction (navigability expresses the ability of a class to call the methods of another class). The classes are represented as boxes divided into three parts defining the name, the attributes and the operations of the classes. The class diagram also shows the relations between actors and objects of the application.

On figure 2(b), the class diagram represents an application composed of one object (a purse) and two actors (the user and the administrator). The purse object has two attributes (*Balance* and *MaxBalance*) and three methods (*Credit*, *Debit* and *SetMaxBalance* - an administrative operation).

Sequence diagrams and collaboration diagrams show the interactions among a set of object collaborating to achieve one operation. In the sequence diagrams, objects participating to the collaboration are laid out horizontally and time is represented on the vertical axis. Arrows from the sender to the receivers denote the messages exchanged during an interaction. One can use sequence diagrams to express test purposes.

On figure 3(a), a simple sequence diagram shows a credit and a debit done successively.

Statechart diagrams can be used to describe the evolution of a model element such as an object over its lifetime. A statechart diagram is composed of states and labeled transitions. A labeled transition is composed of three parts: *Event [Guard] / Action*. A guarded transition occurs only if the guard is resolved to true.

Figure 3(b) represents a simplified statechart for the object Purse that is depicted in figure 2(b). This statechart is composed of two states and four transitions. The states are "ST" and the initial one (which has no name and is depicted by a black circle). The transitions mean that a debit is possible only if there is enough money in the purse, although the credit is always possible.

The UMLAUT tool that translates UML models into labeled transition systems used for test case generation relies on statechart and class diagrams [JLP98].

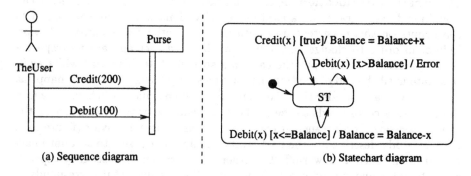

(a) Sequence diagram   (b) Statechart diagram

Fig. 3. Simple UML sequence diagram and statechart for the Purse object

2.2   An Approach for Modeling

There exists more than one process to develop UML models. Booch, Jacobson and Rumbaugh suggest one [BJR98b], which defines a complete guideline for UML use. In this guideline, the test workflow that is proposed identifies human responsibility concerning test goal elicitation. However, a human tester can forget test purposes or can define redundant test cases. Modeling an application in a particular way, in accordance with a systematic or automatic test generation process, can help the human tester to avoid these problems.

Modeling an application consists in building an abstraction of it. Firstly, building an abstraction necessarily requires making some hypotheses that will correspond to test hypotheses [Pha94] for the test generation. These hypotheses have been studied in case of object-oriented programs [Bar97] and more particularly for Java Card applications [Mar99]. They are important to determine the abstraction level required for the UML model. From a methodological point of view, they correspond to the fact that the designer will have to integrate rigorously in the model all the features that will need to be tested. On the other hand, the other entire subsidiary features or properties will be integrated informally, in accordance with developer understanding. Secondly, UML provides different diagrams and notations to describe different point of view of one application.

A recurrent question is to identify which kind of representation should be used. Validation process provides one answer to this question, using the test generation process to drive the UML specification step. Our approach consists in using conformity testing to verify implementation. We consider that objects are entities that encapsulate data, states and operations. In order to specify data and operations, we use class diagrams. In order to represent states and their evolutions, we use statechart diagrams. Of course, the UML models we use are not restricted to these diagrams, but these ones are in our case necessary for the validation purpose.

Statecharts identification. A card can be seen as a secure container. It can contain end user data, or data used for security. Some states can correspond to constraints on this persistent user data and some others to security behavior. Indeed, in order to change end user data, the card user an have to respect a secure protocol that will put the card in a specific state. The card will stay in this state until the end of the transaction, unless any unexpected event happens.

Then, we can consider that there are two different kinds of behaviors within the card. One corresponds to the application behavior, without considering the security aspects. For instance, it can be the purse balance behavior (figure 6) of the case study described in the next section. It does not take into account unexpected events such as power-off. The other one corresponds to security aspects, and integrates unexpected events. It specifies the behavior that corresponds to the security protocol. It can be, for instance, a secure messaging initialization or an identification before communicating with the purse balance (figure 4 of the next section).

In the implementation code, developers can decide to mix application and security behaviors in only one class. One reason to implement in this way could be memory size constraint. However, as our purpose is to validate the application considering a black-box approach, we produce tests independently from implementation static structure.

Constraints identification. In our specification, we distinguish two kinds of constraints, as we do for Statecharts. Some constraints correspond to the semantic of application operations. For example, we consider that it is not possible to debit more money than we have in our purse. Some others constraints are dedicated to security constraints on application behavior. For example, it is not possible to credit our purse without being authenticated. These last constraints can correspond to a card state. In case of authentication before credit operation, the purse first verifies that the object *User* within the card is in the state *UserAuthenticated*.

In our modeling approach, we identify these constraints separately, in order to verify a priori that we cover both application and security requirements. We then introduce these constraints together on the UML model, by attaching them to transitions. Finally, for each state, we manually evaluate output transitions in order to verify that we have covered all possible cases. For instance, if we have the two constraints *(A and B)* and *((not A) and B)*, we must model a new output transition with the constraint: *((A and (not B)) or ((not A) and (not B)))*, which can be simplified in *(not B)*. This last step often implies to detail behaviors corresponding to unauthorized applet use. We then enhance the model with error messages. The resulting UML model includes both normal uses and unauthorized uses of the applet. As a consequence, the conformity verification can validate the applet behavior for both uses.

Communication with other embedded components. In Java Cards, an applet can communicate with other embedded applets and use Java Card services. When specifying one applet, it can be useful to specify these other elements of the system, as they interfere with the applet behavior. However, developers do not have to code them and testers should not have to verify them. Modeling these elements requires defining an abstraction level that is often nontrivial. For example, if the user authentication is provided by another applet, do we have to model that the user object within the applet is blocked after three consecutive failed authentications ?

In our opinion, the abstraction level depends on the confidence we have on this external element and the confidence we have on the communication implementation with this element. Then, in the previous example, we can consider that the applet supporting the authentication mechanism is valid, and that the communication with this applet is not corrupted. We have a statechart with only three states, which does not take into account the security policy of a limited number of failed attempts. This statechart is described in figure 5 in the next section.

As a consequence, when testing our applet, we only test the authentication mechanism, and we do not test the security policy of the authentication applet. One should remark that our choice for this authentication example is arguable, but it corresponds to a more general problem of risks taken when performing test.

2.3   A UML Model for the Purse Application

The UML model presented here illustrates a subset of the purse applet. This subset has been selected to show how some security aspects are taken into account.

In order to credit the purse, the user has to perform two actions. The first one is an initialization (*appInitCredit*, see figure 4), which aims at configuring a secure communication between the purse and the card reader. This operation represents a cryptographic key generation. The second operation is the "acknowledgement" of the credit operation (*appCredit* operation). It consists in performing the credit operation while verifying the correctness of the secure communication.

For security reasons, the *appInitCredit* operation succeeds only if the user is authenticated. Moreover, a key computed when performing an *appInitCredit* operation has a limited lifetime. It is invalidated by the application if another operation than *appCredit* is performed just after an *appInitCredit* operation, or after an *appCredit operation*. This protocol has been introduced to prevent malicious purse utilization. Another verification is done during initialization: a credit can be performed only if the resulting balance value is not higher than a predefined value stored in the *maxBalance* variable (or *MB* in the following figures).

In order to represent this behavior, we use a UML model composed of three objets, which represent the secure messaging protocol of the operations (named USM), the user authentication (UB) and the balance of the purse (BAL).

Figure 4 depicts the statechart corresponding to the behavior associated to the credit secure messaging protocol. This statechart is composed of three states: the initial state, the *IDLE* state and the *InitCredit* state. This last state is reachable only after a valid *appInitCredit*. An *appCredit* is valid only if it is done in the *InitCredit* state and if the key corresponds to the current key of the system (*Ckey* on the diagram) is correct. Every other operation leads to the *IDLE* state. The internal management of the key *Ckey* of the system is not depicted in figure 4.

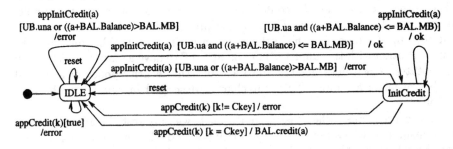

Fig. 4. User Secure Messaging behavior limited to the credit operation

A credit can be done only if the user has been previously authenticated. This is represented by the condition UB.ua (which is true if the statemachine of *UB* is in state *ua* - user authenticated) and if the resulting amount is still less or equal to the maximum amount possible in the purse ($a + BAL.Balance <= BAL.MB$). The secure messaging is simply represented by a test on the key value k. This abstraction can of course be detailed in a next step in the incremental modeling process.

The user authentication is performed by another applet within the card. A first approach can be to consider that the security policy applied to the user authentication is in charge of this other applet. We do not consider the fact that after three failed authentications, the authentication applet is blocked. Then, the purse authentication behavior can be as presented in the figure 5.

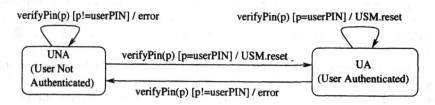

Fig. 5. Purse User Authentication

A next step in the incremental model development could be to detail the purse authentication mechanism. As said before, we consider that we do not have to test other applets, even if we communicate with them. But, when detailing the expected behavior of the purse authentication applet, the tester can verify the correct implementation of the communication between the purse applet and the user authentication applet.

Finally, the balance value is constrained between zero and the maximum value $MaxBalance$ (MB in figure 6). The evolution of balance with respect to the different operations is modeled by a statechart. This one characterizes two important states of the purse: if it is full or not. In order to have a more understanding diagram in this article, we have not represented all the transitions.

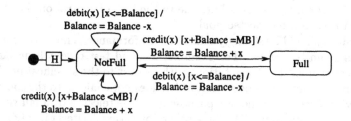

Fig. 6. Balance behavior

3   Java Applet Validation

3.1   Conformance Testing

We choose to perform the applet validation with testing. Testing is an operational way to check the correctness of a system implementation by means of experimenting it. It increases confidence in the quality of a computing system, especially when proof is not possible or too expensive.

There are many different kinds of testing. Several aspects of the system behavior can be tested: Does the system have the intended functionality and does it comply with its functional specification (functional tests or conformance tests)? Does the system work as fast as required (performance tests)? How does the system react if its environment shows unexpected or strange behavior (robustness tests)? How long can we rely on the correct functioning of the system (reliability tests)?

A common distinction between tests is the one between black box and white box testing. In black box testing (or functional testing), only the outside of the system under test is known by the tester. In white box testing, the structure of the system is also known and used by the tester.

In this paper, we focus on a black box functional testing called conformance testing [Tre99]. The key points are that there is a specification and a system implementation exhibiting behavior. The specification is a prescription of what the system should do. The goal of the testing is to check whether the implemented system satisfies this prescription.

The usual theoretical approach is to consider a formal specification of the Implementation Under Test (IUT) intended behavior. According to attended security level, the tester identifies a conformance relation (or a fault model) that is used to define an implementation correctness criterion, with respect to the formal specification. This conformance relation also allows to formally define test cases, their execution on an IUT, and the notion of verdict associated to this execution.

Three verdicts are generally distinguished. Informally, "fail" means rejection by the test case, "pass" means that the goal of the test experiment (described by a so called test purpose) is reached, and "inconclusive" means that the implementation correctly behaves but, due to the lack of control on the IUT, does not allow to reach the expected goal.

As verdicts should be strongly related to conformance, a notion of correctness of test cases can be defined. For example, a sound test case will declare "fail" only non-conformant implementations with respect to the specification. We may also require that any implementation which does not conform to the specification in a behavior targeted by the test purpose might be rejected by a fail verdict (we call it "partial completeness"). Some other correctness criteria involving "pass" and "inconclusive" verdicts can also be defined.

3.2   TGV

During the last decade, conformance testing theory and algorithms for the generation of tests have been developed. TGV is such a tool. It is developed by IRISA [JM99].

TGV needs as inputs a specification and test purposes. The specification can be expressed as a Labeled Transition System (LTS). A LTS is a structure consisting of states with transitions between them, where transitions are labeled with actions or events. An example of a coffee machine specification is given figure 7. This specification indicates that the coffee machine should receive one or two coins, and an order (tea or coffee, with or without sugar). Then, the coffee machine should emit the right product(s).

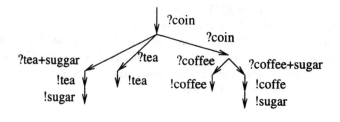

?i: specification input
!o: specification output

Fig. 7. Specification of a coffee machine, expressed in LTS

A test purpose is used to select a part of the specification, for which a test case will be generate. A "good" test purpose should be simple (typically, much simpler than the specification) and should select exactly the scenarios that the user has in mind. Two test purposes (TP) are given figure 8.

Given such a specification and such a test purpose, TGV generates an abstract test case. Let us study the figure 8. If the test purpose TP1 is used, TGV will produce non-deterministically one of the two test cases (TC1 or TC2). If it is the test purpose TP2 that is chosen, TGV will generate only TC2. This one indicates that after the insertion of two coins and a "coffe+sugar" command, the environment should obtain some coffee and sugar.

As one can notice, the test case actions have not the same orientation as the specification ones. Indeed, the specification expresses the system under test viewpoint. On the contrary, a test case specifies what the environment (here the coffee machine user) should do and observe during the test.

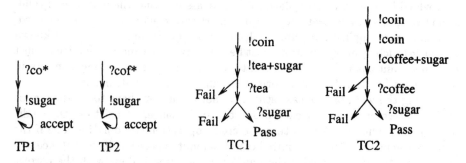

Fig. 8. Test purposes and test cases

TGV relies on efficient algorithms that are based on adaptations of on-the-fly model-checking algorithms [JM99]. "On-the-fly" means that the test case generation is done on a lazy way. During the computation, the specification state space is not completely stored, so the state explosion problem is limited.

subsectionTGV and UMLAUT connection

As we said before, for the present work, we express the specification with a UML model. The specification is **automatically** translated into a labeled transition system thanks to the UMLAUT tool [JLP98]. So TGV can produce the test cases from a UML specification and from test purposes produced by hand. Figure 9 depicts this connection.

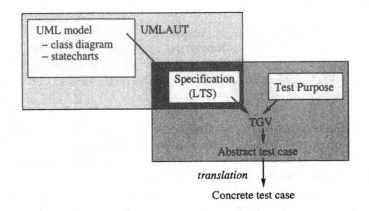

Fig. 9. UMLAUT and TGV connection

3.3   Case Study

Test Generation. To use TGV, we have to exhibit a set of test purposes. Considering smart card validation, the number of test purposes can be very large compared to the application size, depending on the abstraction level of the model. In case of Java Card application, an important part of security features is provided by the Java Card platform. As we assume that the platform is valid, some tests purposes dedicated to specific smart card constraints can be removed.

Smart card applications, and so Java Card applications require well known properties such as every function must be valid, available and every misuse must have been anticipated. One test strategy for conformance testing consists in testing each function for every normal use and every possible misuse.

During the work on the case study, we notice that we have to produce a lot of similar test purposes, for each property. For instance, let us study the credit functionality. One property is that the credit operation can only be done if the user is authenticated, if the required credit amount is positive, if the balance will not exceed *MaxBalance* and if the *appCredit* operation is done with the correct key. Like the credit functionality, the authentication requires a key exchange.

Each operation can be done with correct or incorrect parameters: correct or incorrect PIN and key for *appVerifyPIN* operation call, correct or wrong key for *appCredit*. For *appInitCredit*, the amount can be positive, null, negative, or greater or equals to *MaxBalance*.

To check the credit property, we found interesting to generate one test case for each combination of the different parameters values, thus 4*2*4 test purposes. Those test purposes differ only from the value of the parameters. The process of creating the test purpose by hand is repetitive. So we have the idea to automate it.

To do so, we have created a program, BuildTP, which is able to generate a set of test purposes satisfying a defined high-level test purpose. For instance, to test the credit functionality, a high-level test purpose can be "HTP1 =(*appVerifyPIN(*) . appInitCredit(*) . appCredit(*)*)", where "*" means that the parameters should be completed and "." stands for concatenation. Figure 10 presents a test purpose produced by BuildTP from HTP1. In the textual representation, "des()" indicates the initial state, the transition number and the state number. The expressions "lec!" and "lec?" identify the environment emission and reception events. The user PIN is 9999, and *MaxBalance* is equal to 300.

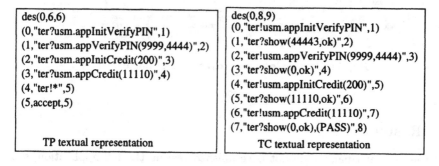

Fig. 10. Example of a test purpose and its corresponding test case

BuildTP can generate a set of 500 test purposes in less than one minute. More information on BuildTP can be found in [MdB00].

Test execution. Test cases obtained with TGV are expressed in a textual and non executable format (Figure 10). Moreover, they have the same level of abstraction as the specification. Two steps have to be done before executing the test cases: decrease the abstraction level and translate the test cases into Java programs.

In fact, the two steps are realised at the same time. We made a program that automatically produces a Java program from the textual representation. This program is composed of a card initialization (to initialize parameters such as *MaxBalance*), and a sequence of procedure call. Each of these procedures prepares a APDU message, sends it to the applet, waits for the applet answer and compares the expected result with the actual answer (see Figure 11).

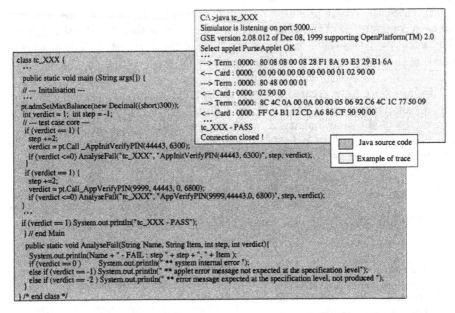

Fig. 11. Java code source extract and example of trace

4   Results

At the present time, we do not have finished testing the full application; some mechanisms involving other embedded applets and the communication with these other embedded applets have not been tested yet. However, more than 80% of the application has been taken into account.

In order to evaluate our approach, a manual process has been performed at the same time, in order to compare quantitative results, and to analyze the added value of our methodology.

The quantitative results are:

Process	Manual	Automated	Both
Errors found	39	38	49
Number of test suites	95	1800	NA
Time spent	25	15	NA

Considering qualitative analysis, some differences appear between the two sets of test suites. As for manual tests that have been generated, we have noticed that:

- It does not perform any abstraction. It then tests all the data.
- Some tests are missing, due to omissions at the implementation step.
- It enables to take into account implementation choices that are left for free in the specification.

Considering the automated tests suites that are generated, we have noticed that:

- It uses abstractions, and so do not test the full application. However, by spending more time, it is possible to build a concrete model with fewer abstractions.
- It does not miss any tests that are specified in the specification.
- It enables to automatically generate test purposes. Some combinations of events have been elicited by this generation, which was missing in the manual test purposes specification.

Considering the applet shareable interfaces, we have developed applets that are embedded with the Purse inside the card. This applet is used to transfer data from the Purse to the card environment and from the card environment to the Purse. We can then test the shareable interface from the card environment. Indeed, as we suppose that the memory administration of the Java Card is valid, we can suppose that the behavior of the tested applet is independent from the other applets that are embedded in the Java Card.

We use the same test generation process as for the interface delivered to the end user. Indeed, as we have said previously in the article, we do not take into account malicious attacks of the applet under test. We then expect that the results will be consistent with those detailed in this chapter.

5   Conclusions

In this article, we have summarized a solution to verify properties on the Java Card embedded platform, using an automated testing process. By assuming the validity of this platform, we have proposed an object oriented testing methodology that integrates software- engineering practice and smart card security needs. This methodology is based on an incremental approach that consists in expanding a UML model in order to increase the conformity verification. From our point of view, this approach allows to offer different conformity levels, in accordance with a UML model usable by both developers and testers. By doing it, our goal is not to exclude UML specifications that use both formal approaches and natural languages, but on the contrary to integrate theses approaches in a common methodology.

The experimental result obtained with our case study indicates that our methodology could fulfill industrial requirements for applet behavior verification. New experimentation on industrial products, using less abstract UML model could allow to certify that our methodology fulfills security verification needs of Java Card applications.

References

[Bar97]   S. Barbey. *Test selection for specification-based unit testing of object-oriented software based on formal specification.* PhD thesis, Ecole Polytechnique Fédérale de Lausanne, Switzerland, 1997.

[BJR98a]   G. Booch, I. Jacobson, and J. Rumbaugh. *The Unified Modeling Langage - User Guide.* Addison-Wesley, 1998.

[BJR98b]   G. Booch, I. Jacobson, and J. Rumbaugh. *The Unified Software Development Process.* Addison-Wesley, 1998.

[JLP98]   J.-M. Jézéquel, A. LeGuennec, and F. Pennaneach. Validating distributed software modelled with UML. In *Proc. Int. Workshop UML98, Mulhouse, France,* June 1998.

[JM99]   T. Jéron and P. Morel. Test generation derived from model-checking. In *Computer Aided Verification (CAV).* LNCS 1633, Springer-Verlag, 1999.

[Lan98]   J.-L. Lanet. Using the b method to model protocols. In *Approches Formelles dans l'Assistance au Développement de Logiciels (AFADL),* pages 79–90, Poitiers, France, September 1998.

[LS99]   P. Lartigue and D. Sabatier. The use of the b formal method for the design and the validation of the transaction mechanism for smart card applications. In *World Congress on Formal Methods,* volume LNCS 1708, pages 348–369, Toulouse, France, September 1999. Springer Verlag.

[Mar99]   H. Martin. Using test hypotheses to build a uml model of object-oriented smart card applications. In *International Conference on Software and Systems Engineering and their Applications (ICSSEA),* Paris , France, December 1999.

[MdB00]   H. Martin and L. du Bousquet. Tools for automated conformance testing of java card applets. Technical report, Gemplus, September 2000.

[Mot00]   S. Motré. Réalisation et spécification du modèle formel du firewall de la java card en utilisant la méthode b. In *Approches Formelles dans l'Assistance au Développement de Logiciels (AFADL),* Grenoble, France, January 2000.

[Pha94]   M. Phalippou. Relations d'implémentations et hypothèses de test sur des automates à entrées et sorties. Thèse, Université Bordeaux I, France, septembre 1994.

[Tre99]   J. Tretmans. Testing concurrent systems: A formal approach. In J.C.M Baeten and S. Mauw, editors, *10th Int. Conference on Concurrency Theory (CONCUR'99),* volume LNCS 1664. Springer-Verlag, 1999.

[UML99]   Unified modeling language specification, version 1.3, June 1999. Information available at http://www.omg.org/cgi-bin/doc?ad/99-06-08.

[VV99]   J.-J. Vandewalle and E. Vétillard. Developing smart card-based applications with java card. In *Third European Research Seminar on Advances in Distributed Syst ems (ERSADS),* Madeira Island - Portugal, April 1999.

Formal Specification and Verification of JavaCard's Application Identifier Class*

Joachim van den Berg, Bart Jacobs, and Erik Poll

Dept. Computer Science, Univ. Nijmegen,
P.O. Box 9010, 6500 GL Nijmegen, The Netherlands.
{joachim, bart, erikpoll}@cs.kun.nl
{http://www.cs.kun.nl/~{joachim, bart, erikpoll}

Abstract. This paper discusses a verification in PVS of the AID (Application Identifier) class from the JavaCard API. The properties that are verified are formulated in the interface specification language JML. This language is also used to express the properties that are assumed about the native methods from the Util class that are used in the AID class. These properties include invariants for classes and behaviour specifications for methods; the latter give pre- and post-conditions describing the functional behaviour, and also specify when exceptions may be thrown.

1 Introduction

This paper describes the obvious next step after the formal specification of the JavaCard API [16,17] in the specification language JML [13,12], namely actual verification that the current reference implementation (version 2.1.1, [1]) satisfies these specifications. This verification is done with the proof tool PVS [14], using the translation of Java and JML to PVS, as incorporated in the LOOP tool [11,3]. This verification forms a test, both for the JML specifications, and for the Java implementations (and of course also for the LOOP tool). Here we concentrate on a small part of the API, involving essentially only the classes Util and AID. In an earlier version of this work only lightweight specifications were verified, but here more complete functional specifications will be studied. This is the first major case study in verification of JML specifications. (An earlier verification case study [8], on the Vector class from the Java API, did not use a formal semantics of JML.) The case study presented here heavily uses the tailor-made Hoare style logic developed especially for JML [10], in combination with dedicated proof strategies in PVS.

The JavaCard API specifications in JML make many implicit assumptions explicit, see [16,17], and provide very precise (and hopefully readable) documentation which should be useful for applet developers. But one can also make mistakes in writing specifications, so it is important to actually verify them, if possible. One option is to use so-called extended static checking, with ESC/Java [18],

---

* Extended version of [4]

I. Attali and T. Jensen (Eds.): Java Card 2000, LNCS 2041, pp. 137–150, 2001.
© Springer-Verlag Berlin Heidelberg 2001

which can automatically spot potential violations of specifications. This is certainly very effective and useful, but it can only deal with relatively "simple" properties—which do not include the properties with universal quantification used in this paper; and though ESC/Java can detect many errors it never guarantees the absence of any errors. We see our approach as complementary, providing additional certainty: our verifications are based on a mathematical semantics of Java and JML (expressed in the logic of PVS) that allows in principle arbitrarily complex assertions to be used in specifications. But proving such assertions is interactive, and far from automatic. The fact that both automatic checking using ESC/Java and interactive verification using PVS are possible for JML is a strong advantage of this specification language. Additionally, it is possible to do run-time checking of JML assertions [5].

This paper cannot give more than an impression of some of the issues in API specification and verification. It does include the full JML specifications of the AID class (that have been verified) in Section 3, and also the specifications of the two relevant (native) methods from the Util class (in Section 2) that are used in AID. Section 4 highlights some of the interesting issues that came up in the specification and verification of the AID class; in particular it discusses exceptions and invariants, and the important role they play in the verification. Finally, Section 5 draws some conclusions.

2   JavaCard's Util Class: Specification

The AID class makes use of two methods from the Util class, namely **arrayCopy** and **arrayCompare**. Both these methods are static, final and native: 'static' means that they can be invoked without a receiving object, 'final' that they cannot be overridden, and 'native' that no actual Java code is provided, but their implementation is given in some other (low-level) language.

The behaviour of these methods is described in informal comments in the Util.java file [1]. We quote these explanations:

arrayCopy: "Copies an array from the specified source array, beginning at the specified position, to the specified position of the destination array (non-atomically)."

arrayCompare: "Compares an array from the specified source array, beginning at the specified position, with the specified position of the destination array from left to right. Returns the ternary result of the comparison : less than (-1), equal(0) or greater than(1)."

More information is given in the informal (but very detailed) specifications included as javadoc comments in the code [1], especially about when exceptions may be expected. Such information is important for correct use of the JavaCard API in applets.

We shall use the formal specifications in JML given in Figures 1 and 2 (see also [16]), which closely follow these informal specifications. What we add are

```
/*@ normal_behavior
  @    requires: src != null &&  srcOff >= 0 &&
  @                srcOff+length <= src.length &&
  @                dest != null && destOff >= 0 &&
  @                destOff+length <= dest.length &&
  @                length >= 0;
  @ modifiable: \nothing;
  @     ensures: \result == -1 || \result == 0 || \result == 1;
  @     ensures: \result == 0
  @                 <==>
  @                \forall (byte i) 0 <= i && i < length
  @                            ==> src[srcOff+i] == dest[destOff+i];
  @ also
  @ behavior
  @    requires: true;
  @ modifiable: \nothing;
  @     signals: (NullPointerException)
  @                src == null || dest == null;
  @     signals: (ArrayIndexOutOfBoundsException)
  @                (src != null &&
  @                  (0 > srcOff || srcOff + length > src.length))
  @                ||
  @                (dest != null &&
  @                  (0 > destOff || destOff + length > dest.length));
  @*/
public static final native byte arrayCompare(byte[] src,
                                             short srcOff,
                                             byte[] dest,
                                             short destOff,
                                             short length)
throws ArrayIndexOutOfBoundsException,
       NullPointerException;
```

Fig. 1. JML specification for arrayCompare from Util

```
/*@ behavior
  @   requires: src != null && srcOff >= 0 &&
  @               srcOff+length <= src.length &&
  @               dest != null && destOff >= 0 &&
  @               destOff+length <= dest.length &&
  @               length >= 0;
  @ modifiable: dest[destOff..destOff+length-1],
  @               TransactionException.systemInstance.reason;
  @   ensures: \forall (short i) 0 <= i && i < length
  @               ==> dest[destOff+i] == \old(src[srcOff+i]);
  @   signals: (TransactionException e)
  @               e.getReason() == TransactionException.BUFFER_FULL;
  @ also
  @ behavior
  @   requires: true;
  @ modifiable: dest[destOff..destOff+length-1],
  @               TransactionException.systemInstance.reason;
  @   signals: (TransactionException e)
  @               e.getReason() == TransactionException.BUFFER_FULL;
  @   signals: (NullPointerException)
  @               src == null || dest == null;
  @   signals: (ArrayIndexOutOfBoundsException)
  @               (src != null &&
  @                (0 > srcOff || srcOff + length > src.length))
  @               ||
  @               (dest != null &&
  @                (0 > destOff || destOff + length > dest.length));
  @*/
public static final native short arrayCopy(byte[] src,
                                           short srcOff,
                                           byte[] dest,
                                           short destOff,
                                           short length)
throws ArrayIndexOutOfBoundsException,
       NullPointerException,
       TransactionException;
```

Fig. 2. JML specification for arrayCopy from Util

the explicit distinction between normal and exceptional termination, plus the precise information about items that may be modified by the methods.

Instead of explaining JML in general, we explain only the meaning of these specifications. The **behavior** keyword indicates that if the precondition as given by the **requires** clause holds, then either the method terminates normally, and the "normal" postcondition after the **ensures** keyword holds, or the method terminates abruptly because of an exception of the type indicated after **signals**, and the ensuing "abrupt" postcondition holds. The keyword **normal_behavior**, instead of just **behavior**, indicates that the method must terminate normally if the precondition holds. The **behavior** specifications are translated into *partial* Hoare formulas, and the **normal_behavior** specifications into *total* Hoare formulas, in a special version of Hoare logic adapted to JML [10].

The **modifiable** clauses tell which items may be changed by the method, and thus also, implicitly, which are left unaltered. The method **arrayCompare** does not modify anything, and thus has no side-effect. The **arrayCopy** method can modify certain entries of its parameter array **dest**, namely those in the range **offset**, ..., **offset + length - 1**. The need for **TransactionException.systemInstance.reason** is discussed in Section 4.2. The **TransactionException** may occur when an overflow arises in JavaCard's transaction buffer—which is used to enable rollback of operations in case of failure. The **ensures** clauses describe the postconditions, and thus the functional behaviour of these methods. Notice that we did not describe everything: it is not made explicit what it means when the result of **arrayCompare** is -1 or 1. This is possible, but cumbersome and these cases are probably not often needed. The various signals clauses of the form **signals: (E e) Q** express that when an exception **e** is thrown which is an instance of (exception) class **E**, then the postcondition **Q** must hold. These are useful for distinguishing the various possible causes for abrupt termination.

A subtle point is the use of **\old(...)** in the **ensures** clause of the **arrayCopy** method. This is needed to allow for aliasing, *i.e.* for **src == dest**. In this case **src** may be modified, and so we have to refer to the original entries of the **src** array to explain the copying. The informal javadoc specifications explicitly state that this is what happens if **src** and **dest** are aliases.

3   JavaCard's AID Class: Specification and Verification

In the JavaCard platform each applet instance and package is uniquely identified and selected by a so-called application identifier (AID)—and not, as usual in Java, by a string possibly in combination with a domain name, see [6, §§3.8]. AIDs are used in loading and linking. As prescribed in the ISO 7816 standard, each AID consists of an array of bytes, ranging in length from 5 to 16. The first five bytes form what is called the resource identifier (RID), which is assigned by ISO to a company. The possible remainder (between 0 and 11 bytes) forms the proprietary identifier extension (PIX), which is under the control of individual companies.

Before giving the specification of the `AID` class together with the current implementation[1] we describe the essentials of the `AID` class. Its field, constructor and five methods, without their implementations, look as follows.

```
public final class AID {
  byte[] theAID;
  public AID(byte[] bArray, short offset, byte length);
  public byte getBytes(byte[] dest, short offset);
  public boolean equals(Object anObject);
  public boolean equals(byte[] bArray, short offset, byte length);
  public boolean partialEquals(byte[] bArray, short offset, byte length);
  public boolean RIDEquals (AID otherAID);
}
```

Our JML specification of this class adds a class invariant, a history constraint and pre-/post-conditions for its constructor and methods.

Unlike the pre-/post-conditions, the invariant and history constraint are not explicitly stated in the informal documentation, but especially the invariant is crucially needed to prove that the implementation meets the specification. Since the array `theAID` of an AID consists of a 5-byte RID possibly together with a PIX of up-to 11 bytes, our invariant is

```
/*@
 @ invariant: theAID != null &&
 @                5 <= theAID.length && theAID.length <= 16;
 @*/
```

The proof obligation is to show that this property holds after normal termination of the constructor, and also that it holds after termination (both normal and abrupt) of each method, assuming it holds in the state in which the method is invoked[2].

Another class assertion is a so-called constraint:

```
/*@
 @ constraint: theAID == \old(theAID);
 @*/
```

It says that the `theAID` field never changes. Again, this property should be established for all methods. Class invariants and constraints are included in the semantics of (pre- and post-conditions of) methods specifications.

The `AID` class with JML specifications looks as follows.

```
public final class AID {
/*@
 @ invariant: theAID != null &&
```

---

[1] The implementation has revision number 1.19, written by Ravi, under Sun Microsystems copyright (1999)

[2] What is surprising is that the `theAID` field is not declared as `private`. As it stands, it can be modified from the outside (but only within its package), making it vulnerable to a breach of the invariant. We consider the omission of the `private` access modifier a bug.

```
  @                5 <= theAID.length && theAID.length <= 16;
  @
  @ constraint: theAID == \old(theAID);
  @*/

  byte[] theAID;

/*@ behavior
  @    requires: 5 <= length && length <= 16 &&
  @              bArray != null &&
  @              0 <= offset && offset + length <= bArray.length;
  @ modifiable: theAID, theAID[*],
  @             TransactionException.systemInstance.reason;
  @     ensures: length == theAID.length &&
  @             (\forall (short index) 0 <= index && index < length ==>
  @                     theAID [index] == bArray [offset + index]);
  @     signals: (TransactionException e)
  @                  e.getReason() == TransactionException.BUFFER_FULL;
  @*/
public AID( byte[] bArray, short offset, byte length )
    throws SystemException {
  if (length < 5 || length > 16)
    SystemException.throwIt(SystemException.ILLEGAL_VALUE);
  theAID = new byte[length];
  Util.arrayCopy( bArray, offset, theAID, (short)0, length );
}


/*@ behavior
  @    requires: dest != null && dest != theAID &&
  @              0 <= offset &&
  @              offset + theAID.length <= dest.length;
  @ modifiable: dest[offset..offset+theAID.length-1],
  @             TransactionException.systemInstance.reason;
  @     ensures: (\forall (short index)
  @                  0 <= index && index < theAID.length ==>
  @                  dest [offset + index] == theAID [index]) &&
  @              \result == theAID.length;
  @     signals: (TransactionException e)
  @                  e.getReason() == TransactionException.BUFFER_FULL;
  @ also
  @ behavior
  @    requires: true;
  @ modifiable: dest[offset..offset+theAID.length-1],
  @             TransactionException.systemInstance.reason;
  @     signals: (TransactionException e)
  @                  e.getReason() == TransactionException.BUFFER_FULL;
  @     signals: (NullPointerException)
  @                  dest == null;
  @     signals: (ArrayIndexOutOfBoundsException)
  @                  dest != null &&
  @                  (0 > offset || offset + theAID.length > dest.length);
  @*/
public byte getBytes (byte[] dest, short offset) {
  Util.arrayCopy( theAID, (short)0, dest, offset, (short)theAID.length );
  return (byte) theAID.length;
}


/*@ normal_behavior
  @    requires: (anObject instanceof AID) ==> \invariant_for((AID)anObject);
  @ modifiable: \nothing;
  @     ensures: \result ==
  @              (anObject instanceof AID &&
  @              ((AID)anObject).theAID.length == theAID.length &&
  @              (\forall (short index) 0 <= index && index < theAID.length
  @                  ==> theAID [index] == ((AID)anObject).theAID [index]));
  @*/
public boolean equals( Object anObject ) {
  if ( !(anObject instanceof AID) ||
```

```
                ((AID)anObject).theAID.length != theAID.length) return false;
      return (Util.arrayCompare(((AID)anObject).theAID, (short)0, theAID,
                                (short)0, (short)theAID.length) == 0);
}


/*@ normal_behavior
  @   requires: bArray == null || (0 <= offset &&
  @                                 length >= 0 &&
  @                                 offset + length <= bArray.length
  @                /// the extra condition below is needed to prove that
  @                /// the (apparently unnecessary) assignment on testByte
  @                /// never fails.
  @                /// The 3 conjuncts above are not strong enough.
  @                          && offset + length >= 1);
  @ modifiable: \nothing;
  @   ensures: \result ==
  @            (bArray != null &&
  @             length == theAID.length &&
  @             (\forall (short index) 0 <= index && index < length ==>
  @                  theAID [index] == bArray [offset + index]));
  @ also
  @ behavior
  @   requires: bArray != null;
  @ modifiable: \nothing;
  @   signals: (ArrayIndexOutOfBoundsException)
  @                offset + length < 1 ||
  @                0 > offset             ||
  @                length < 0             ||
  @                offset + length > bArray.length;
  @*/
public boolean equals( byte[] bArray, short offset, byte length ) {
  if (bArray == null) return false;
  // verify the array index
  byte testByte = bArray[(short)(offset + length - (short)1)];
  return ((length == theAID.length) &&
    (Util.arrayCompare(bArray, offset, theAID, (short)0, length) == 0));
}


/*@ normal_behavior
  @   requires: bArray == null || (0 <= offset &&
  @                                 length >= 0 &&
  @                                 offset + length <= bArray.length);
  @ modifiable: \nothing;
  @   ensures: \result ==
  @            (bArray != null &&
  @             length <= theAID.length &&
  @             (\forall (short index) 0 <= index && index < length ==>
  @                  theAID [index] == bArray [offset + index]));
  @ also
  @ behavior
  @   requires: bArray != null && length <= theAID.length;
  @ modifiable: \nothing;
  @   signals: (ArrayIndexOutOfBoundsException)
  @                0 > offset ||
  @                length < 0 ||
  @                offset + length > bArray.length;
  @*/
public boolean partialEquals( byte[] bArray, short offset, byte length ) {
  if ( bArray == null || length > theAID.length ) return false;
  return (Util.arrayCompare(bArray, offset,
                            theAID, (short)0, length) == 0);
}


/*@ normal_behavior
  @   requires: true; /// implicitly: \invariant_for(otherAID)
  @   ensures: \result ==
  @            (otherAID != null &&
  @             (\forall (short index) 0 <= index && index < 5 ==>
```

```
  @                       theAID [index] == otherAID.theAID [index])));
  @*/
public boolean RIDEquals ( AID otherAID ) {
  if ( otherAID == null ) return false;
  if ( Util.arrayCompare( theAID, (short)0, otherAID.theAID,
                          (short)0, (short)5 ) == 0 ) return true;
  return false;
}
}
```

The LOOP tool translates the Java implementations to certain (complicated) structures describing their semantics in PVS. The JML specifications become predicates on such structures. The actual verification task then consists of showing that the structures arising from the given Java implementation satisfy these predicates. For the methods that are called in these implementations (like **arrayCompare** or **getReason**) their JML specifications are used, and not their Java implementations (if any). In this way, all of the above specifications have been proven in PVS, for the given implementations. The proofs are done interactively, by using the JML proof rules from [10]—following the structure of the (translated) Java code—together with appropriate powerful proof strategies.

On average, constructing such a proof takes about one hour—assuming the specification is correct. But during this case study we frequently had to go back and adjust a minor detail in the specifications. It is surprisingly hard to get specifications precisely right. This fact makes actually doing the verifications so important.

4   Some Special Issues

Due to space restrictions we cannot discuss all aspects of the **AID** specification and verification, so we concentrate on several special points.

4.1   behavior and not exceptional_behavior

Our **Util** and **AID** specifications contain **normal_behavior** (for total correctness) and **behavior** (for partial correctness, when exceptions may be thrown). When specifying under which conditions methods throw certain exceptions as we have done using **behavior** specifications, one has to be very careful with the subtle difference between specifying when a method *may* throw an exception and specifying when a method *must* throw an exception, especially when there is the possibility of throwing more than one exception. The **signals**-clauses in the **behavior** specifications state that an exception *may* be thrown (and that some-thing special condition is then the case). In the JavaCard API documentation it is explicitly stated that when different kinds of exceptions may be thrown, then there are no guarantees about which one will actually arise if conditions overlap. This excludes **exceptional_behavior**, because it is used for specifying that an exception *must* be thrown if a given precondition is met. In our experience it is extremely tricky to specify when a certain exception *must* be thrown, and, moreover, typically one is not so interested in such properties.

4.2   No Exception Object Creation

Because of the limited resources available on smart cards, exception objects are not created during run-time [6, §§6.2]. Instead, an already existing static exception object, typically called systemInstance, is thrown via the throwIt method, see the AID constructor. The different exceptions are distinguished via a reason field. That is why there are so many (qualified) reason's in the modifiable clauses: any method that can throw a TransactionException can modify the reason field of the static exception object TransactionException.-systemInstance.

(Since static initialization does not take place during the execution of Java-Card programs, we have a semantics which is different from Java programs. In [2] it is described how the underlying memory model in PVS involves for each class with static initialization a special Boolean telling whether static initialization for this class has already taken place. Whenever a member from this class is used, the value of this Boolean is checked. We have disabled such a check for JavaCard programs, and thereby disabled static initialization.)

4.3   Class Invariants

The preservation of invariants in an object oriented setting is a notoriously complicated issue, see for instance [7,9,19,15]. The hardest problem is caused by aliasing: an object can hold references to other objects and its invariant can depend on the states of these other objects, and vice versa. Another problem is that of callbacks, also known as re-entrance.

Ideally, the way to deal with invariants is to assume that *all* objects—not just this—satisfy their invariants at beginning of a method body, and to prove that *all* objects satisfy their invariants at the end of the method body[3]. Invariants can then be temporarily broken during the method invocation. However, note that if our method body contains a method invocation then all invariants should be re-established at this point, because this is required by the precondition of this method that is invoked.

However, a fundamental problem with this idealized approach above is how to prove that a method of an object does not break the invariants of some other objects. For example, the method getBytes changes the contents of the byte array dest it gets as an argument; how can we possibly prove that this does not break the invariant of some other object that also holds a reference to this array? To do this we would have to know all other objects and class invariants that exist. It should be clear that this approach is not really feasible.

In light of this problem, what we currently do when verifying methods in PVS is that we assume at the beginning of the method body

- that the precondition holds,
- that this satisfies its invariant, and

---

[3] For private methods we can drop the requirement that invariants are maintained, but, since all methods of AID are public, we ignore this here.

– that any objects the method receives as parameters (if any) satisfy their invariants;

then we prove

– that the postcondition holds,
– that the invariant of this hold at the end of the method body, and
– that the appropriate invariant for a result or exception object, if any, holds[4].

What actually happens is that the LOOP tool strengthens all pre-conditions with the assertion that this satisfies its invariant, and with assertions that the parameter (if any) satisfy their invariants. So, for example, the pre-condition of RIDEquals is strengthened to include an assertion that its parameter otherAID of class AID satisfies the AID-invariant. This can then be used during verification of the method. (And in fact this is needed in the verification, namely to establish that otherAID.theAID is not null and has a length of at least 5 in the invocation of arrayCompare in RIDEquals.)

In a dual fashion, when a method specification is *used*, to prove a property of some invocation of the method, then this strengthened pre-condition has to be established; this includes proving that all parameters meet their invariants.

However, this implicit strengthening of preconditions does not suffice for all cases, and sometimes preconditions have to be strengthened further, explicitly. For example, if we have an object obj of class Object, and (down)cast it to an arbitrary class A, then we would like to use that (A)obj satisfies the A-invariant, and not just the Object-invariant. This actually comes up during verification of the equals method from AID with parameter Object anObject. After a check that the parameter belongs to class AID, it is used as an AID object, and the AID-invariant must be assumed for it. At the moment this problem is dealt with manually by adding an extra clause in the requires clause, namely

```
(anObject instanceof AID) ==> \invariant_for((AID)anObject)
```

which states that if anObject is an instance of class AID, then is satisfies the AID-invariant. This can then be used to prove the method correct, but of course has to be established for any invocation of equals. How to handle this in general still has to be elaborated.

4.4   Class Invariants and Exceptions

Our semantics of JML requires that invariants are established by every normally terminating constructor and maintained by every method, regardless of whether the method terminates normally or terminates abnormally by throwing an exception. Invariants (for this) are implicitly included in all postconditions, both in the ensures and in the signals clauses, of all methods. Requiring that invariants are maintained even if an exception is thrown may seem an overly strong

---

[4] In the end, the invariants of the parameters should still hold, if all methods applied to them preserve invariants—as they should.

requirement. However, it is needed, because if the exception is caught later and normal execution of the program resumes, then the invariants should still hold. Inside method bodies the invariants may be temporarily broken; care must be taken that no exception can be thrown while this is the case.

For constructors the situation is more subtle, because the invariant typically does not hold until right at the end of the constructor body. But if an exception is thrown, one cannot retrieve a partially constructed object via catching. So there is no need to require the invariant for abrupt termination. Therefore, only the ensures clauses are interesting for constructor specifications. For the AID constructor we do not write a normal_behavior instead of a behavior specification because the Util.arrayCopy method may still throw a Transaction exception (when the transaction buffer becomes full). Trying to exclude this in the precondition is not so easy.

5   Conclusions

We have sketched the verification of the formal JML specification for the AID class in the JavaCard API using the theorem prover PVS, based on the semantics of Java and JML provided by the LOOP tool. In the end, what we have obtained is a fully verified formal specification of a small part of the JavaCard API. This is of course not a major example, but it does show the possibility of such validation efforts for class libraries.

One interesting—and sometimes frustrating—aspect of doing this kind of formal verification is the continuing discovery of ever more subtle mistakes in the formal specification. The verification of an individual method typically involves dealing explicitly with many possible cases, some of which are easily overlooked. Indeed, everything in Java can throw an exception, which creates many possibilities to be explored. But handling all of them is important, because unexpected exceptions form a notorious cause of (run-time) errors in programs.

Work on formally specifying and verifying more classes of the JavaCard API is continuing[5]. Our aim is to obtain a fully verified formal specification of the JavaCard API that can serve as the basis for actual applet verification. Initial goals for these applet verifications will be proving the absence of runtime exceptions and non-termination, and proving the absence of unwanted side effects (notably side effects on other applets) expressed by modifiable clauses. Achieving all this will still require the development of more proof rules and PVS tactics to further reduce the effort required for verifications.

References

1. JavaCard API 2.1. http://java.sun.com/products/javacard/htmldoc/.

---

[5] The work on the JavaCard API is part of European IST-project "VerifiCard", see www.verificard.org.

2. J. van den Berg, M. Huisman, B. Jacobs, and E. Poll. A type-theoretic memory model for verification of sequential Java programs. In D. Bert, C. Choppy, and P. Mosses, editors, *Recent Trends in Algebraic Development Techniques*, number 1827 in Lect. Notes Comp. Sci., pages 1–21. Springer, Berlin, 2000.

3. J. van den Berg and B. Jacobs. The LOOP compiler for Java and JML. Techn. Rep. CSI-R0019, Comput. Sci. Inst., Univ. of Nijmegen. To appear at TACAS'01., 2000.

4. J. van den Berg, B. Jacobs, and E. Poll. Formal specification and verification of JavaCard's Application Identifier Class. Techn. Rep. CSI-R0014, Comput. Sci. Inst., Univ. of Nijmegen. Appeared in: Proceedings of the JavaCard Workshop, Cannes. INRIA Techn. Rep. Updated version will appear in: I. Attali and Th. Jensen, editors, *Proceedings of the Java Card 2000 Workshop* (Springer LNCS 2001), Sept. 1999.

5. A. Bhorkar. A run-time assertion checker for Java using JML. Techn. Rep. 00-08, Dep. of Comp. Science, Iowa State Univ. (http://www.cs.iastate.edu/~leavens/JML.html), 2000.

6. Z. Chen. *Java Card Technology for Smart Cards*. The Java Series. Addison-Wesley, 2000.

7. D. Detlefs, K. R. M. Leino, and G. Nelson. Wrestling with rep exposure. Technical report, Compaq Systems Research Center, Palo Alto, 1998. Research Report 156.

8. M. Huisman, B. Jacobs, and J. van den Berg. A case study in class library verification: Java's Vector class. Techn. Rep. CSI-R0007, Comput. Sci. Inst., Univ. of Nijmegen. To appear in *Software Tools for Technology Transfer*, 2001.

9. K. Huizing, R. Kuiper, and SOOP. Verification of object oriented programs using class invariants. In T. Maibaum, editor, *Fundamental Approaches to Software Engineering*, number 1783 in Lect. Notes Comp. Sci., pages 208–221. Springer, Berlin, 2000.

10. B. Jacobs and E. Poll. A logic for the Java Modeling Language JML. Techn. Rep. CSI-R0018, Comput. Sci. Inst., Univ. of Nijmegen. To appear at FASE'01., 2000.

11. B. Jacobs, J. van den Berg, M. Huisman, M. van Berkum, U. Hensel, and H. Tews. Reasoning about classes in Java (preliminary report). In *Object-Oriented Programming, Systems, Languages and Applications (OOPSLA)*, pages 329–340. ACM Press, 1998.

12. G.T. Leavens, A.L. Baker, and C. Ruby. JML: A notation for detailed design. In H. Kilov and B. Rumpe, editors, *Behavioral Specifications of Business and Systems*, pages 175–188. Kluwer, 1999.

13. G.T. Leavens, A.L. Baker, and C. Ruby. Preliminary design of JML: A behavioral interface specification language for Java. Techn. Rep. 98-06, Dep. of Comp. Sci., Iowa State Univ. (http://www.cs.iastate.edu/~leavens/JML.html), 1999.

14. S. Owre, J.M. Rushby, N. Shankar, and F. von Henke. Formal verification for fault-tolerant architectures: Prolegomena to the design of PVS. *IEEE Trans. on Softw. Eng.*, 21(2):107–125, 1995.

15. A. Poetzsch-Heffter and P. Müller. A programming logic for sequential Java. In S.D. Swierstra, editor, *Programming Languages and Systems*, number 1576 in Lect. Notes Comp. Sci., pages 162–176. Springer, Berlin, 1999.

16. E. Poll, J. van den Berg, and B. Jacobs. Specification of the JavaCard API in JML. In J. Domingo-Ferrer, D. Chan, and A. Watson, editors, *Smart Card Research and Advanced Application*, pages 135–154. Kluwer Acad. Publ., 2000.

17. E. Poll, J. van den Berg, and B. Jacobs. Formal specification of the JavaCard API in JML: the APDU class. *Comp. Networks Mag.*, 2001. To appear.

18. Extended static checker ESC/Java. Compaq System Research Center.
    `http://www.research.digital.com/SRC/esc/Esc.html`.
19. C. Szyperski. *Component Software*. Addison-Wesley, 1998.

Security on Your Hand :
Secure Filesystems with a "Non-Cryptographic" JAVA-Ring

Rüdiger Weis[1], Bastiaan Bakker[2], and Stefan Lucks[3]*

[1] cryptolabs Amsterdam
convergence integrated media GmbH
Berlin, San Francisco, Amsterdam
ruedi@cryptolabs.org
[2] Delft University of Technology / LifeLine Networks BV
Bastiaan.Bakker@lifeline.nl
[3] Theoretische Informatik, University of Mannheim
lucks@th.informatik.uni-mannheim.de

Abstract. In this paper we present the first implementation of high-speed filesystem encryption with a slow JAVA card. Using new "Remotely Keyed Protocols" designed by Lucks and Weis we can use the highly tamper-resistant JAVA ring, and even restrict ourselves to a version of the ring without built-in encryption.
We have implemented this protocols on the ring and give a first performance comparision.

Keywords: i-Button, tamper proof, Remotely Keyed Encryption

1 Introduction

Many security-relevant applications store secret keys on a tamper-resistant device, a *smart card*. Protection of the valuable keys is the card's main purpose. Although in recent years some interesting cryptographic [Weis97] and many very dangerous hardware attacks [WKT97] have been mounted, smart cards provide much higher security than other storage systems.

The i-Buttons from Dallas Semiconductor are fully inter operable JAVA cards in the form of a finger ring. This unusual form provides reasonable security against hardware attacks, compared to that provided by ordinary chip cards [WKT97]. Two problems remain, however with regard to using this device for bulk encryption.

The first lies in the physical limitations of smart cards which make them typically slow. Especially JAVA devices are *too slow* to provide an acceptable bandwidth. Fortunately, remotely keyed encryption schemes are designed to allow "High-Bandwidth Encryption with Low-Bandwidth Smart cards" [Blaz96]. (This is accomplished with the help of a fast but untrusted host.)

* Supported by the Deutsche Forschungsgemeinschaft (DFG) grant KR 1521

I. Attali and T. Jensen (Eds.): Java Card 2000, LNCS 2041, pp. 151–162, 2001.
© Springer-Verlag Berlin Heidelberg 2001

The second major problem is posed by the restrictions on encryption hardware. Our legally exported JAVA rings do not offer native support for encryption. However, authentication tools such as cryptographic hash functions are not considered "encryption" [LuWe99]. Protocols developed by Lucks [Luck97] and Weis [Weis99] can be used with an underlying hash function, even without a native encryption function and are well suited for bandwidth-greedy cryptographic services, such as file system encryption.

We use JAVA cards because we can program them easily, we can provide vendor-independent applications, and finally we like the fancy, secure and very practical i-buttons.

2   Secure File System Encryption

For many fielded systems, the key management seems to be the weakest link. Perhaps the biggest problem is the fact that there is no "safe place" to store the secret keys for a computer connected to the internet. If someone uses a Windows system there does not seem to be even a theoretical chance of avoiding attacks over the network. Known attacks with "Trojan Horses" (e.g. Back Orifice), are very hard to prevent, since we have no open sources.

Also swapping of sensitive memory to the hard disk is difficult and often impossible to prevent. If key bits or even only intermediate values can be located on the swap areas of the hard disk, the security of the system may be compromised.

2.1   Attack Scenarios

In this section we discuss our standpoint that in open systems, smart card supported systems represent the only practicable solution for encrypting sensitive data.

We want to discuss two main attack scenarios. In an *offline-attack* the attacker gains physical control of the hard disk. In an *online-attack* the attacker takes control of the host system and is able to communicate with the smart card.

2.2   Security Problems of a Software Solution

A software-only solution is not secure against both kind of attacks.

Offline Attack: If the attacker gains control of the hard disk (e.g. steals the notebook computer) she can try to perform a *dictionary attack*. Most humans use passwords with a very poor entropy.

Additionally she can search "random looking" data in the swap areas. Note that this strategy of "Playing Hide and Seek with Stored Keys" [ShSo99] was suggested by Shamir and Someren and has helped to find the Microsoft "_NSAKEY".

Online Attacks: If an attacker can take control of the host during the encryption she can read the secret key.

2.3   Security of Smart Card Supported Solutions

Offline Attacks: Given a sufficiently high entropy and length of the secret key in the smart card, a Brute Force Attack seems to be infeasible. An attacker has to steal both the hard disk AND the smart card AND crack the smart card PIN.

Online Attacks: The security proof of our protocols show that an attacker who has control of the host system can only read those files that are decrypted while she is in control.

3   Remotely Keyed Encryption

A *remotely keyed encryption scheme* (RKES) distributes the computational burden for a block cipher with large blocks between two parties, a *host* and a *card*. We think of the host as being a computer at risk of being taken over by an adversary, while the card can be a smart card, protecting the secret key. The host knows plaintext and ciphertext, but only the card is entrusted with the key.

An RKES consists of two protocols: the *encryption protocol* and the *decryption protocol*. Given a B-bit input, either to encrypt or to decrypt, such a protocol runs as follows:

The host sends a *challenge value* to the card, depending on the input, and the card replies with a *response value*, depending on both the challenge value and the key. Exchanging callenge and response values can be iterated.

Since we want to integrate our smart card supported encryption protocol into a file system in a transparent way we focus on length-preserving schemes. In a length-preserving scheme the ciphertext is exactly the same size as the plaintext.

3.1   The First Security Model for RKE Schemes

Lucks [Luck97] pointed out some weaknesses of Blaze's scheme and gave formal requirements for the security of RKESs:

(i) *Forgery security:* After having controlled the host for up to $q - 1$ interactions, the adversary cannot produce, the adversary she cannot produce q plaintext/ciphertext pairs.

(ii) **Inversion security:** An adversary with (legitimate) access to encryption only must not be able to decrypt and vice versa.

(iii) **Pseudorandomness:** The encryption function should behave pseudorandomly for someone without access to the card, nor knowledge of the secret key.

While requirements (i) and (ii) restrict the abilities of an adversary with access to the smart card, requirement (iii) is only valid for *outsider adversaries* without access to the card. If an adversary could compute forgeries or run inversion attacks, she could easily distinguish the encryption function from a random one.

3.2   The RaMaRK Encryption Scheme

In this section, we describe the _Random Mapping based Remotely Keyed (Ra-MaRK) Encryption scheme_, which uses several independent instances of a _fixed size random mapping_ $f : \{0,1\}^b \longrightarrow \{0,1\}^b$.

The scheme is provably secure if its building blocks are, i.e., it satisfies the requirements (i)–(iii) above, see [Luck97]. Note that b must be large enough to make performing close to $2^{b/2}$ encryptions infeasible. We recommend to choose $b \geq 160$.

By "$\oplus$" we denote the bit-wise XOR, though mathematically any group operation would do the job as well.

We use three building blocks:

1. Key-dependent (pseudo-)random mappings

$$f_i : \{0,1\}^b \longrightarrow \{0,1\}^b.$$

2. A hash function

$$H : \{0,1\}^* \longrightarrow \{0,1\}^b.$$

   H has to be _collision resistant_.

3. A pseudorandom bit generator (i.e. a "stream cipher")

$$S : \{0,1\}^b \longrightarrow \{0,1\}^*.$$

If the seed $s \in \{0,1\}^b$ is randomly chosen, the bits produced by $S(s)$ have to be indistinguishable from randomly generated bits.

In addition to pseudorandomness, the following property is needed: If s is secret and attackers choose $t_1, t_2, \ldots \in \{0,1\}^b$ with $t_i \neq t_j$ for $i \neq j$ and receive outputs $S(s \oplus t_1)$, $S(s \oplus t_2)$, $\ldots$, it has to be infeasible for the attackers to distinguish these outputs from independently generated random bit strings of the same size. Hence, such a construction behaves like a random mapping $\{0,1\}^b \longrightarrow \{0,1\}^{B-2b}$, though it is actually a pseudorandom one, depending on the secret s.

Based on these building blocks, we realize a remotely keyed encryption scheme to encrypt blocks of any size $B \geq 3b$, see the following figure.

We represent the plaintext by (P, Q, R) and the ciphertext by (A, B, C), where

$$(P, Q, R), (A, B, C) \in \{0,1\}^b \times \{0,1\}^b \times \{0,1\}^{B-2b}.$$

For the protocol description we also consider intermediate values

$$T, U, V, X, Y, Z \in \{0,1\}^b, \text{ and } I \in \{0,1\}^{B-2b}.$$

The encryption protocol works as follows:

1. Given the plaintext (P, Q, R), the host sends P and Q to the card.
2. The card computes $U = f_1(P) \oplus Q$ and $T = f_2(U) \oplus P$, and sends $X = f_3(T) \oplus U$ to the host.

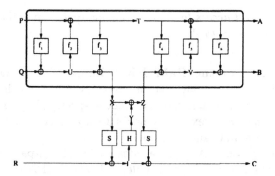

Fig. 1. The RaMaRK encryption protocol

3. The host computes $I = S(X) \oplus R$ and $Y = H(I)$, sends $Z = X \oplus Y$ to the card, and computes $C = S(Z) \oplus I$.
4. The card computes $V = f_4(T) \oplus Z$, and sends the two values $A = f_5(V) \oplus T$ and $B = f_6(A) \oplus V$ to the host.

If the block size B of the cipher it realizes is not too small compared to the parameter b, the RaMaRK scheme is efficient. The card itself operates on $2 \cdot b$ bit data blocks, and both $3 \cdot b$ bit of information enter and leave the card.

3.3   The Security of RaMaRK

Lucks has proven that the RaMaRK scheme is secure in the first security model [Luck97]. The RaMaRK scheme is Forgery secure, Inversion secure and Pseudorandom in the sense of [Luck97].

Extended Security Model. Blaze, Feigenbaum (AT&T) and Naor (Weizmann Institut) [BFN98] published a paper at the EUROCRYPT'98 which has showed a new formal model for RKES, found a problem in the RaMaRK protocol, and suggested a new RKES that fulfills the new security model.

It is theoretically desirable that a cryptographic primitive always appears to behave randomly to everyone without access to the key. In any RKES, the amount of communication between host and card should be less than the input length, otherwise the card could just do the complete encryption on its own. Since (at least) a part of the input is not handled by the smart card, and, for the same reasons, (at least) a part of the output is generated by the host, an insider adversary can easily decide that the output generated by herself is not random.

Blaze, Feigenbaum, and Naor [BFN98] found another way to define the pseudorandomness of RKESs. Their formal definition is quite complicated. It is based on the following scenario: *Adversary A gains direct access to the card for a certain amount of time and makes a fixed number of interactions with the card.*

Onces A has lost direct access to the card, the encryption function should appear to behave randomly, even to A.

Security Problems of the RaMaRK Scheme. Regarding the RaMaRK scheme, the authors pointed out that an adversary A who has had access to the card and lost the access again, can later choose special plaintexts where A can predict *a part of* the ciphertext. This makes it easy for A to distinguish between RaMaRK encryption and random data.

The intermediate value X only depends on the (P, Q)-part of the plaintext, and the encryption of the R-part only depends on X. If A chooses a plaintext (P, Q, R), having participated before in the encryption of (P, Q, R'), with $R \neq R'$, the adversary A can predict the C-part of the ciphertext, but not the P nor the Q part, corresponding to (P, Q, R) on her own. Thus, according to the definition of [BFN98], the RaMaRK scheme is not pseudorandom.

"Decryption" of the Ciphertexts. Blaze, Naor, and Feigenbaum [BFN98] also mentioned that after an online attack it may be feasible to decrypt parts of the ciphertext. We argue that such an attack is not possible (cf. [Weis99]). that this statement does not apply.

The authors of [BFN98] pointed that there is a possibility to attack files with the same $2b$ bit header.

> "However, because the encryption key depends only on the first two plaintext blocks, an arbitrarily large set of messages all of which start with the same two blocks will always be encrypted with the same key. This is not a hypothetical situation: A set of files in a computer file system, for example, might always start with the same few bytes of structural information."

The above describes a *known plaintext* distinguishing attack that is actually feasible. The authors of [BFN98] continue:

> "An adversary that controls the host during the encryption or decryption of *one* file in such a set could subsequently decrypt the encryption of *any* file in the set."

We argue that this attack ist *not* feasible. Note that the second intermediate key Z (resp. X for decryption) depends on all bit of the plaintext (P, Q, R) (resp. ciphertext (A, B, C)).

$$Z = X \oplus Y = X \oplus H(I) = X \oplus H\left(\boxed{R} \oplus S(X)\right)$$

Thus the knowledge of the intermediate value X (resp. Z) is *not* sufficient to decrypt of *any* file of the mentioned set of files.

On the other hand it is a not satisfactory cryptographic property that an attacker can peel off one of the two stream cipher encryptions if she knows the intermediate key X.

$$C = I \oplus S(Z) = R \oplus S(X) \oplus S(Z)$$

3.4 Improved RaMaRK

Motivated by the discussion described above, Weis [Weis99] proposed a slight modification.

Protocol Modification. We want to make sure that also the intermediate keys X and Y depend on every plaintext bit. Instead of P and Q we submit

$$\bar{P} := P \oplus h(R) \text{ and } \bar{A} := A \oplus h(C)$$

where h is a cryptographic hash function.

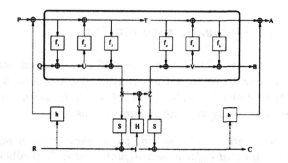

Fig. 2. Improved RaMaRK

The *Improved RaMaRK scheme* is interface-compatible with the unmodified RaMaRK scheme. So no hardware modifications to the smart card are necessary.

Characteristics and Limitations. If we choose a standard hash function with 160-bit output, a *known plaintext attack* against the pseudorandom property seems to be infeasible.

A *chosen plaintext attack* in the BFN scenario to distinguish the output of the protocol from random output is still feasible. So even the improved RaMaRK scheme fails to meet the stronger security model of [BFN98].

Furthermore, it is not possible to peel off one stream cipher encryption as discussed in the last section.

The modification requires two expensive hash function calls for the big block B. We do not expect this to cause a problem for most applications since the main bottleneck seems to be the communication with the card.

3.5 Implementation Aspects

In this section we discuss how to choose the building-blocks for our protocols. In order to combine the big block of data with the small blocks in the card, we need a *collision-free* hash function. The calculation is performed on the host, so we can simply choose a well-tested hash function like SHA-1 or RIPE-MD160. Both produce a 160-bit output, which seems to provide sufficient security.

In [Luck97] the use of a stream cipher was suggested. But we can also use a well-tested block cipher in the OFB or CFB mode (e.g. CAST-5 performs very well even on small packets [WeLu98]).

Now we discuss how to realize Pseudo Random Mappings (PRM) with a Non-Encrypting smart card. One promising method is to use a hash-based MAC function. HMAC [BCK96] uses an iterative cryptographic hash function $\mathcal{H}$ as a black box. This approach has several advantages. Cryptographic hash functions have been well studied and they are usually faster than encryption algorithms. It is easier, in many countries, to export or import an authentication tool, such as a signature system, than to export or import an encryption system.

4   i-Button by Dallas Semiconductor

The i-Button is a standard JAVA "card" in a 16 mm, stainless steel case. Some accessories enable one to to wear the i-Button, like watches, metal cards, or finger rings. Note that the "wearability" is not a a funky feature as user friendly constructions are absolutely vital for secure systems.

> *"While cards are fine for playing poker, they're not a safe place to keep a fragile chip that defines your digital identity."* [Dall99]

The unusual form of the i-Button provides reasonable security against hardware attacks, compared to the security of ordinary chip cards [WKT97]. Furthermore the case provides clear visual evidence of tampering.

Dallas Semiconductor [Dall99] gives the following summary of the physical security:

- Armored with stainless steel for the hard knocks of everyday use
- Wear tested for 1 million insertions and more than 10 years of life
- ESD protection is more than 25,000 volts for wash-and-wear dependability
- Three-layer metal technology and flip-chip bonding form barricades to protect data
- Opening of the physical perimeter generates a tamper response
- Tamper response causes rapid zeroization of NV SRAM to prevent disclosure of secure data.

The 6 kB of SRAM included on the monolithic chip has been specially designed so that it will rapidly erase its contents in the event of an intrusion.

The following instances are treated as intrusions:

- Opening the case
- Removing the metallurgically bonded substrate barricade
- Micro-probing the chip
- Subjecting the chip to temperature extremes.

There are several design elements against Differential Fault Analysis. Thus if excessive voltage is encountered, the sole I/O pin is designed to fuse. This will render the chip inoperable.

Fig. 3. i-Button ring and Blue Dot reader

5   Practical Results

We have implemented the RaMaRK and the Improved RaMaRK protocols based on SHA-HMAC. The SHA hash function is provided as a native function in the non-cryptographic JAVA1 ring we used in our tests. We tested our first implementation with different packet sizes. The performance numbers are given in milliseconds. As a first test, we enrypted a file with the size of 23,508,492 byte as one single block [WEL00]. Note that we have no security problems since our security proves that the security of our protocols is (under meaningful assumptions) only determined by the small block.

In Table 1 and Table 2, we describe the following values:

Communication time Time consumed by sending and receiving 320 bit to the ring

Total (excluding file-io) Time for the full protocol

Stage 1 Time for receiving 320 bit and the first 3 Feistel rounds $\{f_1, \ldots, f_3\}$ with SHA-HMAC on the ring

Local Calculations Time for bulk encryption on the host (SHA / RC4 / SHA)

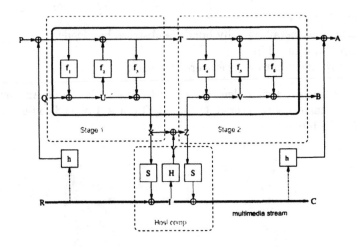

Fig. 4. The different protocol steps

Table 1. RAMARK and IRaMaRK Encryption for 23 MB blocks

Protocol Steps	RaMaRK	IRaMaRK
Communication time	2,470	2,470
Total	15,420	15,430
Stage 1	4,610	4,610
Local Calculation	6,200	6,210
Stage 2	4,610	4,610

Table 2. Performance of IRaMaRK for 3 block sizes

Protocol Steps	8kB	8 MB	23 MB
Stage 1	4,670	4,670	4,610
Host comp	110	2,470	6,210
Stage 2	4,610	4,620	4,610
Total	9,390	11,760	15,430

Stage 2 Time for sending 320 bit to the host and the second 3 Feistel $\{f_4, \ldots, f_6\}$ rounds with SHA-HMAC on the ring

As expected, there is no significant performance difference between RaMaRK and Improved RaMaRK. So if we want to use a protocol of the RaMaRK family, we suggest to use the Improved RaMaRK.

The performance is mainly influenced by the speed of communication between the host and the i-Button reader and the calculations on the ring.

And this communication is painfully slow. According to iButton support <
jibsupport@dalsemi.com > "1.5-2.0 seconds per hit are normal." [BWL00].

For the standard files system block sizes we can neglect the time spent on
the host operations.

Table 3. RaMaRK Encryption with typical filesystem block sizes

Block Size	1kB	2kB	4kB	8kB
Total	9,400	9,450	9,470	9,490

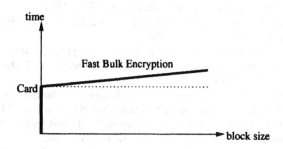

Fig. 5. Performance of RaMaRK protocol family

Note that the Host step is done in JAVA, so we will get a significant speed-up
if we switch to C++.

6   Conclusion and Outlook

We have hacked the protocols in the JAVA ring to show that it works in principle,
even though our implementations are too slow for practical usage. Now we want
test other hopefully faster JAVA cards and implement a lot of speed-ups to make
the system usable for real systems.

Further we are inventing fast length-increasing schemes with a weaker security model for realtime file encryption [Weis00] and multi media applications
[WVE+00]. We also want to solve the more theoretical problem to build an
efficient system with the stronger BFN security model without resorting to dedicated encryption functions.

Copyleft

We have not patented the protocols or algorithms presented. The required software will be published as Open Sources under GPL.

References

BWL00.   Bakker, B., Weis, R., Lucks, S., "How to Ring a S/WAN. Adding tamper resistant authentication to Linux IPSec", SANE2000 - 2nd International System Administration and Networking Conference, Maastricht, 2000.

BCK96.   Bellare, M., Canetti, R., Krawczyk, H., "Keying hash functions for message authentication", Crypto 96 Springer, 1996.

Blaz96.   Blaze, M., "High-Bandwidth Encryption with Low-Bandwidth Smart-cards", Fast Software Encryption, Springer LNCS 1039 , 1996.

BFN98.   Blaze, M., Feigenbaum, J., and Naor, M., "A Formal Treatment of Remotely Keyed Encryption (Extended Abstract)", Eurocrypt '98, Springer LNCS 1403, 1998, pp. 251-265.

Dall99.   Dallas Semiconductors, i-Button Hompage: http://www.ibutton.com/

Luck97.   Lucks, S., "On the Security of Remotely Keyed Encryption", Fast Software Encryption, (ed. E. Biham) Springer LNCS, 1997.

Luck99.   Lucks, S., "Accelerated Remotely Keyed Encryption", Fast Software Encryption, Springer LNCS, 1999.

LuWe99.   Lucks, S., Weis,R, "Remotely Keyed Encryption Using Non-Encrypting Smart Cards". USENIX Workshop on Smartcard Technology, Chicago, May 10-11, 1999.

LWH99.   Lucks, S., Weis, R., Hilt, V., "Fast Encryption for Set-Top Technologies", Multimedia Computing and Networking '99, San Jose, 1999.

ShSo99.   Shamir, A, van Someren, N., "Playing "hide and seek" with stored keys", Financial Cryptography '99, Anguilla, BWI, 1999.

WeLu98.   Weis, R., Lucks, S., "The Performance of Modern Block Ciphers in JAVA", CARDIS'98, Louvain-la-Neuve, LNCS, Springer, September 1998.

Weis97.   Weis, R., "Combined Cryptoanalytic Attacks against Signature and Encryption Schemes" (in German), A la Card aktuell 23/97, S.279, 1997.

Weis99.   Weis, R., "A Protocol Improvement for High-Bandwidth Encryption Using Non-Encrypting Smart Cards", IFIP TC-11, Working Groups 11.1 and 11.2, 7 th Annual Working Conference on Information Security Management & Small Systems Security, Amsterdam, 1999.

Weis00.   "Cryptographic Protocols and Algorithms for Distributed Multimedia Systems", PhD Thesis, Universität Mannheim, 2000.

WEL00.   Weis, R., Effelsberg, W., Lucks, S., "Remotely Keyed Encryption with Java Cards: A Secure and Efficient Method to Encrypt Multimedia Stream", IEEE International Conference on Multimedia and Expo, New York, July 2000.

WKT97.   Weis, R., Kuhn, M., Tron, "Hacking Chipcards", Workshop CCC'97, Hamburg 1997.

WVE+00.   Weis, R., Vogel, J., Effelsberg, W., Geyer, W., Lucks, S., "How to Make a Digital Whiteboard Secure - Using JAVA-Cards for Multimedia Application ", IDMS2000, Enschede, Springer, LNCN, 2000.

Author Index

Lecture Notes in Computer Science

For information about Vols. 1–1976
please contact your bookseller or Springer-Verlag

Vol. 2020: D. Naccache (Ed.), Topics in Cryptology – CT-RSA 2001. Proceedings, 2001. XII, 473 pages. 2001

Vol. 2021: J. N. Oliveira, P. Zave (Eds.), FME 2001: Formal Methods for Increasing Software Productivity. Proceedings, 2001. XIII, 629 pages. 2001.

Vol. 2022: A. Romanovsky, C. Dony, J. Lindskov Knudsen, A. Tripathi (Eds.), Advances in Exception Handling Techniques. XII, 289 pages. 2001

Vol. 2024: H. Kuchen, K. Ueda (Eds.), Functional and Logic Programming. Proceedings, 2001. X, 391 pages. 2001.

Vol. 2025: M. Kaufmann, D. Wagner (Eds.), Drawing Graphs. XIV, 312 pages. 2001.

Vol. 2026: F. Müller (Ed.), High-Level Parallel Programming Models and Supportive Environments. Proceedings, 2001. IX, 137 pages. 2001.

Vol. 2027: R. Wilhelm (Ed.), Compiler Construction. Proceedings, 2001. XI, 371 pages. 2001.

Vol. 2028: D. Sands (Ed.), Programming Languages and Systems. Proceedings, 2001. XIII, 433 pages. 2001.

Vol. 2029: H. Hussmann (Ed.), Fundamental Approaches to Software Engineering. Proceedings, 2001. XIII, 349 pages. 2001.

Vol. 2030: F. Honsell, M. Miculan (Eds.), Foundations of Software Science and Computation Structures. Proceedings, 2001. XII, 413 pages. 2001.

Vol. 2031: T. Margaria, W. Yi (Eds.), Tools and Algorithms for the Construction and Analysis of Systems. Proceedings, 2001. XIV, 588 pages. 2001.

Vol. 2032: R. Klette, T. Huang, G. Gimel'farb (Eds.), Multi-Image Analysis. Proceedings, 2000. VIII, 289 pages. 2001.

Vol. 2033: J. Liu, Y. Ye (Eds.), E-Commerce Agents. VI, 347 pages. 2001. (Subseries LNAI).

Vol. 2034: M.D. Di Benedetto, A. Sangiovanni-Vincentelli (Eds.), Hybrid Systems: Computation and Control. Proceedings, 2001. XIV, 516 pages. 2001.

Vol. 2035: D. Cheung, G.J. Williams, Q. Li (Eds.), Advances in Knowledge Discovery and Data Mining – PAKDD 2001. Proceedings, 2001. XVIII, 596 pages. 2001. (Subseries LNAI).

Vol. 2037: E.J.W. Boers et al. (Eds.), Applications of Evolutionary Computing. Proceedings, 2001. XIII, 516 pages. 2001.

Vol. 2038: J. Miller, M. Tomassini, P.L. Lanzi, C. Ryan, A.G.B. Tettamanzi, W.B. Langdon (Eds.), Genetic Programming. Proceedings, 2001. XI, 384 pages. 2001.

Vol. 2039: M. Schumacher, Objective Coordination in Multi-Agent System Engineering. XIV, 149 pages. 2001. (Subseries LNAI).

Vol. 2040: W. Kou, Y. Yesha, C.J. Tan (Eds.), Electronic Commerce Technologies. Proceedings, 2001. X, 187 pages. 2001.

Vol. 2041: I. Attali, T. Jensen (Eds.), Java on Smart Cards: Programming and Security. Proceedings, 2000. X, 163 pages. 2001.

Vol. 2042: K.-K. Lau (Ed.), Logic Based Program Synthesis and Transformation. Proceedings, 2000. VIII, 183 pages. 2001.

Vol. 2043: D. Craeynest, A. Strohmeier (Eds.), Reliable Software Technologies – Ada-Europe 2001. Proceedings, 2001. XV, 405 pages. 2001.

Vol. 2044: S. Abramsky (Ed.), Typed Lambda Calculi and Applications. Proceedings, 2001. XI, 431 pages. 2001.

Vol. 2045: B. Pfitzmann (Ed.), Advances in Cryptology – EUROCRYPT 2001. Proceedings, 2001. XII, 545 pages. 2001.

Vol. 2047: R. Dumke, C. Rautenstrauch, A. Schmietendorf, A. Scholz (Eds.), Performance Engineering. XIV, 349 pages. 2001.

Vol. 2048: J. Pauli, Learning Based Robot Vision. IX, 288 pages. 2001.

Vol. 2051: A. Middeldorp (Ed.), Rewriting Techniques and Applications. Proceedings, 2001. XII, 363 pages. 2001.

Vol. 2052: V.I. Gorodetski, V.A. Skormin, L.J. Popyack (Eds.), Information Assurance in Computer Networks. Proceedings, 2001. XIII, 313 pages. 2001.

Vol. 2053: O. Danvy, A. Filinski (Eds.), Programs as Data Objects. Proceedings, 2001. VIII, 279 pages. 2001.

Vol. 2054: A. Condon, G. Rozenberg (Eds.), DNA Computing. Proceedings, 2000. X, 271 pages. 2001.

Vol. 2055: M. Margenstern, Y. Rogozhin (Eds.), Machines, Computations, and Universality. Proceedings, 2001. VIII, 321 pages. 2001.

Vol. 2056: E. Stroulia, S. Matwin (Eds.), Advances in Artificial Intelligence. Proceedings, 2001. XII, 366 pages. 2001. (Subseries LNAI).

Vol. 2057: M. Dwyer (Ed.), Model Checking Software. Proceedings, 2001. X, 313 pages. 2001.

Vol. 2059: C. Arcelli, L.P. Cordella, G. Sanniti di Baja (Eds.), Visual Form 2001. Proceedings, 2001. XIV, 799 pages. 2001.

Vol. 2064: J. Blanck, V. Brattka, P. Hertling (Eds.), Computability and Complexity in Analysis. Proceedings, 2000. VIII, 395 pages. 2001.

Vol. 2068: K.R. Dittrich, A. Geppert, M.C. Norrie (Eds.), Advanced Information Systems Engineering. Proceedings, 2001. XII, 484 pages. 2001.

Vol. 2072: J. Lindskov Knudsen (Ed.), ECOOP 2001 – Object-Oriented Programming. Proceedings, 2001. XIII, 429 pages. 2001.

Vol. 2073: V.N. Alexandrov, J.J. Dongarra, B.A. Juliano, R.S. Renner, C.J.K. Tan (Eds.), Computational Science – ICCS 2001. Part I. Proceedings, 2001. XXVIII, 1306 pages. 2001.

Vol. 2074: V.N. Alexandrov, J.J. Dongarra, B.A. Juliano, R.S. Renner, C.J.K. Tan (Eds.), Computational Science – ICCS 2001. Part II. Proceedings, 2001. XXVIII, 1076 pages. 2001.

Vol. 2091: J. Bigun, F. Smeraldi (Eds.), Audio- and Video-Based Biometric Person Authentication. Proceedings, 2001. XIII, 374 pages. 2001.

Vol. 2092: L. Wolf, D. Hutchison, R. Steinmetz (Eds.), Quality of Service – IWQoS 2001. Proceedings, 2001. XII, 435 pages. 2001.